LETTERS TO HAZEL

from

Douglas Gifford

1943 – 1947

LETTERS TO HAZEL

LETTERS TO HAZEL

from

Douglas Gifford

1943 – 1947

Edited and published by Hazel Gifford

DECEMBER 2004

Letters to Hazel
Edited by Hazel Gifford
First edition copyright © Hazel Gifford 2004

Typeset in Plantin
Printed and bound by the Printers to the University of St Andrews

Frontispiece Douglas and Hazel on leave in Madrid, 1947

FOREWORD

Douglas was born on 21 July 1924 in Belgrano, Buenos Aires, Argentina, the only child of Augusta Louisa and Laurie Gifford (in fact the unacknowledged 'natural' son of Augusta and W.C. Gentry – 'Unk' in these letters). I was born on 21 November 1921 in Upper Norwood, London, S.E.21, fourth and youngest child of Muriel and Stanley Collingwood. Douglas and I met in Oxford in November 1942, and were engaged within the year.

In deciding which extracts to publish from our intense-though-distant courtship correspondence, I have tried to keep in mind: 'what will interest the Family?' It has been fascinating for me to go back 60 years; we learned so much about each other (and maybe were wiser and cleverer then, than ever after), through those four years of separate–belonging during the Second World War. We wrote almost daily, and posted 2 or 3 times a week. I hope the reader will understand that much therefore has been left out.

I warmly thank Heather Simpson for her meticulous typing and Nate Suda, her husband, for overseeing the scanning-in of Douglas' wee drawings; our daughter, Frances Grant, who oversaw all the technicalities of text and layout; and our third and youngest son, David Gifford, who also brought his expertise in to create the cover and photographic pages. Without all of them, and the courteous competence of the University's Printing Department, I am sure this enterprise would never have been completed. My gratitude goes deep indeed.

HAZEL GIFFORD
St Andrews, November 2004

1943

*Douglas' first posting was to the Primary Training Wing, Quebec
Barracks, Northampton. At this time Hazel was living in Kettering,
Northamptonshire, as an evening class lecturer for the WEA (Workers'
Educational Association).*

[*16.12.43*]
Darling,

Here I am in the barracks – I felt terribly miserable after I'd left
you, but the nostalgia is somewhat lessened now by not being able to
think about it because of strange happenings and odd surroundings. I
met a bloke in the train who was going to Quebec Barracks. We waited
for years in the station for a lorry to take us out there. They are in quite a
different place to where you said they were. A very pleasant surprise
from what I thought they would be – very modern and neat. I don't
know how much I'm allowed to say at all, but I suppose it's all right.

Darling, yesterday was a day, wasn't it. I loved every moment of
it. I think that your little room [in Kettering] is just heaven – I shall
be terribly happy to get to it. Oh sweet. I love you so.

... Food here (from what my lunch was) is rather like college, so
I'm quite happy. There is a lot of row going on all over the place
and people are shouting nearby. I have received masses of kit and
things and have a heap of socks to gaze at. Sweet, I don't think we
are allowed out on Sunday – new people aren't anyway. But
normally the amount that we can be out is very reasonable – every
day 6-11, Saturday 1-12 (midnight) – and I have a 36 hour leave to
travel in before Jan. 30th or so.

[*17.12.43*]

I love you so. And I'm going to see you next Sunday. 'Ooray! I'm getting a pass to be made out for Kettering, and I'll be out at 1.0, not 3.0, so I shall see you earlier. I just do so want to see you before Christmas.

Sweet, I was told I would probably be O.K. for a commission if I 'behaved myself' and I have a v.good chance to get into the Intelligence. In that case I'd probably be at Northampton another 10 weeks after these six! And I'd be in N'ton proper, not three miles out! But it'll be hard grinding too, so I mustn't get twittery and excited.

... We've been inoculated today, and have a free day tomorrow, though alas we're not allowed out. Next week we have intelligence tests and things. I'm scared stiff I'll come out 214 or something and be shoved into the pioneer corps! All the blokes here are quite decent – one old lad next to me (they're mostly about 35-40) has a family, a little girl of 11 years old, and is a non-smoker and non-drinker. Sweet, I'll rush, & perhaps this'll get to you by to-morrow.

[*undated*]

Here's rather wonderful news: The Officer in charge here has given permission for leave from Friday night Christmas Eve till Sunday night! So I'm reckoning on travelling to Kettering – changing into clothes, and coming down to London. Gawd knows what might happen if I got asked for my identity card, but the risk is definitely worth it. I don't know quite when I should arrive at home – probably sometime early Christmas morning, and I would have to leave either Christmas night or very early Sunday morning because I have to be in by 12 Sunday night, and I'm scared stiff of the trains running late! Still, it's marvellous to be able to come home for Christmas day.

[*Douglas and Hazel's engagement was officially announced during this leave.*]

[*28.12.43*]

I'm writing this while waiting for our little band of brothers to finish their dental treatment. Scene: a dark room with wooden forms and fidgeting men, about-to-be-vaccinated, dentalized, or just writing letters and waiting for the others. I'm one of those. I had three teeth filled and am coming again twice more. The dentist was a decent bloke with a very pleasant chair-side manner. We marched the 4½ miles down here and will presumably march the three miles back. (Horror). Still, I'd march anywhere to get my grub...

... No, you're not the ship, but I love you just the same.

... I have had a very tiring day. There were 4½ miles to march down into Talavera barracks, 2 hours to wait, and another 4½ miles back. Then after that we were on parade again crawling about in the mud and running behind cover. Ooof! Oh well – I just dream of home half the time.

My humorous rifle is now all oily and natty, and looks quite reasonable. But it has a silly idiotic habit of trying to slip off my shoulder on the march.

[*29.12.43*]

... Since our Corporal is in hospital, we have been issued with another one – this time a non-swearing one, a great change and pleasure to work with. I wonder what you would say if you saw me carving great chunks of mud off my boots with my knife, then cheerfully wiping it on my trousers and going and eating with it!

... I forgot my gym shoes on parade today. Alas, me.

... Also, having left my gloves in Kettering, I was the one in the squad without them for the Company Sergeant Major's Parade. That is a very special parade in which the whole company of 300-odd men take part, and are marched in great pomp about and around the barrack square. Everyone has to be natty to the point of shininess. And of course, I hadn't my gloves. So I pulled my army pullover sleeves down over my hand and hoped they looked like gloves. Cor was I scared as I marched by the officer! He was blaring away (or rather bleating) at everyone for being dopey.

... Our Sergeant is also on the sick list, and everyone is happy (I fear). The new non-swearing Corporal we have been fitted with is a very good bloke – he gets good results with us while never shouting at us.

... We went through the gas chamber today. That is, we filed reluctantly into a chamber full of gas, with our gas-masks on and came out; went in again (more reluctantly) and (even more reluctantly) had to take 'em off. The thing was to inspire us with confidence in our gas-masks so that we should always have them, and how horrid it was without them. Still it was only tear gas, so it didn't matter. Ah me.

1944

[*2.1.44*]

Thanks Infinite for yesterday. Gosh was it sweet 'n perfect every moment of it – and it'll last me the week till Saturday. Gosh I enjoyed it: it lies warm & fragrant in me now. All those lovely memories do; they're all invaluable bits of treasure in the great and boundless treasure chest of our lives. Coo... Wa! I say, I have a horrible disclosure to make, but I need three items of wash by next Saturday. I really am very sorry indeed, but you see, it's a kit inspection. So I shall need the Army Vest and pants and Army socks, I fear. But look, sweet, if you haven't time to do them, could you just send them and I will demonstrate them, and bring them again on Sunday.

[*4.1.44*]

... There was another Company Sergeant Major's parade this afternoon and as usual I was in agony lest one of the officers should notice that one of my gaiters was upside down and the other the wrong way round. Still, all went well. In P.T. there was a "game" of rugger without rules of any kind, i.e., you picked up the ball and hurled your way through; about 25 a side. I scored one try.

[5.1.44]

... I am now writing this in the NAAFI: a lot of new raw recruits have just come in; still wearing civvies – gosh, poor things, I wonder if they felt like I did when I first came in! We had a toilsome afternoon, full of things like Bayonet practice.

... Coo, only another two whole weeks, and I will be shifting. I shall be very sorry to leave the place, I think, what with breaking up our happy barrack room. We do have such fun, and discuss and roar with laughter over the day's events. The highlights today were 1. Harry Chapman's face when bayoneting a sandbag (seen from the other side of the sandbag), and 2. Me giving a demonstration in front of the Light Machine gun class, on what I knew about the barrel and main body (which, wasn't an awful lot). Apparently my lecture-demonstration consisted mainly of the word 'gosh'!

Then Ern was haggled at on parade and taken aside by the corporal (the greatest possible indignity), and shown how to about-turn. The sergeant, too, made a priceless remark: "You've got the ambitions of a —— field marshal and the brains of a —— field-mouse"! Which I thought rather good! Then there was ABCA period (Army Bureau of Current Affairs), in which the young lieutenant taking us got completely out of his depth when the three Oxford men (inc. me!) began a learned discussion on the racial prejudices of Germany, and the traditions it held (with frequent allusions to Wagner of course!). Oh it was fun.

Now shall I have "Rabbit Pie Peas and Potatoes – 6½d" – or shall I go upstairs to the writing room? No. I will exercise self-control. Anyway I've just had cup of tea, chocolate cake, ginger cake, scone, jam and treacle tarts, so I can't grumble.

[*9.1.44*]

... We've had about the toughest day ever today – this afternoon was amazing. The P.T. nearly laid us out. Everything seems to have become harder all of a sudden – drill, more shouting, more hurrying, more energetic rifle exercises, terrible P.T., in fact everything's just about twice the pace it was before! So I said to Peter Marto, "Hoy-Hoy", he said "You wait till the 5th week!"

... I couldn't finish last night 'cos I was assailed upon to play the piano. But I wrote a letter to Mother, quite a long one, and posted it.

Playing the piano meant playing all the few (very few) dance tunes or waltzes I can play and also that horrid prelude of Rachmaninoff – still, if they liked it, it was quite well worth it!

(After parade, in break) I had to be fitted for army glasses – they're a silver (colour) rims. But I needn't wear them off duty.

We had a wicked parade of drill – I was sent to run round the barrack square twice! Oh well, I'd better change for some mud-slugging – Cheerioh, sweet... Oh, it wasn't mud-slugging after all. Just a lecture, then some very gentle P.T.; 'Ooray!

[*10.1.44*]

... I say, when and if you receive wash or find a pair of pyjamas, could you send me some? Please? Also, if you could send me my writing pad and envelopes, I should be very grateful...

... P.S. Could you send me too a shaving brush – you'll find one in a dark red little case in my knapsack. Thanks, sweetheart.

[*On 11 January 1944 Douglas was successfully interviewed for the Intelligence Corps.*]

[*undated*]

... To-day we're doing a Bren gun practise. Out of fifteen shots I got two on target. hm... I rather think it's because I close my eyes when firing, and of course that does things from the aiming point of view.

[*18.1.44*]

... I got into various spots of bother all day, beginning with dirty-boots, and going on with shoutings and ravings through the day, so I just haven't had a chance to sit down once. I was put down for cookhouse scrubbings-about as a punishment, but seem to have evaded it somehow.

Cor, but I have been shouted at to-day and have been the bête noir of the flock, through my dreamings and dopeyings. "Dreaming about that girl of yours, you — — —, are you? Blast you, wake your ideas up" is the sort of stuff I've got all the time.

[*20.1.44*]

... I boxed last night (Thursday night)...

So, I'm a sap am I??? Well, as a special punishment, I'm not going to tell you what happened till Sunday, see! (!!)...

... And I'll tell you about the boxing (said he imperiously "but no doubt a bit pathetically" said she, jumping at a very possible conclusion). Yes, well, but I'm still alive. [*Douglas actually knocked his opponent out!*]

We had quite a normal day yesterday, and for once I wasn't shouted about on the drill parade – only did I hear "You're overdoing it Gifford", which of course was a bit better. Ah well.

[*23.1.44*]

... [*Following a brief time out in N'hpton.*] I got into slightly hot (or hottish) water on arrival back for having slipped away in such a slippery way and not having asked permission etc. etc... One thing, if I had asked for permission, I know I shouldn't have received it!

[*25.1.44*]

... We leave on the 9.10 train to-morrow morning, and are to be carried down in trucks. On the kit inspection we had the C.O. (Lt. Colonel) coming round. "Gifford's going into the Intelligence Corps" mumbled the Major to the Colonel.

"Wey? Eh! Is that the bloke who knows seven languages, Eh?"

"No Sir, only three" says I.

"What d' ye speak?"

"French, Spanish, and German, Sir."

"Eh? Well, say that in French." (I say it in French)

"Hrrrmph! Now in German." (I say it in German)

"Mmph." He passes on to the next bed.

"Eh... " He comes rushing back with Ern's pay book.

"Eh – translate this into French!" (I translate it into French)

"Hmmph." He goes on again – thank goodness for the last time.

... Well, the time is nigh, and I'd better put all my junk and strappings on. I inevitably end up looking like a bundle of rags.

[*Douglas was next sent to G.S.C. Depot and Training Centre, Bradford.*]

[*27.1.44*]

Hallo Sweet,

Ah! I am a happy man once more relieved and happy-as-a-cod-equipped-with-a-very-superior-fin. FOR – I haven't got to do my Primary Training again after all. All the blokes (with the exception of the two sergeants), who were waiting for the interview with me in London (in the Intelligence Recruiting Centre) are with me, and we have been moved to the Headquarters Company which is full of people waiting to be posted. All the Intelligence Corps men are there waiting too (as I said), and it is the normal thing to happen, so I'm quite as merry as usual. I really did think though that I would have to do all my training again, and was pretty miserable for a few hours. Still, that's over. Our life now will consist in trying to dodge fatigues and cookhouse washing etc., which the H.Q. Company men have to do to fill up their time.

[*28.1.44*]

'Tis only yesterday when I wrote you a miserably short note, in the Y.M.C.A. I am now in another rest room, the Cathedral Canteen. It's wonderful the amount of comfortable rooms and brightly furnished chairs etc. there are about Bradford; Y.M.C.A.s, Y.W.C.A.s, canteens galore – people really are most kind.

... To-day? We had orders to sweep out the billets (which are very bare, unfurnished and awfully dilapidated civilian houses), over which we took nearly all the morning. Then after lunch we (Peter the artist), Charles (a Dutchman bound for the Intelligence Corps too), Nicky (a German bound for the Intelligence Corps), and myself, changed, washed, and preened ourselves and hastily left the billets before any Sgt. could nab us for fatigues. We wandered round the town, being shown the sights by Peter, and then had a cup of tea at Anglo Polish Rest-room, then tea at the Y.M.C.A. We then all divided.

... Sweet, I've been having an awfully agonizing mental struggle over this savings business – I mean. I've got £1-1-6d – and I want to send you the £1 for saving, but since I don't get paid for another week, I don't see how (with the life I'm leading at present) I can do on 1-6d, 'cos it's so different to N'ton; we have such a lot of free time, that we're bound to go to Y.M.C.A.s and have cups of tea an awful lot – not really wasting money, or anything, but such a lot of cups of tea and cakes. So alas I'm not saving it this week-end!

... And I'm sending my clothes to a laundry here (Chinese one).

[*1.2.44*]

... Hallo sweet, how are you? I wrote you a dreadfully scrappy letter in a great hurry last night. I haven't seen if there's any post to-day yet, but will soon. The thing is, it's inadvisable to go near the office at lunchtime, 'cos they generally nab people for duties 'n things. But I'll see before I post this off, and write more later.

... Thanks terrifically for the washing. I can now go about less like the Rhinoceros in the Just-so story! I'm sure my nose is broke: it clicks every time I tap it with my finger. It must have been that beastly bloke wot I knocked out, when he hit me on the nose. What shall I do? Shall I leave it to recuperate or what? Ern might be in shreds for all I know! Anyway it clicks, and it never used to before.

... Dearest, it seems more and more certain that I shall be going to North Wales; isn't it awful! The place is in Anglesey, of all the potty places. And we seem to do "Intensive Infantry" training there. It seems an Intelligence man is supposed to be a good soldier amongst other things (in case of being left to his own resources). The whole period of training they say lasts six months.

... After that, I just don't know: we're sectioned off: that is, we are put somewhere and do our job there. The somewhere might be anywhere, however, from John O'Groats to Calcutta. Oh sweet, aren't I depressing! Never mind, never anticipate or worry. (Helpful, aren't I!). No darling, don't get upset or worried or anything. Just watch events.

[9.2.44]

... I have been a lazy fellow to-day! I dropped off to sleep and slept in my chair (in the C.S.[1] rooms) till about ¼ to 5! And then remained in a sort of dope till 6.0 or so. Then I did some more work on something-or-other; had supper at 7.0, back to the C.S., more work, then was ejected at 9.0. Now I'm in the Y.M.C.A. with a cup o'cocoa for company.

... I 'thort' today another 'thort'. 'Twas about the Relative and Absolute agin', I was saying to myself how important it was to only have the Absolute ahead of you in your mind. Then I 'thort'; Yes,

---

[1] C.S. – Christian Science

but if it weren't for the relative, how would we know about the Absolute? How could Jesus have demonstrated the power of good and love if he had talked then in an absolute way, and not in parables?

What then I am trying to work out is, that we're shown God and the Absolute in a Relative kind of way (parables, and in Christian Science for instance). The truth is demonstrated by healings (again relative things), and whether we should also look for and look at God through Relative channels.

Ooo, aren't I getting involved. But just as we wouldn't ever know about the sun were it not for its rays, we probably wouldn't know about God and the Absolute were it not for his thoughts, rays if you like, us-ward.

I suppose we should have to look at the absolute through the relative channels, but what we must be terribly careful to do is to look at the absolute and not the relative channels. Oh dear, I haven't got anywhere. But I mustn't be too hard on the relative; at least the relative between us and good, as it's really our relation to God. Ah, I've got it. It's the relative between the human and human as opposed to the relative between human and good that's wrong.

I hope you got the gist of all that. Not to think Sam-Smith-drinks-PIMM's No.1-Why- shouldn't-I, but; it's wrong to drink it, so I won't never mind what Sam Smith does. We must look UP, and not across. Looking up, we gravitate upwards, Godwards, looking across, we slither about one way and another.

[*10.2.44*]

... Mother seems definitely happier, and things seem easier; though her chief concern during the letter seemed for my state after injections and teeth pulling! Bless her she's the greatest character I know – and the most powerful stream of love and consideration that I have ever known in any one; she's always thinking of other people, and doing things.

You know, sweet, if there's anything in me that is good, it is what she has brought out in me; I mean, I haven't had a father ever to educate me; it has all been Mother's work; she has never punished me or drilled anything or forced anything into me & has always tried to spoil me! (A tendency which I defeated when I was about 14! But the defeat was by no means final, and the dear thing still doggedly tries!).

We've been very good friends, and, I think I can say, better companions than a lot of Mothers & sons – in fact, perfect companions – mainly because we've only had each other since I was six. She says I make her happy, and that's why she loves me so, and I wish I could really believe it, though God knows I've been irritable & cross many a time, a thing for which I've always cursed myself savagely for. I know I'm right in saying that Unk has also made her happy for the last eight years and more; and he has educated me too, and taught me to be honest and not to deceive. He's very honest, and I refuse to say "was", 'cos I think that things'll be all right in the long run.

... Sweet, your letters were nice; yes of course it's the way you look at things, and the path is laid out for us, and all we have to do is to think & live aright and we'll be guided along the path by the hand of God.

[*Douglas now moved to Rhosneigr, Anglesey, for the next part of his training.*]

[*16.2.44*]

Darling,

Here I am, it's a lovely place – as far as country goes, at any rate; I haven't been here long enough to know anything more. I am living in an empty house again, but much bigger this time, much nicer, and with a real bed with real spring things cris-crossing it.

'C' Coy is all Intelligence Corps, and all my roommates (seven or so) are I. Corps, all of whom speak Oxfordish kind of English (if ye get wot I mean), so it is all very pleasant to the ear.
But my dear! The things I shall have to do here:

... all sorts of awful courses, assault courses, throwing noisy objects, bangs, marches. Cor, it'll lay me flat. (If I let it.)

[*17.2.44*]

My first day here. Waah, we got talked to by various people – the Captain pointed at me during his talk & said I don't care whether you be the biggest Cockney ever and can't speak any languages and have never been to a place like Oxford or Cambridge as long as you're a good soldier you can get a chance of a commission – which is about the biggest set of oppositely-true remarks I've ever heard. They pick people for OCTU here, but I don't want an Infantry Commission, and would shun it like the plague if it ever came near me. Sorry, sweet, but I'd rather be a

Lance/Cpl in the I. Corps (he said for the 15th time) than a lieutenant in the Infantry.

But there are pleasanter aspects revealed to-day. I find there are play readings on Sundays, gramophone recitals, and all sorts of interesting things. There is also a radio, and I've been listening to Schumann's piano concerto to-night.

[*19.2.44*]

... My sweet, if you don't stop twittering about me and a commission, I'll bean you one! Anyone who has been to a university and who is A1 could get a commission in the Infantry – honestly, they're two a penny, and I really promise you that is true. They desperately need Infantry Officers nowadays, anyway. And this place is one of the most dangerous places for that kind of thing, for you get a very much higher standard of characters and everything than you do anywhere else. So they are on the lookout for possible officers. They notice you, and after a time (not here, but later on) offer you a chance of going to an Infantry O.C.T.U. You go (if you accept) and get an Infantry commission. You have then lost your place in the Intelligence, and nothing on earth can get you back into the I. Corps. So there you are. A commissioned man may look twice the man, to many in amongst the civilians (ones' families, and friends), but in reality he is exactly the same; a commission is just a commission: a Lieutenant is something to talk about and be proud of, and get wallowed in patriotic sentiment over.

... Darling I'm not trying to give you a lecture or anything, but to show you how to explain things to people if they wonder why I am only a private or N.C.O. Mind you, I probably will get one one day, perhaps, but there are only two ways of getting them. One way is rushing at the word "commission", and grabbing at the nearest one you can find, which will land you up in the Infantry, or the other one is sticking to your job and working your way up, like a clerk in a bank (he said, unpicturesquely) does to become a manager.

[21.2.44]

... Civilization is indeed quite near – the Irish mail passes within a mile; there is a station from where one can get to London, by changing at Crewe; then there is quite a little shopping centre; to-day I bought: ½ lb of margarine, one packet of Ryvita, one tin of dried milk, one bottle of pickled beetroot, one bottle of Ovaltine tablets... ! 'ad enough? And 4 oranges. Now will you come up here for a weekend?

[22.2.44]

I had such a lot o'things to-day – a letter from your Mother, one from Monica; & three parcels! The ones you sent on were washing, and a cake from the very kindly Mrs. Evans – your Mother sent me an enormous bar of chocolate!!

It was good of her, wasn't it! They have been having beastly raids on London lately, haven't they though. How are you? My blessed sweet old one. Yes, I will write to Ern – apparently he narrated to your gentle Mother and family all the awful details of that boxing match!! And apropos of gore, don't think that that is blood – it's merely pickled beetroot [*referring to a reddish spot on the letter*]. I am in the Information Room in our Battalion rest room, and intellectual people are sitting round reading deep works on politics, etc, while I, poor mortal, am endeavouring to eat (as secretly and furtively as possible), some hard ship's biscuits, margarine and pickled beetroot. Awful crunching noises split the air, and I am afraid they are all aware of one in their midst Who is Not a Pure Ascetic. I intend a bit later on to eat an orange... I'm quite sure nobody has ever eaten in here before, anyway.

... To-day has been utterly beautiful weather, though it has also been very tiring. Wherever we go, we have to run there, and when there is all ones' equipment-and-a-rifle to carry, it is all very 'ard. Still I expect it's doing me good, to move about a bit, and it's really not too bad at all, and we are given plenty of breaks in the between periods.

[24.2.44]

... We had a route march this morning – only about 6 miles – quite easy; it seems it was so 'cos the company commander didn't come. He generally makes everyone run and double about the countryside! Then there was a lecture by a Commando Lieutenant on fighting etc; quite interesting. By the way, re: commissions, you may always say that I was recommended for one ('cos I was), if that is anything. I think it was done at my P.T.W. Actually, I only found that out to-day.

... I told the Captain of our company that I didn't wish to go on OCTU, and he was extremely pleased! Said he didn't agree with them, and so forth. So instead of getting a terrific dressing down as I expected, all was quite O.K.

Now I am in the midst of a gramophone recital; the overture to Borodin's Prince Igor is being played. About the classes etc. here – there is an educational officer here, a very chummy sort of cove, who procures all the books for playreadings etc., but most of the things themselves are organized by us, and he gives us the wherewithal to run them.

[*26.2.44*]

... Gosh, I've just been thinking of our early letters – of July & August & September – it all seems like a symphony; what with the lovely Oxford weather, and my little room...the strolls at night along the Parks Rd, the tennis, the boats and punts, the glorious Cherwell, from Magdalen bridge, up to the rollers, Mother coming every day to tea, the noise of Victor outside in the quad, shouting and running about, the warmth and freedom of a perfect summer, with perfect memories and a harmony which was the same throughout; these things are gone only to come back in a different combination, a different harmony, and perhaps a different setting. But the same things in that same way are gone indeed, never to return. And the ever-increasing crescendo of You was electrifying, and vivifying too; a theme running through the everyday glory and harmony.

[*28.2.44*]

... About the 2nd point – sweet, the greatest help you are is by the love which you give to me. But I know what you mean. But just at present, and very often – in fact, most of the time, I'm not worried or anything by any problems. You see, life here is so enormously simple: we go out, bound about healthfully all day, come in with raving appetites, and in the evenings – well, I generally read my Bible & Science & Health, write to you, write my diary, and listen to music. It's so beautifully simple in a way, and very happy so far. But what I might, and ought to tell you, are the frequent little glimpses of things, which are so easily forgotten unless I develop them and pass them on.

... The blokes here? No, they're not too intellectual at all – most of them just like sitting mildly at a play reading or a gramophone recital, and being very Quiet generally. They are a bit reserved, as I think I already said, and don't put forward opinions unless you dig them out of them! But they're very very "unarty" and not at all loud-voiced or anything. They're a bit like coal-mines with coal very near the surface; sort of green fields with trees & things, but if you go to a bit of trouble, with a bit of persistence, you get marvellous surprises, for there's the richest coal imaginable to be found, just with the 'elp of an axe (or pick).

They are just terrifically appreciative, and the best lot I've ever come across. The reason for their reserve is not only because they are English, I think, but 'cos of the Army life – You see, they are all bundled together for ten weeks, and it really takes more than that to completely thaw them (if not to-wards each other – they thaw there), but towards people outside their squads, and new arrivals. (I've the Christmas Oratorio on now – just discovered some new records here, with some lovely things. I've been sticking doggedly by the gramophone all evening and have played the Grieg P. Concerto again, the Beethoven No. 3 Leonora, the Comus ballet music by Purcell, some piano works by Chopin, and – oh it is lovely.)

... But that about C.S. Lewis, I think... You know, the way we look at God & man is important, because it is a sort of foundation for so many things, and a sort of axiom for many thoughts; and just as you apply axioms in geometry, and theorems in geometry to the life and things and problems around us. And you've got to work things out like that – they've got to be worked out sometime for the picture to be completed.

[29.2.44]

... I went over an assault course yesterday, all sorts of exciting things. All quite potty except that it makes one fitter I suppose!

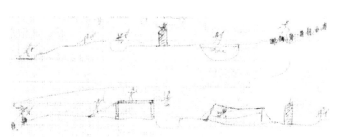

[*9.3.44*]

... I'm dead tired. We had a route march this morning, which developed into schemes, and moving entirely over country, jumping walls and being Energetic. Then a break in which I had time to read your letter – then another scheme toward the middle of this, when Bladworth and I were feeling quite exhausted, albeit quite carefree & irresponsible, not being platoon commanders (which have to rush about a lot) or anything. Then the Sergeant suddenly dropped on us, and made Bladworth platoon Commander, and me the Runner! Horror – so we finished up in style. Then this afternoon we went over the assault course. Which was quite the end.

[*12.3.44*]

... Yesterday morning I was publicly chastised for the state of my rifle. It wasn't clean enough, the Sgt. said. I argue that what use is a rifle? I mean, bayonets are very useful. One can make excellent toast with the help of a bayonet, or one can get stones out of horses' hooves with bayonets (if one is inclined that way), but whatever can one use a rifle for? No use at all. So I was ordered to present my rifle at 2.0, all clean and natty. But as luck would have it, we all gave our rifles to the armourer's, so tee hee.

[*Hazel hitched and trained to Rhosneigr for the weekend.*]

[*20.3.44*]

Here I am in the C.R.S. (Company Reception Station). A sort of Battalion sick room or a very little hospital, with about 50 beds. I reported sick this morning. My temp. was only 98.4, and the M.O. said he was sending me because he thought I was short-winded! And I would have to be examined. An odd kind of complaint, and one defect which I have never regarded as such. When I always get puffing after running I don't think that's a physical defect, do you? Joe is very short winded too, and he's Al too. All a bit queer. Still, this is a very fine place, wot with real sheets and baths & things and good food. My bed is up against a radiator. There is a radio and a piano in the room, too, and flowers & comfortable chairs, and a general atmosphere of homeliness (and happiness).

Sweet, that was a marvellous weekend – thank you so terribly much. It was so flawless – from my point of view, anyway (did you mind nursing a dopey sleepy child all day long?). Oh it was all just right n'est-ce-pas? Perhaps it might have been so much better had I not been dopey? Bless you. I haven't finished my diary of it yet, and I spent two hours this morning doing it, oh it was a lovely dream – I say a dream 'cos it was so perfect, absolute and harmonious. Thank you a million times for coming, sweetheart and for having made me so happy – and for doing my diary! I will write to you again to-morrow. God Bless you my angel, All my love.

[*21.3.44*]

...I am still snug in Bed, and have been asleep nearly all this morning. This is a very comfortable dormitory, what with spring beds and warmth. But my dear, the radio... ! It is put on at about 8.0, and blares through the whole day till 9.0 at night. Vast quantities of hot "music", patriotic and sentimental programmes... Oh, 'orror...

... The Army chaplain is oozing round the place – he is a very fat fellow with an unfortunate knack of sounding insincere.

[*10.4.44*]

... Darling about your queries concerning what I think. I'd better say what I think instead of arguing or anything.

I think that this world is God's & God's only. O.K.?

I believe that God is good – perfect Love, truth, Life, beauty, and all.

God made man in his own image, and so he created him – an idea of himself, and therefore perfect. He did not create things like suffering etc.

All that God made is spiritual, the Kingdom of God is spiritual, also as Jesus said, the Kingdom of God is within you.

The Godly You, the You that dwells in God is the reflection of Him, that is, the creation which he makes, which is, as an expression of Him, perfect.

Now, as far as we go, we acknowledge the Kingdom of God to be the real kingdom (or the one that really matters), therefore the real you is the true expression of God.

(Sorry to be going so slowly, sweet, but I am putting 'em down slowly)

The you that suffers is the part of you that still clings to the material beliefs and fears that are, in the eyes of God, just unreal – not pertaining to his kingdom. And in the eyes of God, so in the eyes of our spiritual selves.

... and the 'mind' which causes all the discord is called Mortal mind. Well, according to whether Mortal Mind (which shuts out the light with doubts etc.) or Divine Mind governs the person (i.e. whether there's more darkness or light in him) – in consequence transforms his body.

... What I'm getting at is very simply this. The H.M.C. everyone loves, the sweet & woozily & kindly & Godly you is the real you – the expression – or reflection of God in you. The you that may suffer is the you that lets itself be assailed by fears, or lets thoughts of fears come into your mind. The one is incorruptible, the other is corruptible. One is spiritual, the other worldly.

So. Then, Jesus. Surely (say I), he is the very embodiment of that spiritual Godly Man that I've been talking about – he it was who is God's perfect image, and he came on earth to show us what God's image really was, and to help us (or perhaps 'help' is too feeble a word) to see the Christ in ourselves, the Kingdom of Heaven within us. "That which I have done ye shall do also." We can be like Jesus – (but gosh, how hard it seems!). You see, he proved (or showed, if you like) that every mortal pain can be conquered, that every mortal pain is unreal to the spiritual man – and every mortal pain – even death itself! And it was at Eastertide that he reached the culmination of his teachings, that Death can be to the Christ as every other material thing – unreal.

You might say, "But what of his suffering" – sweet, he had to go through every mortal pain to show how He (and we) could rise above it. That's the wonderful part about his love – like a tender parent or teacher who goes through all the possible obstacles that might present themselves to the child in the problem he is setting him. Jesus overcame everything, so that we might well say He has borne everything, and there is no mortal pain he did not endure. Therefore let us do likewise & try to follow his example. And that is what C.S. people have endeavoured to do; and it's marvellous what results they've had by just plain downright Right thinking – I mean results in healing, in helping, in the return of friendship & love. There is no hypnotism or mesmerism or anything like that – in fact, we might call it "The Efficacy of prayer & love". It's so deeply simple and strong that I haven't the slightest doubt that it is the same feeling that Jesus & the early Christians had.

... It's up to us to show up that belief to be wrong and become more & more Godly. This we do by just praying & trying to be better Christians & understand more – just like you do. It's a struggle O.K., but a struggle upwards, to rid ourselves from the unreal dream of mortality. And our mortal minds don't like it a bit; they kick & screech & in short, they suffer. And if we dwell in them, we suffer too.

... Therefore it is that we recognize the Beauty in Cathedral in Castle, and in landscape. Also in the small things we personally know; in the garden of 45 Fairdene Rd – Why? Because you know it & love it, & it is beauty to you. What I am getting at is, that the things themselves may be material & (?) neutral, but the Love & Godliness in your soul & your mind gilds them with that immortal thing, Beauty.

That is perhaps why I can pray better in a little plain C.S. church, which to me is very very beautiful. You see, as long as Love is there, Beauty is there also. As long as I have Love in me, I can see beauty in things, and I think that plain little oak wooden seats, with two plain oak desks, with a bowl of flowers between them, are the very dearest & beautiful things. So it is, that wherever you can pray best, do it there, and if you can pray best in a mighty Cathedral, then it is the best thing for you to do so – there is all the Good & godliness attached to it. But did Jesus, & Paul & the disciples have to have these things to help them pray. They prayed in the midst of Beauty, yes, but it was the Beauty of Love about them – in the little room or wherever it was.

Then later on, good Christians who were also good artists presented their talents before God, and prayed in the midst of them & so did other people, deeming the artist's beauty more conducive to prayer than anything they had known. And so it grew & grew.

Perhaps another thing is that Jesus and his disciples themselves made the atmosphere they prayed in, by their sacred presence, while to-day people use other peoples' atmosphere's created by the beauties in the churches?

But please don't think I am saying anything against churches at all. I only put my own view very humbly, and say that I can pray better in simple & plain surroundings. If we had a little room of our own to pray in, then we should pray best there, I know, cos it would be our atmosphere.

[*April 44*]

... To-day has been quite fun – very energetic afternoon – "crawling" it was called – our section had to crawl up behind cover, and that entailed crawling along a nasty hard road on our hands & knees for about half a mile.

[*12.4.44*]

... I've had a very exciting day – it was called 'Battle Inoculation'. We fired mortars, of all things, Imagine little Douggie firing 4 mortar bombs (which he did!) – gee whiz, do they make a row. We fired three mortars at a time, in salvoes! Then we were stuck in the middle of a piece of ground and a machine gun was fired at us, or rather, just over our heads! A funny sensation, like nothing on earth. Then in the afternoon we did a scheme, firing live ammunition, with machine guns and the like pattering away. I was a rifleman, and so had to take part in the assault on the objective. And the specially exciting part was that we very nearly ran into the line of fire from the machine guns! Again a very curious sensation, like being naked in the middle of the street! Sort of!

[*April 44*]

...I feel beautifully comfy & restful, as I played Rugger yesterday, against a team in an aerodrome. It was a jolly good game; we lost, 'oweffer to the R.A.F. Most of our team were from our platoon – young lot of toughs that we are. Always the day after an energetic game of Rugger one feels peaceful even if a bit stiff! We had a shower afterwards, and tea at their N.A.A.F.I., then sailed home in truck. Then in the evening I played the piano for a long time & composed a noo toon! – Actually, I'd been humming it for a long time before.

[*22.4.44*]

... I talked to a bloke who had been in Casablanca and in a Vichy Concentration camp – one gets all sorts of people in the I. Corps!

[*28.4.44*]

... On Thursday I went to the specialist – Ha... Hee Hee, like to know wot happen, wouldn't you. Bless you my angel, and then I'll tell you.

Well, I went to Bangor, then out to a lovely country mansion standing in hundreds of acres of most beautiful country – I had to wait for my interview with the specialist, so I went for a walk – oh darling, would you had been there, carpets of primroses and bluebells. Gosh it was terrific! Then I waited some more, and the C.O., a Lieutenant-Colonel – who was most nice, and completely informal and chatty – he was the Ernie Crayford type of fellow – very kindly & nice. Anyway, he read the M.O.'s report, which said I was a bit short of breath – like, and all that.

And then he said that being short of Infantry Officers and all that, there was a danger of my being picked out for infantry, and he didn't think that I was the type of person for an Infantry Officer, being an imaginative kind of person, and rather peaceful etc – so he was going to grade me down – not that there was anything wrong with me at all, but the Army had a tendency to be a bit crude, and any A1 person might be picked on and shoved goodness knows where.

So he changed me (horror) to B1 (!) – which I now am. (Still love me?) – I'm B1 for 12 months, which he said, will stop me from being either shoved down 1 grade or being put into something like commandos... (I suppose after a year I'll get another medical). And then he held an official board – which was quite informal anyway, for the witnessing officer spoke German, so the Colonel made him speak German to me, and made me speak German back, and we all had quite a merry time, quite forgetting what the issue was, for a time! It seems the Colonel was at New College! And he was by far the nicest officer I've ever met in all my Army career – I mean the account of it all hardly seems possible for the Army, does it!

... Then to-day we had to move from a comfortable Billet to a hutted camp, where we arranged ourselves. I followed my usual practice of carrying about half a ton of things on my back – 4 blankets, a pillow, a mattress, and two full kit bags (kit bags are about 3ft 6 long and a foot wide each) – and arrived rather dead.

Then in the afternoon we doddered about and had desultory lectures on various odd things.

Then at 5.0, with a scrappy team of only 14 men we went and played Rugger against the R.A.F. Needless to say, we lost! Then a cup of tea and I played a grand piano which was in the sort of hall in which we changed, and back here.

[*1.5.44*]

... To-day I've been cruising round at a high speed, doing things, and "Blanco-ing" my equipment and polishing my mess tin – there are all sorts of inspections to-morrow, from Health inspections to kit inspections. We say goodbye to our rifles & bayonets, Hooray! Then Wednesday off we go. Then three weeks on a motorbike. Wheeee!!

[*Douglas was next sent to I. Corps Depot, Wentworth Woodhouse, Rotherham, Yorks.*]

[*8.5.44*]

... To-day we went careering about in the morning and went out on the road in the afternoon, 'n did various things & had great fun.

I say, it was a scream last night after I came in, for I suddenly found myself in an awful pickle: (a) There was to be an inspection of gaiters in the morning; and I hadn't got mine, as you know! And (b) our (identity card arrangement) and Service Books had had to be collected that morning (Sunday morning), and I hadn't taken mine, and everybody else had – and what was worse, I had gone out without it, which is a great crime in the army, as it serves as one's identity card: So there I was in a dashed great pickle! But everything turned out all right in the end: I borrowed some gaiters of someone who had two prs. and I went to ask the quartermaster sergeant for my paybook whilst he was shaving, and thus got it without much fuss & pother!

[12.5.44]

... Well, well, what have I done to-day... We went over slag heaps & things – all sorts of rough riding – extremely diverting. And we charged through a thickly treed wood, which caused much mirth and merriment, as the trees nearly came off second best! But it is really terribly funny sometimes. (Gunner Smith, who has stalled at the bottom of a slope 'midst a clump of bluebells):

"This damn thing 'as stopped, Cpl"

Cpl: "For Christ's sake 'urry up, I want my lunch, I do!"

Gunner Smith tries feebly to start up his engine, but is interrupted by an irate Corporal.

"Take yer 'and off the throttle!"

"Take yer foot off the brake!"

"Take yer – Oh Gawd!"

And he trots down in a heated way towards Gunner Smith. But when he is halfway there, there is a great bang, and a bike zooms up the incline, at the top of which five other fellow bikers are cackling to their heart's content. Gnr. Smith, overcome by all this movement, clutches at his clutch brake, front pedal, rear pedal, ignition switch, exhaust valve lever, changes gear, and gets his foot caught in the clutch fulcrum. Then, like an exhausted duck, the bike runs back in a withered way in reverse down the slope again, the engine dead.

The Cpl. Marches up in a stern way, looks at the bike, looks at Smith, looks at the bike again, then, looking at Smith and staring at him steadily, he stoops down & turns on Smith's petrol.

[14.5.44]

... The bike I have been riding up to nah is an "Ariel!" – but that has just gone wrong with something or other, and I have now a "Matchless" which I rather dislike. I'm not specially frightfully keen on motor-bikes, and infinitely prefer a bicycle – but my "Ariel" was very comfortable & nice.

[*16.5.44*]

... To-day I have been doing fatigues all the time – N.A.A.F.I. ones – i.e., sweeping out the N.A.A.F.I., cleaning the tables, sweeping out the quiet room – and, grrr, removing two tons of coal from one spot to another with the help of a shovel – all in the pouring rain.

... As you know, I was born in Belgrano, a suburb of Buenos Aires. It's about like Coulsdon or Purley is to London – quite a way out. Shortly after that, I think, we moved to Bahia Blanca, which is a port some way down the coast. When I was two we went to England for a holiday (my father was an electrical engineer) – then came back. When I was four we moved back to Belgrano, and, evil days having come upon us (Daddy having lost his job), Mother became a general housekeeper and caretaker of one of the Christian Science churches in Buenos Aires – quite a big church. Also, before that, she was housekeeper for a family who lived on one of the islands in the delta of the Paraná River.

Things financially didn't get much better, and Mother & Daddy unfortunately had one or two rows, and disagreements – but not very bad ones – I only mention them because I happen to remember one of them. Some time after that, Daddy suggested to Mother that she should take me to get my education in England, while he got a job – in Chile. – By the way, I had been to England again when I was four, for another holiday.

I was now six. So Mother and I set off on our travels, to England. There's a lot I don't understand about it all, but it has never been told me, so I didn't ever ask any more about it. In England, Mother bought a wee cottage near Bognor Regis, and I attended a kindergarten school there – of which I was at one time (a), the only pupil, and at another time (b), the only male member

– the rest being a lot of little girls who rather thought me a little tick. But things weren't too well financially; no money came from the Argentine, and though all her friends rallied most kindly, funds ran low.

Then Unk came very much into the scene. For about twelve years he'd been our best friend, and was also Daddy's best friend, and he offered Mother a sort of informal position of housekeeper. (He had been in the Argentine in the bank – then he'd been transferred, in the course of promotion, to Spain). Mother went to Spain, then, as his housekeeper, and somewhat reluctantly left me at a boarding school in Brighton, which, she had been assured, was very good. But good or not, I was very unhappy there – I was 8 by now – and one holiday (I spent the holidays with the Aunts Gifford at Bassett Rd) I wrote a miserable letter to her, depicting with aids of drawings, the frightful time I was having. (I was a little horror, and I suppose boys couldn't help bullying me & biffing me about). Mother, like the sweet soul she is, rushed up from Spain. Then I got measles, and she just arrived the day after. From then on, she decided not to let me go, bless her heart, and took me back to Spain with her.

That was 1933. I had a very happy time in Spain – as a carefree irresponsible infant would do in a country with a glorious climate, and I attended the Berlitz School there. Every year for a month or so we would come to England for our holidays, Mother & I. We once stayed with Auntie Ethel in Sherwood Forest, or Ollerton, rather – but generally with Mother's brothers & sisters in North London. In 1934-5 I went to a larger school in Valencia, and in 1936 I started Boarding Schools afresh. This was Park Lodge, Pau, Basses Pyrenees, France, and I had a wonderful time.

Even so, I was still a tick, a little horror etc. I went to Spain for my holidays, going home in a joyous crowd of other boys who went to that school, and who lived in Valencia. It was a very small private school, the headmaster being a retired English Major – but the boys were all (except me) American. We used to go skiing in the Pyrenees in winter, and had a very good time generally.

Manners were very strictly emphasized there, and one dressed into dark blue suits for dinner.

Well, in 1936 the Civil war broke out, and after a few months, I had to leave, by order of the British Consul. Unk was just Bank manager then. I went onto the "Repulse" which was just outside the harbour, then onto the "Maine", a hospital ship. That took me up to Marseilles, from whence I travelled up to England. Mother had to follow a month or so later. When school started again in September, I went back to France. Mother went back to Spain in January and after a while went to Madrid with Unk. (Gosh, I forgot to mention, they got married in August 1935). They had a very exciting time there, and had a few narrow squeaks – but were very happy; they'd been happy all along, anyway, being great companions. Well, I stayed my holidays at school, and went to England once, with the Headmaster & his family. In February of the next year Mother & Unk came back, and all was terrific excitement. In 1938, Unk couldn't get away for a holiday, but Mother & I went for a wonderful holiday to Scotland. And cruised around there around the Clyde.

We three had had some terrific times in the Pyrenees that spring, and Unk managed to come to Pau again for Christmas, when we had a great time again. Then he went back. Mother & I spent the Easter holidays at St. Jean-de-Luz – which was awfully good of her, since it was near Biarritz, where a girl lived with whom I was deeply in love. (The love affair, dear, before my third & last – and I was only 16!) Still, we managed to have as good a time as ever. Then Mother went off back to Unk – and I went to England to take School Cert. – & failed.

I then tootled back to Spain, and was very glad to be home once more. January of next year (I had been having French, German & Spanish lessons with a girl called Jean Bastide, with whom I was deeply in love, but who had other ideas, evidently), and a young Dutchman who I suspected of being one of the other ideas. His father later on was decorated by Hitler for the 5th column work he had done in Spain. In January then, I came up straight to Wycliffe (Jan. 1940 – I was 15), and at Wycliffe I stayed most holidays, or with Fred. I took school cert in July (1 Dist. 6 credits rather feeble – I suppose, to a Brainy Person like you!) – and Higher in 1942. Mother & Unk had come back in August 1941, and we had a very enjoyable and happy time together, in Bristol, Cheltenham, Lampeter, & London. Unk went back to Spain in January 1942 – and that is the last we have ever seen of him. Mother as you know, wanted to stay with me till I was called up – but in the end went in October, having handed me over to you, Bless you both.

And so there I am!

A very happy though difficult (at times) past, one or two heart-tugs nowadays when I remember them, but a lot of happiness and hope from my own point of view, for the future. Mother and I were the greatest of friends always, and shared in everything, and Unk was always happy to share with us, for he adored Mother, and loved me a lot. I think he still likes me, and of course, still likes Mother, though in that tragic inadequate & vague way. Oh dear...

[25.5.44]

... Hazel, this is a hopeless letter – I don't know what's the matter with me – it's not just being tired – I think it's something to do with being Rushed & – Got-to-clean-my-equipment-tonight-must-hurry-up-&-finish-this feeling, and I'm danged if I want to finish it. Time to think is what is needed.

... Oh I do want to do something in life & not feel a failure – 'cos I should think the worst thing is to let down your family – for you feel so ashamed of yourself that you tend to excuse yourself and vent your annoyance on other people... mmm... though it's amazing how cheering a black hour can be – you see (Oh I'm getting muddled – you'll have to sort this out). Pride is the foulest thing out – selfishness, Pride and Fear are all related in a way, and Pride is a horrible thing. It's a false sense of strength, that is what it is – and in marriage it is an awful "contra-lubricant" (if you excuse the word). You could call it resentment, too. But kindly give and take is surely one of the most essential things.

Then "scoring" is another bad thing. I've played golf which isn't my game really – all in give & take for you, and now you don't want to play croquet which is my game etc. etc. – see?

But softspokenness & honesty, as gently and courteous as possible, go a long way to alleviate any kind of Thing. And we two are funny sort of birds – without being vain or anything, I'd say we had the most wonderful material in us, which we must try & build up (and which I think we shall succeed in building up – even if in a rather muddled way just at first!). You see, apart from having all the Best, we also have a lot of things which go to making the whole thing far from an easy walkover (which of course would be horrid anyway) – we're both sensitive to an enormous degree, and "you-know-that-I-know-that-you-know-that-I-know-that-you-know" type! N'est-ce-pas and we're both rather liable to moods – not nasty moods, but different ones! Darling, it will be fun! And as you always say, always laugh at each other. Laughter is like water running over dry caked mud. In a short time it melts it down & washes it all away!

[29.5.44]

... My time is completely full now with work, learning notes and summarizing lectures – work rather after my own heart, actually: but then there is constant maintenance in brasses, bayonets and webbing to be carried out, as we are practically measured with tapes and inspected with magnifying glasses! Sentences are heard like:

"Ere, You!! On Report for being H'idle!! Cor blimey! My little kid o' three slopes her rifle better than you!!"

[*30.5.44*]

... We've been having terrifying periods called "Close Combat" in which we are shown how to push an enemy out of action without firearms etc. Dreadful periods they are, since we have to practise the things on each other. All very exciting. I'll teach you it when I see you next!!

The Drill we're doing now is just nothing short of – well, '!' We get so wet & thticky, and are dropping by the end of the period.

... But even if after all that we have a very wee house with nothing at all, it'll always be Home, won't it. One thing is rather important, though sounds a bit daft. Such a lot of homes (not yours 45 F. Rd) are spoilt by smells. Not Big smells, but faintly sickly stale cooking smells and stale cigarette smoke, and sweets & things. If we have to have a smell, let's cultivate our own! That's one very surprising thing about here in the T.C.D., the barrack rooms generally have no disagreeable smells (of cigarette smoke or anything) – and if anything, tend a bit towards a faint soapy smell, which is rather nice!

[*31.5.44*]

... But – sweet – I'm afraid I can't come this weekend – the stinkers – just won't give 36 hour leaves. Apparently it's quite universal, and no one in England can do it (?), so perhaps they're not stinkers... Our unhappy sergeant just managed to scrape one, then had it cancelled the next day!

[*1.6.44*]

... Drawing maps all the rest of the morning before break – then this afternoon we had our three ¼ hr periods, in the first of which I was in frightful agony, trying not to go to sleep. Every few moments the sergeant would undergo a fading vista in my eyes, and then suddenly reappear as I jerked awake! Then pay, then people came in with long faces saying, how they hadn't been able to get weekend passes -even-though-it was only for a few miles away. They are stinkers these army people, some of them. Fancy not letting a Father go home to see his wife after she has had a child – I'd like to write to the Times, I would! The silly thing is that the Army has some queer notion about owning you body & soul – which is rather an awful delusion for it to have! I don't see that it can expect a man to lose his freedom just because he has joined a cause which is supposed to be fighting for the preservation of that Freedom!

... Ooo, & did I tell you that I ought to be getting 6d extra soon 'cos I'll be Class I soldier, having served 6 months? Oh, I saved a £1 this week – I was hoping to come home, and was saving it for that, but since I'm not, here it is, with my love.

[*D-Day, the invasion of France, was 6.6.44.*]

[*6.6.44*]

...Today, I almost got put on a report for a dirty rifle! In fact, I did get put on one, but got taken off it again when the Sergeant softened his heart! Isn't the news exciting! 2nd Front and Rome all in one short space! Phew!

[*15.6.44*]

... I've been undergoing a change of Company – "2" to "3". The exam failure didn't make any difference after all, so I went up the normal way, and so did Bartlett. We've got little bunks – in a corner of a Nissen hut, and hundreds of pegs to hang our things, and photos hung up of our various wives & sweethearts.

... Line in 3 Company consists in very energetic training, but the discipline is much easier; things don't have to be as formal, the instructors are human, and drill parades are heaven compared to before. We work from 9.0 till 12.20; 1.35 till 4.40! So the hours are very easy. Yes (he said, anticipating), less than wot you do! But we double all over the place... though I'm B1 I can (I reckon) run faster & longer than any one else in our squad★ (vain fellow). And yesterday I came in 2nd in the half-mile race!! (We 'ad athletics.) (Everything is very schoolboyish here though, isn't it!)

★which isn't surprising as I'm easily the youngest by about 7 years!

[*19.6.44*]

... But I'm having rather a merry life at present: running about always suited me, and we have plenty of it, and bags of jumping, and some snoozing in the sun, and all kinds of things. This afternoon really was first class. We went to a large deserted and empty house where there were about five "booby traps" hidden in each room, and little groups of us went into different rooms and had to find them and not tread on them, or pull them, or anything, or else they would go off with a fearful bang (only caps, but they did, just the same!). Anyway, it was amazing where they'd been set. When you pull the cupboard down, it pulls a wire, which pulls the thing which lets off the boobytrap! And ones which are like this – when you tread on there [the loose floorboard] the thing goes off.

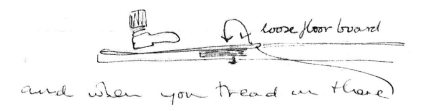

loose floor board

and when you tread on there)

Well, you'd probably think I did everything wrong and everything I touched went off (Oh you did, did you! – You Thing!!!).

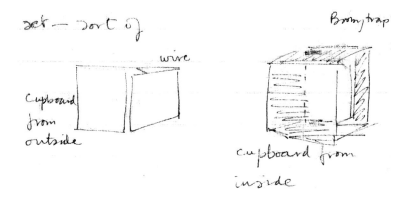

set — sort of

wire

Cupboard from outside

Booby trap

cupboard from inside

But not one went off, and I dismantled all the ones I found, and I found ever such a lot!! So There!! Neither did any of my squad, probably because, being nervous, we were all very conscientious.

[21.6.44]

... Watcher think? 1st piano concerto of Brahms – I rushed all the way to the wireless as soon as the strains first caught my ear across the distance. I listened to it, then two songs by Haydn, then (now) variations on a theme of Haydn by Brahms. (I think I was music-starved and that was why I was 'fed' – I am so wholly in love with music, that I suppose if I never heard any for a time I'd feel it without realize it! And now I realize that I haven't heard any for a very long time – about 4 weeks!)

[*25.6.44*]

... Sorry not to have written Thurs. Fri. & Sat. – but – well I was more like a caveman during those three days! And it was nice to hear you last night, but what a shock when the Man wouldn't let us have any more time! And we hadn't said half of what we had wanted, had we!

... I must tell you about Thurs. & Fri. We had a TERRIFIC time – in every sense! On Thursday morning we set out by truck, and were dumped on the moors west of Penistone. Bartlett & I were together, and off we went to a wee village on the moors. We made a map of it, knocked at doors and asked a lot of questions as to the local landowners & how many soldiers could they possibly billet if they had to? (All this was part of an exercise – not real thing!) – and some kind ladies asked us in to cups of tea. Then we made our way across the moors to a place called Snittlegate Inn – a terribly exhausting walk.

Then down into a valley, where all the others had assembled. Then all the afternoon we were doing a 'scheme' – i.e., we rushed up this huge valley in two parties, and fired across at targets, and finally made an assault on an imaginary position. I wonder whether it's possible to express how utterly done in we were??? We just gasped and felt awful – though it soon wore off. Then – the worst part, we had to retrace our steps –which meant climbing up all the way we had rushed down in the assault etc., and picking up empty cartridge cases! Gosh... Well, the afternoon passed somehow, and we went back to Snittlegate Inn and cleaned our rifles.

... Then that night we were to bivouac out & made sort of tents with our gas capes and lit fires and cooked meals. But at 10.30 we all paraded for a "night scheme" – and did a stalking exercise – crawling up to a house guarded by sentinels and trying to read the number chalked on the wall! If the sentinel saw you he could take you prisoner. Bartlett & I did quite well there. Back from the night scheme at 1.30 – and then, as I'd volunteered for guard, I was guard till 2.30. We arose at 5.30 the next morning and de-camped as quickly as possible. Off to Snittlegate Inn and received sandwiches for the day, and also instructions & briefing. Bartlett & another fellow & I had to find our way to a point about five miles away on the hills to the west, and make an enlargement of a map there. This we did with much puffing & blowing. The next objective was a reservoir another eight or ten miles to the west over the hills, so off we went on that. We had to cross some gigantic valleys and climb enormous mountains!:

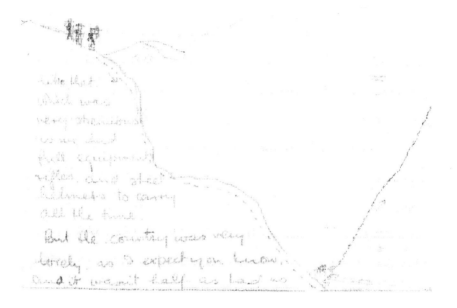

the day before, as there weren't N.C.O.s & the cameraman egging us on. Oh Yes, did I tell you – they were filming all this!

Well, eventually we got to this reservoir, and had a wash & a cup of tea. Then again over five miles of Peat Bog (imagine!), till we came to a little town in a valley. But the Peat Bog was dry – the difficult thing was that it was so uneven.

Anyway, we had a very nice cup of tea here, and cake or two, and then a bus took us all the way back to Wentworth. That evening we were all hobbling about like lost Souls!

The last part of the ordeal was the next day. When we ran in the Athletic Sports! I'd entered in for six events, but only did three, as they didn't require me for the others, having enough people already. But I ran the 100 yds, jumped the High Jump, and ran the ½ mile. That was frightful, as I was running rather slowly, and was in the middle of the rear position, when everyone behind me fell out, exhausted & done in completely! – So I finished the race – last man in! Disgrace... ! Still, our company won the sports, which was a very fine show, considering the scheme.

... I'm on guard tonight – groans! Bartlett & I will probably retire to some lecture hut or other and write letters, or talk! What we're supposed to do is: Perambulate the area (a distance of about 1 mile) three times during the two hours, and see that all is well. Not talk. Interrogate strangers who happen to come in and ask to see their papers.

As far as I can see, the Depot might be invaded by Zulus, for all the guard might know!

[*Hazel went up to Wentworth Woodhouse for two weeks from the 27th June to 12th July.*]

[*12.7.44*]

... Here I am at Matlock in an enormous hotel-cum-sanatorium overlooking a valley rather like Cheddar Gorge. The food so far is exquisite (trifle & peaches for tea!); Aelred (Bundle) and I have been very lucky in getting into a room the only other occupant of which is an R.A.F. corporal! Every bedroom has hot & cold water, and we all have mattresses & pillows, and comfortable camp beds... what else... Oh yes, and a marvellous looking N.A.A.F.I. with Palm Trees in it!! Ho, yes, a very fine place it is. Aelred is thinking (& so am I) that our slightest move is being watched – not seriously, but we like to think we are – microphones under the bed & things like that!!

[*14.7.44*]

... Phew, is it hard work here or is it hard work! We have lectures literally all day long, and I've taken so many notes that my writing's all wobbly! But otherwise, Life is very good here: hot baths in Refined Bathrooms are to be had at any time; beds are very comfy, and it is a dreadful business getting up in the mornings!

[*18.7.44*]

... I've a lot of silly homework to do in the form of exams and what not. I haven't worked so hard since I came into the Army! It's very – in fact – almost too absorbingly interesting – I am steeped in Security up to the neck now! It's all very great fun, though awfully concentrating & exacting.

[*Douglas got leave from 29th July to 4th August*]

[*9.8.44*]

... After this letter don't be disturbed if you don't receive any for a wee while: I am still at sea and living an absolutely lazy life; sunbathing, sunbathing, and yet more sunbathing! I do little else than do my diary, read the Bible, snooze, doze, and wooze (thinking of you).

... All sorts of craft are buzzing about; it's awfully interesting to see them & watch them – they're just like gnats! I've wanted to do some sketching, but it ain't allowed, worse luck, and anyway I couldn't bring my sketch book as there wasn't any room!

[12.8.44]

Hello My Darling!

Here I am at long last, and in rather confusion! We arrived latish and dropped to sleep thankfully in our tents. It was like a pailful of cold water, coming into France: In England, everything is so very different & peaceful (Malgré Les Buzz Bombs!) here, it is what is popularly known as 'stark reality'! But joking aside, it's all very grim: I only wish you could see it all – vast preparations, sunny & tanned soldiers in shirt sleeves & dust... and pervading all a relentless efficiency, operating like an automaton – everything impersonal, everything rather unsmiling yet very helpful – the very famous and great 'mucking in' spirit, where everyone helps everyone else. Ideally rather what one might expect – but the shock is there just the same. Through the dust over pot-holed roads, the roads full of soldiers and vehicles doing their various jobs – through the dust past the pathetic little fields of white crosses – sprung up in the past few weeks, and through the little villages, battered and crumbling in places, where little children squeak at you and people look suspiciously at you... Through mile after mile of the military and hardly a green field anywhere. But once you turn off the main way, you come to a saner France. We are camping in a lovely field in some beautiful country, actually, and it's good to be here, after the stress & strain of the main highway.

There is a canteen nearby, with some things there – I was able to get a few books. Do you remember that King Penguin book I wanted? I was able to get it! Of all the places I least expected to get it, by Jove! I enclose a 5 fr. note for you to look at (all right, I know you don't want it, but surely you are interested in it??)

... Sweet, if you are able to find it, could you send me that steel mirror Thing, as my other one was pinched, alas, and I keep on shaving parts of my face which aren't supposed to be shaved... —

also could you send with it a handkerchief or so, and make a wee parcel of it all, and register it, as I'd like to see if it gets here O.K. Would you please, darling? The things you're not allowed to send, apart from the obvious things like grenades and tanks, are foodstuffs and rationed goods, like butter and meat etc. Food here is the jolly camp food, and very good. One tragic thing is that I've lost my fork and spoon, and have to eat everything with my knife which is somewhat awkward, as you might imagine (Ha yes, I can see you imagining it!... grrr...).

[*14.8.44*]

Sorry not to write yesterday: I became involved in a tornado of fatigues: guard on Saturday night, digging a pit for the tent all Sunday, and also putting up other tents – then today I've begun a job in the office, which will last till I get a posting, I expect.

The weather's absolutely IT, and the sun pours down, warming everything & everybody – how is it with you? How are raids & things? – we're still in our tent, and as I said, dug a large square pit 2 foot deep for us to sleep in, as protection against shells if any should happen to come around, which they haven't yet.

The country round about, as I said, is really lovely – very English, only a little less green. The harvest has just been gathered in so we can't do any damage to the fields. There are (or seem to be) vast quantities of cheese about, of rather promising & tempting type. I must try & get some. One can get quite a good Camembert for a reasonable sum like 1/ -.

Planes are rushing about all the time, but apart from that one would hardly guess that a great battle was being fought less than 100 miles away. It's quite quiet, here, therefore, and very pleasant.

... (Don't forget – you need only put 1½d on your stamps to me!)

[*16.8.44*]

... Yesterday afternoon I went into a nearby town and spent quite a happy time wandering about by myself – I sniffed the smells, drank in all the colours & generally revelled in the glories of the continent. It was a feast day, and all the shops were closed and everyone was in their Sunday best. I went to the Cathedral and arrived in the middle of a service. It was very lovely in its pomp and beauty – I loved the music of the organ, too. And then there was a procession round the Cathedral – a wee provincial sort of procession, with the bishop in magnificent clothes coming just after the choir, and then some sweet little infants (girls) in white, with white flowers round their heads in garlands, wandering along with some semblance of order, and gazing wonderingly at all the people on either side – urged on by a clucking & elderly female...

Then the little boys, in two files, and down between them strode, hands clasped, a magnificent-looking person singing very lustily & deeply but keeping a very vigilant eye on his flock and darting a threatening look at anyone should he transgress in any way! – then all the Girl Guides & Boy Scouts – and finally all the old 'uns. from white-bearded aldermen to collarless (& arty-looking, such are Frenchmen) tramps. Some magnificent beards, egad – forked, tousled, pointed and spade like!

Then I spent the rest of the evening wandering about, and sitting under the trees at the NAAFI (very fine NAAFI! – very continental) – and after that, since there was a thunderstorm, inside, sipping tea & lemonade, & munching buns, biscuits, chocolate & toffee... !

[*17.8.44*]

... Life here is proceeding according to plan and everything. Until I do something I am working in the office & working very hard, too. Camp Life is getting more & more comfortable as we settle down – I now have a little night table ("Macleans Toothpaste" box upside down!), and a ledge onto which I can put my things. All I want now (as I've said before) is my O.C.M. (Oxford Companion to Music) Corlummeluvaduck how I want it!! There are masses of wasps about the place, however – that is the only flaw. Wasps in the tent, in the dining tent, on the farms, in one's bed in one's washing – what a time they have, the dears. Grrrr... Still, what are wasps but big grubs with wings, and what are grubs but little wormy things, and what are worms but caterpillars without feet, and what are caterpillars but young butterflies, and everybody likes butterflies. So we all ought to like wasps.

[*19.8.44*]

... Ho... here I am and the time is about 6.0 – I had a very jolly afternoon – firstly a haircut in a little barbers shop. The barber was ranting (quite intelligently) to the crowd of waiters against the Germans and their ways – all very favourable for us, I suppose, though negative criticism doesn't mean much. The question looms here of what-to-do-with-the-Germans-after-the-war. It's rather dreadful, all the things they seem to have done round here. I rather used to think (and still would like to think) that any German atrocity story was exaggerated beyond all proportions, but reports here show very similar stories to those which we hear to be horribly true. Oh, it's all very nasty indeed and one of the less pleasant things I've come into contact with over here. Oh dear.

But even then I fail to see what right we can take on ourselves to do anything to the Germans... But God only knows in what way we are to do it. The best way, I suppose is by Education. Education, however, will demand such a sacrifice from the Educators. What Englishman (or Frenchman or American) will be ready to give up say 20 years of his life to take part in a giant scheme for re-educating the German people? Then there may well be discussion as to a plan of education – the Pooh-poohers, the cynics, who in turn enrol more pooh-poohers and cynics around them. Yet there has been created in Germany a certain – well,

Energy (What our English bloodcurdlers like to call 'the tasting of first blood') – which surely could be turned in a good & constructive direction? Oh well...

Then after the barbers I scoured the town for a fork and spoon... and could I get them... Ha! (bitter laugh). The fork is precisely 4½ inches long, has a wooden handle, and two minute prongs. The spoon, on the other hand, is over a foot long, and is made entirely of wood. So. And actually it is too big to go in my mouth, it's original purpose being, I believe, to be used as a paddle for canoes. (Anyway, that's the impression it gives me.) Well, well I will have more Fun ahead in the Eating line. Tiddle-um-tum.. . !

After that, I bought two cheeses, one of which I am sending to you. I don't know whether it'll ever get to you, as on sniffing it it strikes me (very forcibly) that it may at any moment get up and walk off. (Yes, that kind of cheese) – Still, dear, it is a very famous brand of cheese, so don't grumble (! !)

... Then I tagged on at the end of a stupendous queue into the NAAFI. It became more and more of a crush as opening time (5.30) approached, and the cheeses (inside my jacket) rather took the strain! Anyway, by dint of the most frightful cheating and by-passing, I got in front of quite half the queue and by speaking nicely to the NAAFI waitress got 3 packets of biscuits, 2 bars of chocolate, 3 pieces of chocolate cake and two cups of tea!

... Yesterday after leaving the NAAFI I went to the cathedral & wandered round it... I saw, too, a reproduction of the Tapestry, which was in the chapter house: it was about 150 feet long, and 1½ to 2 feet high. It dealt with all Duke William of Normandy's exploits against Harold: all depicted and worked by his 'excellent spouse' Queen Matilda!

[*This was Douglas' cunning way of telling Hazel that he was in Normandy and Bayeux...this 'information' made it past the censor.*]

[*20.8.44*]

...Well, it's getting too dark to write anymore just to-night. Ooo, I wrote a Pome – quite a well-meaning Pome, though it looks a bit odd. Here it is...On the Desirability of Shaving.

> Of all things a Woozel likes
> Is perhaps a Pootle without spikes;
> For a spikey Pootle is a source of woe
> To the tender Woozel wot loves him so.
> <u>She</u> never grumbles, snarls or growls
> At the roughish texture of his jowls
> Nor makes true comments on his chin
> Or on the bristly substance of his skin!
> You know, a Woozel is a tender thing;
> You can be sure she feels it sting!
> So remember, as you wield your blade,
> A Woozel's comfort is being made.
> And Her happiness and comfort gained,
> What greater thing could be attain'd?

So there it is, with my best compliments!

... Rather rainy today, and consequently very muddy – quite warlike and life-in-the-trenches-in-1915 style. (Only there aren't any trenches, oh well.)

... It's rather nice, the rain pattering down on the tent – though the enjoyment stops as soon as one pokes one's head out of the tent. And it's a bit cold, too, that's the snag!

We were talking about Feeling in army Life, that is, how one is inclined, by dint of hard work and strenuous days, to lose for a while the aptitude to feel emotions like excitement, pity, remorse: when one has time to think, it seems that the sensitiveness in one has given way to a more passive form of thinking – It's a hard crust forming really, and "Routine Thoughts" are the only ones which seem to pervade, and imagination lies dormant for a while. It was so for me when I was at a harvest camp, once, I remember – and again when I was at Northampton and Rhosneigr – at times (not at the weekends!!) – but do you know what I mean? Perhaps that's why farmers tend to be unimaginative? But a friend of mine (the person to whom I was talking about this) told me a story of how, whilst he was in Greece, he "lost" his feelings; he was tramping miles every day over mountains, and was roughing it quite a lot. He spent the nights amongst the shepherds in their camps as he went along.

One particular camp he approached one evening, very tired, and as I said, he was feeling insensitive as usual. Being a normally sensitive person, he had being feeling rather worried that he had not been feeling anything at all: not feeling glad, nor being thrilled by the sight of the lights of the shepherds' camps over the hills, which were actually a beautiful and famous sight.

Anyway, he came to the tents, and was immediately assailed fiercely by sheep dogs, who barked and snarled at him. So much, in fact, that the shepherds had to pull them away. But he noticed another dog, a little dog, who didn't bark or snarl, but who was very friendly, and wagged its tail at him. He stopped at the camp for the night, and slept in one of the houses, and the little dog which had rather taken to him, slept up against him.

Now, since it was a shepherd's dog, he couldn't possibly take him, so he tried to shoosh him away. But the little dog just wagged its tail, made a little detour, and followed on again. He went on and on, and kept on trying to shoosh the dog away, but it wouldn't leave him. Later on my friend had to throw things at him to get him away. And in the very end the little dog did stop, and sat down on the top of a hillock and looked at him.

My friend went on, and whenever he looked round he saw the dog sitting there, looking after him, for miles & miles. And the thing was, that he felt very upset & sad about it, but suddenly also felt rather happy that he hadn't lost his feelings after all!

[*24.8.44*]

... Isn't the news bewildering and fast-moving? I wonder sometimes how such foul & ghastly wars can ever take place – it's funny, but most people (including me) can get hardened to a thing like war news – hardened, that is, to the stream of catastrophes, victories yes, and even atrocity stories. One can get hardened to them to such an extent that they fall on a thick layer of skin. But – just once in a while – I read a small bit of news or description or something – which is only meant to be insignificant and small, to be perhaps a touch of colour to a description – which makes me dreadfully upset and which more than anything makes me curse the war which brought such a thing, even though small, to pass.

Do you get what I mean, sweet? These bits are generally only little personal things and they might seem quite silly to others – but I find that they affect me very deeply indeed. Things prisoners of war do – not that I've ever met any – that one reads in the papers – men who are at their lowest ebb and who are pitifully in need of the godly things – and the feeble and pitiful things they do – deceits which are so absurdly easy to see through, yet so very moving. Oh I don't know, they may have been the worst atrocity committers in the world, but they're still children of God, and at that moment they're in need of Him. Oh I can't explain it very well, sorry!

[*26.8.44*]

... The last day or so has partly been spent in learning French slang – Ho, what words have I learnt! Truly terrible, really they were... I copied down the expressions at first, but they later on got so dreadful that I stopped! "Argot" it's called, due, I think to the fact that the most popular ending for the words is "-ot".

[*28.8.44*]

... We have heaps of discussions here over "what to do with Germany after the war" still. – Today we had quite an official one

– and people came to the conclusion that Education was the only way; Education and making the nastier types (like the S.S.) go back to Russia and repair all the damage they've done. Mmm, not bad; perhaps better than most. But how to do it?

We finally changed our tent site, and now we luxuriously stretch our bones (or spread our bones, rather) over a large area of tent the like of which we have never been in before. 3 to a tent-comfortably-holding-8! And we have ground-sheets all over the floor, making it nice & dry, and lots of boxes as cupboards and my little night-table just the same! It's such great fun. (Unless one has a Tummy). Oh, I want to go home... ! All the rest are playing poker now, there's so much room that 4 people can sit round a lot in the middle!

Darling one, I must seem like a never-ending demander of bounty – but could you – would you – send me some candles, please? They're absolutely invaluable in this land of no electricity – I'm sorry to keep on asking you for things! Could you wrap perhaps my woollen polo sweater (the one you washed) round them too? As I'd like it to wear.

[*1.9.44*]

... I got posted the day before yesterday, and spent yesterday being rather busy too. We all set off for a certain place, and I somehow got detached and meandered off on to the wrong road! I didn't realize that it was the wrong road until I saw, by dint of signposts & things, that I was getting extremely close to Paris! Which was quite wrong, so off I beetled – and then, to my horror and wrath, my bike stopped and refused to budge another inch. And to cap it, it began to pour with rain! Torrents & torrents and torrents!

There were two other motor cyclists there too who had gone wrong. So we hailed a lorry, hauled the bikes onto it, and buzzed off again, back to where I started. I pushed it to our former billet – (a lovely ivy clad house, very nicely furnished, with beds and what not – and very comfortable withal), and asked one of the section which had moved in after us whether he knew aught of bikes. He just got on it, and it started! So, blushing and hunched up with shame, I made off once more, this time taking the right turning. After a few more small adventures I reached my section, who were having tea. The billet here is very nice indeed, though inhabited, and I have a large box-spring mattress to sleep on. There is also a piano here which is good, as I hadn't touched one since I left 45 Fairdene Rd.!

... Some of the villages & towns I passed through yesterday were dreadfully knocked about – awfully sad, and so unnecessary, too.

[*2.9.44*]

We've been whirling about such a lot that I'm still spinning! Put-put-put-put all day! But it's great fun, believe me! But let me start nearer the beginning: We moved off in a sort of column, and I spent all my time buzzing past cars and things looking Very Important, and then maybe stalling in front of them all, start up again (by which time most of them would have passed), and then buzz past them again! Ho great fun indeed. And the French people! My, my, my, were they pleased to see us – we were pelted with pinks, carnations, roses and every vegetable (pleasant) under the sun! We were cheered, waved at, shaken hands with, and some blokes got kissed! (misericordia!). Not that we were by any means the first, but I suppose after the first scare of fighting had passed and things were quiet again, they felt quite confident and safe when a mere Div. HQ trundled through!

All great fun, as I mentioned before. And here I am resting, in a room of my own (unless bugs chase me out), with an enormous bed and box mattress all kinds of wardrobes and things. I have made it into a sort of office, with a large notice outside: "F.S.W." (Field Security Wing) – which is dreadful cheek, considering that I should be sleeping outside in a tent, not staying in a château which as far as I can see is only inhabited by officers! Still, I'm here, and nothing short of the Supernatural and/or a Major-General will dislodge me! I say, isn't the news good? Or anyway, was three days ago, which is the last time I heard it. All the people round here are extremely keen to divulge their dreadful secrets about How-the-Germans behaved. Which is quite true probably, poor things, but it gets awfully-the-same after about a dozen people. I don't actually mean to sound callous there, but they really do exaggerate a bit. Everyone too wants to dash into Germany and wipe them all out, which is rather bad.

[4.9.44]

... I'm now on detachment [*near St. Valéry-en-Caux*], and having quite a whale of a time, such are the joys of being on one's own away from the military world. But I don't know if it'll last long. Anyway, living for the present & all that, I can safely say that I and another fellow have our awfully nice civilian billet, with rooms of our own, sheets on beds etc. and are having simply terrific food – for lunch today we had an enormous plate of tomatoes, surrounded by eggs – as hors d'oeuvres – then beautifully cooked veal, mashed potatoes & onions, and then bread & some very good jam – plus cider and tea – a very French meal!

... We had great fun today, visiting mayors & people. One place we went to was a lovely little château [St. Laurent-en-Caux], where the mayor of the town lived. He received us into a very luxurious drawing room, and regaled us with glasses of Calvados – of which I had precisely one, and then wished I hadn't... I think it's a wine of the district we're in, hence the name.

We're right in front of the Gendarmerie Nationale, the police station – this afternoon we interrogated a bloke who'd been denounced by another bloke as being suspicious. What made it awfully funny was that we went in and found the denouncer chatting to the denounced one in quite amiable terms! Thence followed a terrific discussion in which everyone talked at the same time (save yours truly, who took notes) – and finally ended by the denouncer bursting into tears and saying that the person he denounced was quite innocent after all! Whereupon we sighed and the meeting eventually broke up...

Anyway, it's good to get away from the army sometimes!

... You know, we have a female with the section who does its cooking and cleaning up etc. We also have a cook, and also a driver. All this service for just 11 men!

[6.9.44]

... Me voilà again in a tent, after leaving my nice digs. Still, it's a big tent, and only one other fellow in it, who's a very nice bloke. [*This was Ivor Furst*]

[8.9.44]

... Sweet don't ever be anxious, it don't do no good, honest, it doesn't – don't! I might be just as anxious about you, and honestly have more cause – you cannot leave it in any other hands but God's, sweet.

[15.9.44, *near Harfleur*]

... Moi, qu'ai je fait? Hmmph... Well, I've been working quite hard the last two days, but of course can't tell You! Bless you... But it's meant standing in a road for six hours at a time! But the things I've been given! Peaches (4), Pears, tomatoes – eee! ho ho. Then every now and again the proprietor of a little café nearby comes & gives me glasses of coffee & cider (& cognac, unfortunately) – and invited me there to lunch today! And I had a famous 'Biftek' – Beefsteak, so wonderfully cooked! – mmm, and buttered beans! And I'm sleeping (so as not to have to come back all the way here) at a house nearby – or am going to sleep there, and have meals there. That is, if I'm not moved or anything before tonight!

... None of your letters or parcels are ever censored, you know. Everything here is settling down after the excitement and confusion, though the Place itself is quite flat... dreadful. People are quite pleased – in fact, very pleased to see us, and all seem to have been waiting for us these four years. Every day, they said, they used to tell each other that "Les Anglais seront là demain", and never gave up hope. The Germans took everything they could lay their hands on down to babies' prams and peoples' shoes!

And of course, spoons, forks etc. you know, we hardly hear anything of De Gaulle. He is mainly (I rather think) a figure-head for the Free French, in which they aren't particularly interested. What they are interested in, mainly, are the French prisoners (about 1 or 2 million) in Germany – which are much more numerous than the Free French, and being that, more likely to belong to someone's family, and not only the prisoners, but the thousands of Frenchmen deported to work in Germany.

They are quite personal, then, and are most absorbed in their own family affairs, without wondering about politics & general elections (except that they all want to 'coupe la gueule à tous les Boches').

[*17.9.44*]

... Ho, and still another day gone on the control post – ah me, and I am very sleepy, especially after supper. It was a pleasant (always is) affair – you know, a big round table with an oil lamp in the middle (no electricity just yet), and about six people all sitting round – making a terrific row (you know what Frenchmen are), all talking at the same time and laughing away – and one had a piano accordion on which he played lots of wheezy tunes – and everyone telling stories of how the Germans Did This & That, & weren't the British Soldiers Lads. (Whereupon I always assure them that with an English Tommy it's always talk and nothing really else!) – Oh, they're a marvellous family – so very French, & open & sincere. They say what they think, but they do it so gracefully that it never hurts or rankles. They treat me absolutely wonderfully and mother me all the time.

... You often hear blokes who've been Brothel-hunting, and "tart-hunting" – one of my CMP (Mil. Police) friends once went into one to see what it was like & sat down at a table (in the sort of buffet-cum-café there), and watched all the rushes and clamouring going on – but he soon came out, being a bit sick! In France they're all medically-controlled to prevent diseases & things.

... Sweet never listen to rumours – they're one of the army's worst banes – as bad as ticks, almost, and very seldom true. I had a many a miserable moment over rumours about leave & things. You know, some people (we had one) just invent them to see what happens!

[*21.9.44*]

... Yesterday I spent all the morning changing the inner tube on my bike! (of the back wheel), and I had to take the back wheel off – all sorts of Horrid Screws

and Things That wouldn't go, and spindles that wouldn't pull out.

So that in all, I got a bit Hot & Bothered. Enfin, I got it all off, and after putting in the new inner tube – a matter of about 45 seconds, I faced up to the problem of putting it all back again – and you know how Pootles don't have brains – only fluff. Well, well, some passing bloke helped with the pushing & squeezing, and we squozed it on again somehow, and the passing bloke went on. When I had tightened the last screw on the last bracket, and was about to say "Glory Be, I've finished", I found that a mysterious gadget had been left out of the inner works, as I found it on the ground, and the wheel wouldn't go round! So after saying one or two things, I had to take it off again!... Oh dear.

[23.9.44]

... Did I tell you I bought a pair of espadrilles yesterday? Ever such nice ones – rope soles, and brown cloth (tough) upper – very comfy. And all for 60 cigarettes!

[28.9.44]

... I also took my bike this morning to be improved with regards to its carrier-stand. Which is all coming to pieces. In a short time it ought to be O.K.-and-not-sound-like-twenty-rattle-snakes-anymore.

[30.9.44, near Dunkirk]

... I did quite a longish run on my bike this morning, on one of the best roads I've been on. You know, the roads round here run dead straight for miles on end, and you can always see the church spire of the next village at the end of the stretch! I think it's built specially so that the spire does look along the stretch of road. It's very pleasant, anyway, to think "Gosh the next village is 9 kilometres away – oh I can see it anyway!"

[*3.10.44*]

... I wrote a letter to Mother this evening & talked about Me & You., & what had she felt about it a year ago, & things like that. I wonder what she did feel about it – after all, yours (bless their hearts) is such an acquisitive family, full of affectionate creatures – but oh so acquisitive (n'est-ce-pas?) that perhaps she did feel a wee bit sad at first. When and if she thought I'd been raked in (!), and she hadn't been, & was left outside in the cold. But she wasn't, was she? Do say she wasn't, sweet, & when you write, tell her that – cos she perhaps feels out in the cold at present... Sweethearts are so apt to go into deep conferences with each other and forget the outer world altogether, that people outside begin to talk to each other, sort of, to pass the time of day, and to have company. But poor old Mother, bless her, hasn't anyone to talk to, or to pass the time of day with or to have company. So she mustn't feel she's left outside. (No one should really) – But Mothers least of all. Anyway, there's such a lot of love that there's plenty to go round (and to have second helpings... !)

... Do you think what I think when I open a letter from you? I wonder. When I'm all bouncy and agitated and not peaceful and fidgety I can hardly ever write a good letter which isn't composed of about two score paragraphs each two lines long, dealing with trivial things. It's only when I can settle down and think and take my time, & not be distracted that I can write at all the right way.

[*6.10.44*]

... I've had a mixed time indeed. It's been so tiring but so interesting... but oh I must begin at where I first did begin. The business, to put it vaguely, deals (it's one of the many jobs) in interrogating. Those last few times I've just been present while someone else interrogated – and terrific it was – and all the terrible things you could think. For getting, say, a confession out of someone is generally a bitter business. The threatening, the shouting, the pleading, the accusing – & then out it comes, and then things become much easier. But it's not pleasant, by any means. Last night I went to another town to be present at a questioning. There were only two of us, or rather three, with the prisoner, and in an empty darkish, cold schoolroom. We had one interrogation, a young boy, which didn't take long. Then a young of woman of 25 years old – which was a sad case, as she had from quite sincere & convinced motives, done great wrong: she was a fanatically convinced person. Also, she was a very lonely creature. All this made us feel rather hounds – Oh Lord, I hope she doesn't get what she doesn't deserve, not that our interrogation would tell either one way or the other, but somehow a sincere person is much more worth saving than one who sells for money things.

Anyway, it lasted till 3.0 in the morning. We were all frightfully sleepy at the end, and giggling sometimes to ourselves – the atmosphere having cleared up after she had got her wrongdoings off her chest, so that things were freer & easier. Yet it was an awful thought to realize the issues at stake, even if one were, for the moment, eased up.

[*8.10.44*]

... I'm getting all very excited because I'll soon be back with the section and so will get a letter(s) from you. I am quite 'appy, after a long day's travelling. Since we're just going through it's all right (I hope) to tell you we're just by Brussels. The C.O. & his merry little detachment trundled along, across the frontier, through the ancient battlefields of Ypres etc, & to a little place (where we are).

... And I must tell you what I did this evening. Making arrangements to meet a friend of mine at 7.15, I set off on my super-speedster to Brussels, getting there when it was quite dark. I felt a bit lost a first, as it's very big, albeit a simply beautiful place (as far as I could see), with merry lights and masses of people everywhere.

We must go there, sweet, in our Tour. I set out, after parking my bike, to find the Cathedral where to meet the friend. However,

I waited 1 hour for him & he didn't turn up, so I decided to gad about & see wot I could see. Sweet, it was grand to be back in a great metropolis, with townish & city people, & that worldly & rather sophisticated atmosphere (all very bad – but it was nice to see them again). There were crowds & crowds & crowds in everywhere. There were cinemas, theatres, cafés (& how!), & restaurants – in fact, it seemed quite peace-time. Well, I put my nose into several cafés, & at last found a quiet one, where I had a coffee ice cream (Café Glace). Then I realized I only had French money to pay for it! Which the waiter definitely refused. So I had to count out all the oddents & coins I had and finally made up to nearly the required amount (6 francs).

Then I tottered out, and was wandering along, when I caught a dim notice with "FIDELIO" written on it! I couldn't see at all properly, but was so excited about it I fluttered off & borrowed a box of matches from a Company Quarter Sergeant with a match I saw that the whole of Fidelio was being done by a Brussels' company! Then a pleasant sort of voice said something or other, & flashed a torch on it for me. We got talking, & when I said how much I'd like to hear it etc., he told me where to go if I wanted to hear some good music and finally invited me into the café where I'd just come from, & we had an iced sort of beer – which was rather nice, I must admit – & talked about music and everything under the sun! He is in the chemicals manufacturing, & is the manager of a works in Brussels, an awfully nice chap; young, & rather like Gil. We talked till 10.0, & then I came back, without crashing into anything and here I am!

... [*The next day*] in the afternoon, and after changing some money at a bank, we all went our different ways: a friend & I went to the Cathedral (St. Gaulle), which is lovely – some wonderful windows with a red & russet & brown colour scheme – then we went shopping & got various things – the shops are packed full of everything – and there's much more in them than in London! Then to a music shop where the good lady allowed us to sit in a while & listen to some records: we had Schumann's piano concerto & C.

Franck's symphonic variations – which was extremely pleasant...
went to the Opera!! eee, & was it nice.

At first I thought I wouldn't get in, and they turned the queue
away, when a boy came up selling two places, one which I nabbed
quickly, & the other was taken by an old lady. Since we found
ourselves next to each other, we got talking, & she told me that her
son had been in the Intelligence Service, & was dropped on
Belgium (after escaping to England), by parachute. But somebody
denounced him, & he was caught, & shot. Isn't that terrible? What
a swine to have denounced him, the denouncer must have been;
then she lost her husband a year or so afterwards, & that was all
she had, & now she is quite alone. Her son's fiancée was English, &
lived in Bournemouth. She showed me her son's letter to his
fiancée in prison the night before his execution – I wish she hadn't
– for it was terribly sad... The Opera was Bizet's "Carmen" – &
you can imagine how I loved the Spanish setting & costumes.

[*12.10.44*]

Wheee! & here I am back at section, & do you know how many
letters awaited me?? Guess?? Seventeen!! Gosh, I couldn't get over
it – eight from you, & nine from others – including two from
Mother... and how can I thank you enough for them all? Sweet, it
was a half hour of great joy, reading them, and I had a big grin (or
smile) right from the beginning to the end; I was so happy...

In the last billet I was at, the sanitary conditions (as usual) were
frightful – and the lavatory was adjoining the pigsty. There was
widish hole in the wall, and whenever I went in there was a
scurrying of trotters and an anxious snout would poke through the
gap, with two extra-anxious eyes above it – no doubt expecting
some food! Oh but it was funny.

... From our billets near Brussels (where we spent two nights &
a day), we were supposed to travel up north, but just as we started,
my throttle cable broke, and so I was left behind, & had to go to a
nearby unit to get it fixed. But all morning they tried to improvise a

throttle, and didn't succeed, & so up a truck took me to another unit, near Antwerp, who fixed me up in about five minutes! Then off I went through Antwerp, which is a fair-sized place, & a big port. There is a tunnel (road), which goes down just outside the city, and comes up miles further on, in the very centre! From there I took a wrong road (there being two places of the same name, and we were supposed to go to one, & I went towards the other) – and off I went, & then all of annoying things got a puncture, so I spent the night there with some very jolly Canadian Tank people, who were extremely kind & helpful. The next morning I took down the back wheel of my bike, and found no hole at all! So I put it on again pumped it up, & it stayed up! I can't think how it went down like that, with out an 'ole.

[*Douglas nearly crossed into No Man's Land during this 'adventure'. He called the 'punctured' wheel his little miracle!*]

[*12.10.44*]

... Today I came out on detachment again, & am with the same lads as those at Dunkerque. We're staying in a house, or two houses, & I have quite a nice little room in one of them. The only thing is that there is no electric light, but still, what am I to complain like that with the front only – er – let's see, well less than a hundred miles away anyhow!

The Dutch people (I think I said?) are rather different to the French or Belgians. It seems a little odd, but they are always asking How Are They Going To Get Paid for the billets, and things like that! That doesn't seem unreasonable, I suppose, but compare them to the French, who get violent hysterics if you ever even mention paying them – & they do seem rather business-minded!

... You know, I've only been away about two months – what must it be like for blokes away for three years! (touchwood) – for them to think of England, of the background behind the family stage – which has changed so much. Dreadful papers like the News of the World contain an awful lot of drivel, but in it today I saw an article by a very disgruntled ex-sergeant, who was finding life a bit difficult in "civvy street" – and you know, it is true: whatever one likes to say about the army it must be admitted that here are so many stand-bys, helps, and supports in it. The complete lack of responsibility of the soldier. He is fed, clothed & looked after almost fastidiously. He is given masses of cigarettes, every effort is made to speed delivery of his mail, his equipment is of the best & most serviceable. He is carried about in lorries & transport vehicles. Whenever the weather is cold he gets warmer meals & rum-rations. In addition to all this, he is made a terrific fuss of & regarded as a hero (& whatever many civilians have of their very best, they give to the soldiers). Then once out of the Army, which he has cursed & sworn at for three years, he finds that what had become almost subconscious in him must needs be rooted out. People aren't all out to assist him; he has to think – & provide for himself.

[*17.10.44*]

... Now that the long evenings are coming, & that there'll be more leisure, I think it's about time I stirred my stumps to do some more Christmas Cards – so, could you send me my paints, and two sketch books, please – next time you go home? Thanks, darling, if you would – and any odd scraps of good paintable paper you see about (I have a lot in a big envelope in my kit bag)? Oh & candles!

... Lots of music is playing inside me – the Mass, "Comus", & lots of other nice things – isn't it funny when music comes to one: I remember often on assault courses I have charged about, bayonet in hand, humming bits of Tchaikowski (I suppose he's suitable for energetic things like assault courses!) – and also quite deep thoughts would wander in, too.

[*18.10.44*]

... A sergeant with whom I am on detachment & I went to a theatre in a Nearby Town, and saw Shaw's "Arms and the Man", with Richard Greene... the production was excellent, when one takes into account the fact that things like scenery & decor are hard to cart around up to Bleak Outposts like this. The acting was good, too, and of course the play itself was extremely funny, & full of wit, as one might expect. We had seats 3 rows from the front, which was rather good. The scenery was all made of somewhat flappy cloth, but the theatre itself was jolly good. It is a theatre belonging to Philips, the wireless people who are from here. They have schools, workers flats, sports grounds, absolutely everything – it's an enormous factory too.

After that we trundled back to section, had a cup of tea, & buzzed home on George's motor bike in the pouring rain. And now am crouching by the paraffin lamp, with George on the other side of the table writing letters.

[*21.10.44*]

... About corruption in High Circles, I don't know much about Belgium – I think they have made quite good strides the other way, but in Holland it seems Definitely Bad, after what people say. And they're not starving in Belgium now – in Holland though they're not far off it alas, in the German occupied part, d'apres ce qu'on dit. Children are very thin, though – both here and Belgium (and France). Holland is a land which must have prosperity, and it is as essential to her as, say, baths are to the English – for the Dutch have such large families that Peace & Plenty is quite indispensable!

... About telling people where I've been, I think not too much unless it's just "in Holland" or places of passage, like Brussels. But you can wriggle & sniff with your snout as much as like – to yourself! You see, if it trickled along to an unworthy person (as it only too often does, with people), it is always useful for him, as the enemy intelligence works in so many queer ways – and also, their main way of getting the most valuable information is by making a big jig-saw out of millions of tiny little fragments. And like us, they are exceedingly patient and painstaking... I expect all that's very obvious, anyway! But still, sweet, be very careful; it's hard not to feel 100% secure & far away from Fritz (as you might well be), but he may be very near to you, just round the corner. Not meaning or intending to do you any direct harm, but just to listen for anything he can get, his snout quivers most sniffingly, almost as much as yours, bless you. There, after that lecture I'll behave myself again.

[25.10.44, from Boxtel, north of Eindhoven]
... I write this from an even different place! Moved even further on. This time we're in a German Mansion – I asked for a spot of help in cleaning up, and the lady who lived opposite asked two young maidens, and they went off and brought back a whole army of more young maidens, with pails, mops, pans, and they soon got to work with the first floor. It was very rowdy at first, as the whole time there was smashing of glass as portrait after portrait of Hitler or Goering or someone was hurled at a wall..! There was a picture of Hitler in every room. But they made a wonderful job of it and to-morrow they are coming to do the ground floor.
... The guns & cannons are going off round here and making an awful din – I don't know how far Jerry is from here.

[28.10.44]
... You ought to see my bed it goes right down in the middle!! It's up in a loft – rather fun, though cold.

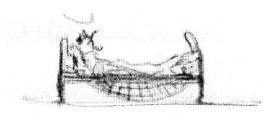

Darling, the High Church does elevate one's cultural self, and that is very right. But it tends to do so to the exclusion of that practical side of Religion which I think is so much more important – by their works shall ye know them: Christians there must be that do things, are examples to their fellows, & who stick to their guns & don't fall into temptations – those are the real Christians – I don't mean people like Auntie Ethel, who would be rather pleased if they had a sword & shield to carry round with them, so that they could slay all non-believers! – but doing things, quietly. ... The Quakers are wonderful people, yet what church could be plainer than theirs. Yes, & the Methodists too, and look what a terrific family you've got. Darling, it is the individual that matters – and when the individual worships, it doesn't matter where he is, though the church does make it easier for him to dwell in that state of mind, that blessed peace, called prayer. And I do think that the so-called low churches, like you, & me, & Quakers, get that atmosphere, and teach Christianity (for all our life we are in the school of Christ) better than the Higher ones. But, my sweet one, though we're all Christians, we must all have our individual way of working it.

[*2.11.44*]
... There is tons of noise going on everywhere – shall I tell you something? When one reads the papers out here, it's awfully funny but it seems so quiet where we are. One hears of massive battles going on, but only through the papers! And just tonight, for the very first time, when I can hear thousands and thousands of bombers flying overhead – I feel a wee bit "in the news" – not that the planes are attacking anywhere near here probably, but it's something "big" which will put me in relation with the news, somehow.
... My bike? er-well, starting from the front, this was the matter with it: the front forks were bent, the handlebars were out of line too, the nuts on the lamp were loose (my fault), the bracket

holding the front brake and air control lever was broken (not my fault), half the cylinder fins had been broken off, things were bent out of shape, the back carrier stand rattle (loose nuts – again my fault), the tyres weren't the correct pressure, and (horror, worst of all)), there was no oil! Also the bike wouldn't start. Oh, & the pillion was missing. The oil & the loose nuts were all I was very much ashamed of... but I would point out that the bike was in perfectly ghastly state when I first received it; half the fins were missing then, even. It had been in the possession of a person like myself before, so that was why. And, of course, another two months with me just finished it off completely, poor thing. Still, it has got out of the army quicker than I have.

... No, I am not in Germany! Every little push or advance we make towards the north or west we welcome with many a hearty cheer, as it takes us a bit further away from the place!... What heroes – I don't think... No, I'll tell you when I get to Germany, if I am allowed to.

[*5.11.44*]

... There are quite a lot of doings going on at present, as you probably will have heard from the papers. It was a terrific sight, to watch from the 1st floor of our house, the battle that was raging: A tremendous and continual thundering & roaring, brilliant flashes of red and white and yellow, a dull red glow over half the sky – and above it all the relentless tat-tat-tat of hundreds and hundreds of machine guns – & the "crumps" of mortars... In all, a very impressive and terrible thing to behold.

... I am sorry for having missed a day – but I was a bit busy – I went up Nijmegen yesterday! Great fun, and saw and went over the famous bridge. I went up there by car, a magnificent one belonging to an officer in our div.

... We've moved again. Oh gosh, what a life – it's not really so bad, and my lot is pretty good, but just as I get settled I have to buzz off again on my little bike (I have one on loan). This evening I went round looking for a billet, and found one very soon, at a policeman's. About an hour after I'd arrived, some CMPs & other policemen came in "because a man was here who spoke very good German, and so he might be a German!" What a scream... so I overwhelmed them with all my vast quantity of passes etc. and they departed quite peacefully, and I speak dreadful German, too! Tee Hee... and there are a lot of jolly Tank blokes as well – you know, Tanks are always marvellous people, ever so obliging & friendly...

... Of course, you silly old thing, all religions have something to offer. Each creed – or rather sect – is the path taken by one particular good Christian –The path he took, which was blessed and worked through to his salvation. He, believing in his path, told others about it. They followed it too, and they found it as wonderful as he said it was. Mind you, they are all Christian paths, and they all end up by God in that perfect state of mind which he first made up. All paths go to the same mountain, then, but they are a bit different to each other in the surroundings they go through. Some have a lot of wonderful views, of valleys, and trees and rivers. Others have nearer attractions, as precious stones by the way-side, others have wild flowers, others are plain – and so on (Bless you). You can always see the Great Mountain whither you are tending, if you only will take the trouble to look – and it's a good thing if you do, as it gives you great heart.

[21.11.44]

... I've been noise-battered today rather, and made very close acquaintance with all sort of cannonades, by having to pass right by them, which is very battering! Plus which shelling as well, and I feel quite tired, though extremely cheerful! (All that in the morning – in the afternoon I painted nearly all the time and Recuperated). I have Acquired a German Wind-jacket, too. It's coloured light blue, so I must get it dyed or something –will light blue dye green? It belonged to a Sgt. Majr, who left it behind when he quitted the place. There was another sight tonight, during a big to-do with noises – across the moonlit sky flew scores & scores of red points, all in orderly rows – flak I suppose but very impressive. A battlefield is generally lit up too at night (so as to help vision), and that is very impressive too.

[*27.11.44*]

... Oh yes, I've been Highly Gadabout – sort of! Yesterday was a glorious day from the weather point of view, & after packing, I asked Truce (the dark-haired girl) to come for a walk. (I also asked Ivor & John, but they were apathetic, rather & wouldn't come), so along we went towards Roermond, along a lovely road, and exceeding nice woods – then we called in at a castle, the lady of whom Truce knew, & had a chat there, and were shown a book with writings & photos of the 40 Allied pilots that had at one time or other been hidden there!! Then we got a rowing boat, and rowed onto the lake there – a nice big one, with woods all round it, and exciting creeks. Even though the winter was on the woods, there were some wonderful colours – in particular, a glorious assortment of mauves – gosh, it was lovely.

Then I rowed back, and we galloped along paths to get warm again cos it was cold in the boat (which had water in the bottom too), & finally went to the hospital where Jo (the fair one), is a nurse, & presented her with half a Mars bar (It was her shift that afternoon so she couldn't come out). I also promised a wardful of men some cigarettes – probably Highly Forbidden! And then back to tea. And in the evening, between air raids, we played Monopoly, & Jo, who had only played once before, won! And I asked them to choose two pictures out of my sketch book, as they'd been so good to us, & two Christmas cards. Jo took the first picture (the snowy one), & Truce took the Arch one. There it's gone... but I can always paint more! And they were sincere & good to Ivor, John & I.

... And we left, & travelled moiles 'n moiles 'n moiles, till we came to Somewhere Else, where we found an empty house, where we installed ourselves. Where it's damned noisy too! (said he, having just jumped 3 feet when some flak burst overhead!). Oh dear, my bed thing is hard! I had a wonder feather bed-cum-box spring mattress, with sheets... alas alackaday. Still, let's hope for a better place somewhere soon.

[*29.11.44*]

... yes, life is quite exciting at times, and all the things I learnt at Wentworth – especially regarding the motorcycling part, and one or two other bits! In fact, the m/c training at Wentworth was quite tame in contrast to what we do now! (all right, I'm quite O.K., and am very careful!). Shells cause fun and games sometimes, too (he said, shivering with fright!), but things like bayonet charges don't happen to us, thank goodness, and we really live extremely well.

I'm off to Brussels for a spot of 48 hour pass!

[*1.12.44*]

And here I am! We travelled down early this morning and nous voilá. A place to stay for two nights we found early on. Then a grape ice cream & a glass of wine, & a terrific dinner at the Sergeants club – and then – we went to the cine & saw "Pygmalion"! Isn't it great fun!

... It's quite amazing what one can get in Brussels now: toffees, chocolate – anything! Martin & I were eating toffee-apples at one point, & jolly good ones, too.

... Gosh, what a day I've had. Shopping... walking all over the place, meeting thousands of people I know, at I. Corps (Field), & the Sgts. Club, & finally the Opera!

... I went with an old friend I'd met here, and after that we had an ice cream & a beer at a very Naughty Ninety Café. Plenty of gilt & looking-glasses – a vast place it was: A terrific ice cream, too!

[*7.12.44*]

... Oh – yes, I had quite a nice motor bike inspection today! "Satisfactory" was very prominent in the remarks. But it didn't stop the workshop rats from keeping my bike for repairs and making me make the 35 miles home as best as I could! Huh! Oh, but it wur a damp day today, it wur... all spotting with rain.

... Friday / There and we've been shifted billets again. But are again very comfortable. I collected my bike, and it works now so smoothly and oilily that it's quite a Different Animal!

I went to a concert-cum-folly-show tonight, given by a Divisional Concert Party, all the Balmorals. Honestly, it was very good, and clean! Which makes a contrast when you think of all the gritty London shows, shown to (seemingly) tranquil people, and then front line shows which are shown to the hardest hit of all troops, the Infantrymen...

[*11.12.44*]

... Brussels is in parts very gorbalish. I was beckoned at, smiled at, leered at, in the dark & narrow streets at the back of the main shopping centres, flashy young barmen laid hands on arms and said "nice cognac in my 'ouse, yes" – oh, very metropolitan... (Ho, and what was I doing in the Dark & Narrow little streets?! – nothing, dear, just wandering about, occasionally getting lost!)

... The Black Market in Belgium is absolutely amazing – people just can't exist on ordinary rations and have to buy off it. In Holland it isn't so blatant, but it still exists. In Belgium they (the Govt.) don't do a thing about the Black Market – it's just tolerated, that's all!

... I'm spending a very lazy morning but also very happy I'm writing this letter, and listening to all sorts of nice things on the radio. I like the Home Service programme, it's wonderfully quiet after that appalling Forces thing.

[*14.12.44*]

... My feet are cold!... We've moved billets again and are now in a palatial billet, but oh – so cold! Brrr... No coal, that's wot it is, none at all – or next to nothing. Warfaring is much more pleasant (wrong word, quite! – less horrible) – in summer than in winter. Not that this here is warfare at all! There, and the fire has gone out.

... There, and another day – mainly spent in getting things like cookers repaired and paraffin stoves to warm our toes in the evening, all the administrative side of things & no work.

... Darling, I love you. I'm thinking of you now at Oxford, attired in an impressive gown, and sweeping across New Inn Hall Street with a lot of books under your arm...(and you didn't recognize me that day either!) – and all sort of brilliant and rushed. Oh bless you, you're a clever thing, you know. They'll say "yes, they get their brains from their mother, of course" (and of course, their unbounded beauty and thickness from their father. hem!) – Oh dear Bear, who would have thought that we'd pair off – when Clive first spoke to me of you? He said "I shall be coming up to Oxford to see you; I have a great friend there, called Hazel Collingwood, a sister of two O.W.s who were at Wycliffe with me – she is very cultured, and likes music and drama; so you ought to have quite a lot to talk to her about.........she will show me round Oxford...." and I said "Beg pardon, but she will show us round Oxford" or something like that! And then he spoke some more about you, and said some very Conceited Things, Too! Ho....

And then I met you, over a custard & pineapple tart – or rather, in Carfax, and then we went to that little snack bar affair, and that was the 5th of November 1942. And on the Sunday you had lunch with us in the Stowaway, and then buzzed off again very quickly...mmm....Gosh, I'd like to read my diary again for those days. You know, I thought the most funny things about you! Reely, I did. Isn't it funny that when we don't see the private lives of some people we know, we often give them vivid and fantastic characters in our mind, whereas their lives and doings are almost the same as our own, their morals and opinions just like ours, and their aspirations and ideals very much akin to ours too. So whereas I thought you (as I did all theatrical people) dreadfully arty, loose-living ('scoosee, dear, remember I don't now!!) and altogether a stranger to my ways (or what I thought were my ways, in my childish – or boyish-priggishness) – there you were, a dear woozel under all your beauty and energetic manner! Ho, but I fished it out, or you fished me out, with your little 'ook...!

Oh sweetest, that was a natural and uninterrupted course of events, and I hope that course will never be interrupted or frustrated in any way. Gosh, how I pray that.

And I've heard Beethoven's 2nd Symphony, too, for the first time! and a Concerto Grosso by Handel. Then Tchaikowski's Nut-cracker Suite, now his piano concerto No 2! I've never heard that before either so I am being very lucky tonight. (Hm... he said, as the concerto proceeded!)

[16.12.44]

... Well, Pooh Mary Bear, the situation 'bout leave is Thus: On Jan 1st (all being well and it not being cancelled), 1000 wallahs will buzz off: Jan 2nd also, but Jan 3rd 3,000 will go: Then from then 3,000 will go every day. Well, naturally, those who arrived first will go first. Then those who came on D day will go first. There are "Batches" – and those over here who've had 6 months by 7 Dec. are in the first batch. There are 5 in our section who are thus. This batch will have to ballot to decide the order of going. One batch done, they'll do another, & so on. Now d' you see? So I might get in in Jan. or Feb (or even Mar. or Apr!). [It wasn't to be until May / June]

... Darling, do you know where I want to take you? Pau, in the South of France. I want to take you to a hotel there where there is absolutely first class food – called Hotel de la Paix, and I want to show you the Pyrenees from the Boulevard. I want to take you up into the mountains – to the Cirque de Gavarnie, to the Pont d'Espagne, to the Pourtalet, to Gourrette, the skiing centre to Lourdes, to St. Jean de Luz, to Biarritz, to Bayonne, where the best drinking chocolate in the world is made, mark my words!

[*Christmas Eve and Christmas Day 1944*]

... A very Merry Christmas, Beloved – and 'twas the first thing I said this morning – to your photo! I have all my cards out on a table in my room – Ivor and I are in some very nice billets, and are very pleased with the way we've managed to be there for Christmas day. And now I await the mail, though goodness knows what right I have to expect any – I had nine yesterday. I made myself a khaki tie out of a shirt (army one, dear!) last night, but it wasn't much of a success, as it was miles too short (wouldn't even go round my neck!), so I had to tack on another bit, which made it all lumpy and Funny.

... There, I spoke too soon when I said we were comfortably ensconced for Christmas, for twixt the last bit & this we've moved – goodness knows how far, too! But here we are, quite happy, with an enormous meal brewing up – in a nice billet again, too!

... I say, though, it's wonderful weather – cold & crisp and clear as crystal. Not much fun on a bike as it's cold, but very lovely indeed. Frost, and things like that. This evening we put ourselves into a hotel, but got kicked out by some magnificent officers.

Dear me, once I've been Moved and Shaken Up & Down, I can't write properly, and write in little bits and dashes. Sorry, old thing. I wonder when this letter will get off – when we're moving it's very hard to get a letter off...

[*26.12.44*]

... Darling I do hope you are having a good holiday and are also resting a lot too. How about air raids? This place here is swarming with all the worst noisiest inventions of the Hun! But what lovely country, indeed – this morning Martin & I went for a wonderful walk through the frost – and this afternoon climbed a mighty hill (or hills) through forests and just terrific country. And what with the Belgians being so nice to us, we are very well off.

[*31.12.44*]

...I say, for goodness' sake don't believe what you see in the papers about the German Report about the 51st – cos it's hopelessly untrue! I don't know where they got the idea at all. (Still keep even the denial to yourself, aye!). We're in Belgium, but – well, the Germans aren't telling the truth there, so there!

... Yes, we are bound together by a Spiritual Contact, sweet it was nice of Deryck to say a thing like that. Oh Bless you darling there are all sorts of contacts as far as I can see – every one I can think of, every side of Life & Love leads to you, in my mind. Spiritual values, ties and contacts are the substantial and real ones

... Gosh, what an enthralling thing "Scheherazade" is – I do wish I could explain that passionate sublimity which flares up in me when certain phrases and successions of notes occur as several do in that wonderful work. Again it's the Love of harmony that gives the igniting spark to the forces of different chords – thus producing a terrific mental and spiritual flare-up which sets my heart beating & thumping and my whole soul radiant. What a Love is music, & what a music is Love!

Douglas' photos of Hazel went with him everywhere

Douglas in Belgium with the Collas family and on detachment

Douglas in France and Germany

Douglas' 21st birthday present, July 1945

1945

[*1.1.45*]

... And the first two lessons of my course have come! The first is called "The Beginnings of English", & is a little sort of pamphlet – dealing with early ballads, Chaucer, early translation of the Bible & so on. Tell you more about it as I do it!

... I think the form for leave is that you get 9 days from when you disembark to when you report back for embarking again, so that will work out nicely, won't it. Working out at an allocation of 3 a month I ought to get it by April or May – but the allocation might well decrease, or anything – I don't see any big offensive coming off while people are buzzing off on leave, and since presumably there'll be one, we'd better not plan (trying to be dismal & pessimistic, I am – but it's as well if we don't plan too definitely, mmm?)

... There's a lovely piano at the billet, in a little room by itself, and I go there most of the day and practise to my heart's content. The owner of the house, a very decent bloke plays the violin excellently, and (horror), wanted me to accompany him today on the piano – which of course I did, or tried to... mmm! I've painted a picture tonight (of the park), and am going to give it to them, as they've been wonderfully kind to us all. It's a nice picture.

Masses & masses of trees, and some terrific wintery colours (hem!) – no but they really are good, blues, red browns, mauves, greens,

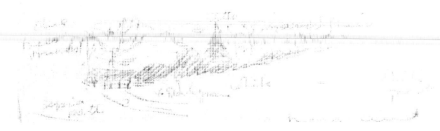

& all the colours between. I hope it won't look different in daylight. [*This was in Tilff, with the Collas family.*]

... These beastly buzz-bombs give me the pip. We've had masses & masses of them, curse 'em.

[*8.1.45*]

... Yesterday & today were spent in sitting in a cab of a 15 cwt truck (thank Heaven it wasn't on a bike) – along roads... Gosh, I've never skidded on so much ice before... Now the snow is mounting up & up and getting whiter and whiter. Everything has lost its shape, and has an eiderdown of pure white over it. The woods are just like Fairyland – absolutely wonderful, what with no colour, but the finest shapes and suggestions of shapes possible, and an unreal look about it.

[*10.1.45*]

... Being strong & definite in conversation is ever so good, bless you – what a sensible one you are. – I'll keep it very much in mind. Sensible Pooh, & you are strong & definite really yourself, for Mummy-Kanga says so! So there! & Deceiving is a wrong word – you're not deceiving yourself that you're clever – you're realizing the Intelligence which is in you – which God gave you, and which is Yours. Bless 'um!

... Today I actually went on my mo'bike to a place – but oh gosh... it was so cold! I had ice forming on my cheeks and eyelashes, absolutely horrid. And Ron Jones also went on his bike, and an icicle formed from his poor nose! And he had to stop to break it off... (the icicle!), EEE, but what a frozen world this is just at present...

... I got very involved with a sentence!! – the captain was arguing about Russia, and the wireless was blaring, and some rather Frightful Remark trickled out of my pen, I was that distracted – so x'coos mess.

[*11.1.45*]

... Then was upbraided by the Captain for having forgotten something in a job. That made me feel fed-up. Then later on at tea all the section (Ivor being on leave and Ron J. being on detachment) began popping little attacks at me on the old subject of women. "Why don't you get experience before you marry, it's hard on the girl etc. etc. etc. if you don't know anything about it." All that kind of tripe, against which I argued and said what I thought etc – the end of it all being the Capt. said he thought it was a very fine thing wot I thought, but he hoped I wouldn't crash down into an abyss of immorality etc. Phew! So it ended well, after all. But what an argument. Generally there is Ron Jones to link with and counter-attack in strength – and if Ivor is there... well, he knows both sides and pours scorn (and how)... oh dear, well, he'll be back soon. And then I thought how I loved you, and there was the best feeling – what a mélange, though...

I had a haircut today... great event, egad!

[*14.1.45*]

... Eee... there's a conversation going on about marriage now. Mmm... Our Field Security Officer married when he was 22, and said he has been terrifically happy ever since... (out of the 6 married men, only 2 have homes of their own – and both of those married before the war)... They think that it was much more fun going through the "Struggling part of Life" with a wife, for wives help not hinder, and it's easier with two... oh now one is saying how he went to prison for two hours for kicking a football at a policeman by mistake – the conversation is veering off.

... You're extremely right when you say that each subject has it's own vocabulary – not only each subject, but each particular branch of thought & life – C.S. certainly has a vocabulary – that's why so many people misunderstand it – because they just don't realize what the words mean, and what C.S. people are trying to put over when they say them.

[*16.1.45*]

... Some days ago, we got a taste of what we were fighting: we came to a village which had been occupied by the enemy – the place was some way behind, and the inhabitants were there. But, the state of it... All the windows were gone – all the furniture in the houses had been burnt, the pictures on the walls smashed, mines everywhere, shells and grenades left lying about, everything filthy and dirty – all food, fuel and things of value gone. And why? There hadn't been any bombardment or fighting or anything, in the village – the Germans had just been there, "stayed & lodged there" – then gone when they withdrew.

Perhaps the saddest thing of all was that they had taken all the menfolk of the village with them. What happened to them, no one knows – we can only pray that their lot was not the same as those unfortunate men, 35 of whose bodies were found in another village, who had been taken from their homes in their villages during the withdrawal, and shot in the back of the head one by one. The German in masses can do the most horrible things, unheard-of and unbelievable acts, which people in England don't believe either. You see, sweet, to combat evil, you've got to know it – turning your back on it is just getting nowhere (I'm not saying that you do!), but a lot of people don't quite appreciate what the population over here has gone through, I'm afraid. And what they are suffering now either. The habit of pigeon-holing nasty subjects has long been a very comfortable trait in the English mind – but it savours a lot too of the line of least resistance, and doesn't further understanding of others' suffering.

[*18.1.45*]

... Today I've been dashing around madly looking for billets – I found enough for the section, with a café to eat in and cook in, so that's all right. Ivor has been indoors or in bed all day because of feeling a bit wuzzy which was fortunate in a way, for looking for billets with Ivor, bless him, is rather dreadful business, as he goes round in circles half the time and can't decide or ask. Still, I expect I do the same if I am with anyone! I called in at a shop to get some aspirins which he had asked me to get, and the chemist asked me in for a cup of coffee! He had a very lovely fair wife and two children (3½ & 2) – and we talked for a long time on Things in general. A lady who was also there said that her husband (a school teacher) painted too (..!), and played the violin – then the conversation veered round to the Flemish people, and the chemist pointed out that nearly all the best painters were Flemish! Rubens, Van Eyck, Rembrandt, etc – and as for musicians, Beethoven was Flemish!! (? was he?). Then I saw some of the pen & wash drawings of the above lady's husband, which were very good indeed – lovely, in fact. (All this, of course, was in French – I can't speak Flemish for nuts!) A very nice family, anyway, and a sweet little puppy too, about 3 weeks old!

[*19.1.45*]

... I've done a dreadful thing! You remember I said I had acquired billets for the section? Well, the eating place was a café, and now it has turned out that it is a Highly Doubtful

Establishment – in fact, there isn't any doubt at all about it! I didn't know it was one, and took them there in all innocence! But as soon as they had been there a few minutes, they knew, being Experienced. Of course, they are vastly amused, being hardened etc., but it's certainly rather a business, and a policeman was with me when went there first, so, really... ! Dreadful... Two of our blokes were in a spare room in the café, and they didn't get any sleep all night! Oh dear.

... Another of our blokes has come back from leave – he says, like Ivor, that the travelling was absolutely awful, but it was great, being home. Apparently, one spends 20 hours in a train getting to Calais. Ho Ho.

... Sweet, I am always having arguments with Ivor on the subject of a Benevolent Influence (a loving God) in life – he thinks there isn't any, and that this world is a frightful place, what with all this suffering in it. But, be that argument what it may, there are certainly one or two things which give glorious and pure feelings in the mind of man – the greatest of these is hope – perhaps it is different for young than for old people, but I know that when I think of you, and hear of events which point to the end of the war and our separation, I get a terrific kick out of that Benevolent Inspiration called Hope. The opposite of Hope is not despair, it is Dudgeon; I'm sure of it – Dudgeon is the enemy of Happiness, Hope, Love, a marriage – everything; existence without life, existence without meaning, existence without Hope. And Dudgeon settles when Things go on without ceasing, without incident, & without ideas of the Future – Hope. I think it is a whiskey night tonight, so I'll be writing letters – crumbs, whiskey night in a brothel... ! Yes, a bit thick, considering it's my fault they're here! I'll definitely be writing letters!! Let's see, Cyrilino, Mac., mmm... aren't friends fun. You know, motor bikes and cars need maintenance, but so do friends (and husbands & wives). Friends are much more important than bikes, but we are never told to be sure to write to them, I wonder why. They're much less messy, too.

[*21.1.45*]

My Darling Pooh,

Just a Beginning to outline the events of the day. Firstly, pending the absence of our cook on three days leave, the section was left cookless and volunteers were needed. (mm!)

Ivor, in a fit of Rashness, combined with weakness and Good Humour, suggested that we (he and I) might conceivably think of perhaps – for a joke, almost – tender a mild offer – purely as a gesture, of course – to help with the cooking. We were naturally expecting (and hoping) for this offer to be hastily turned down and roars of hearty laughter to ensue. Unfortunately, though, someone overheard this conversation, and our Sgt. Major soon learnt that Furst & Gifford had volunteered to be cooks! Imagine, then, our sorrow and despondency when... but enough – needless to say, at 7.30 this morning I started to get up, and from then on the section's appetites Depended on us.

However, contrary to what you might think, Breakfast was a success, and so was dinner. So we decided to actually Do something for tea. So, to a vast quantity of de-dehydrated potatoes, mashed into a sort of mash, we added two tins of salmon, two tins of sardines, one tin of condensed milk, carrots, pepper & salt – and on the top, large slabs of cheese.

Then it went into the oven to bake. In Ivor's billet I wrote a letter to Cyril while it baked, which it did, very well, and was (I think) quite a success at tea-time, for the section ate nearly all of it. (I <u>must</u> say that most of the hard work in all this was done by the excellent cook's boy – who gets up at 6.0 every morning – but we were definitely responsible for making, cooking, & waiting on the others. Also washing up!).

Then after the day was finished, Ron, Ivor & I sat in Ivor's billet and talked & chatted & ate apple tart & drank tea...

[The next day]

... I <u>hate</u> getting up – I'm ever so lazy! – I think "ah, must get up", & shift my position – whereupon I find it is such a <u>much</u> more comfortable position, I stay like that for quite a time! Then I move again to an even more comfy posture, and so on. In the end, when it is getting so late that it is hardly a joke, I sit dopily up and (if it's cold) put my vest on & my shirt without getting out of bed! There, now you know! When it was really very cold, in the Ardennes, I used to take my vest, shirt, socks etc under the clothes, & disappear for quite a time, coming out quite half-dressed! Oh, but you can't be interested in all this, what am I talking about it for. But it all goes to show you that I am a rather (no, very!) lazy Pootle, compared to my Henrietta, bless her sweet heart!

Ivor is asking me how to spell words like "volunteer", & things like "fish", "tinned" and "mess" are slipping out, so I know what he is still writing about!

[24.1.45]

... As I said, we have left our last billet, and are now in a much better one. The Café was an awfully sad place, really – the "girls", whose ages varied amazingly – weren't many, really – about four; but the dreadful lives they led, quite apart from their "profession" – they seemed to sleep on the café floor, eat the left-overs of our meals (which certainly weren't much), and the saddest part were the two youngest were only 17 – just "started" the horrible job – and there was also a little girl of about 10, who was about all the time, and who looks like growing up into that dreadful place, & unless something is done to remove her to a better atmosphere to become one too, if they aren't careful.

But it wasn't really a brothel qua brothel, it was rather a sort of shady meeting place, with the opportunity & all that. But it was sad, terribly sad. And rather pathetic, on Sunday, when some dressed up in their best to go to church! Oh dear, anyway here's hoping the end of the war gives them something better to do.

[*27.1.45*]

... My letter of the 12th was Censored & Sent Back by someone 'cos I'd explained the Morse alphabet to you in it!

[*30.1.45*]

... Ivor is now writing <u>you</u> a letter, and has a grin from ear to ear – I wonder what he's writing about? The Snerge...

My Dear Hazel,

I have been intending to write to you for some little while but the "exigencies of the Service" has made it difficult. Now I am settled (for the moment), in a billet which at times is conducive to letter writing and I thought you might like a short report – Especially on our mutual friend!

Well – he has not changed in spite of the fact that I was almost 15 Days away and therefore unable to look after him. He still writes umpteen letters – strums away at the piano whenever he gets a chance, paints pictures and reads – gets up horribly late and goes to bed in the early hours of the morning – all this whilst Russian Armies thunder across the East and the British American & Canadian freeze in the line.

At the moment I am sitting in the living room of our billet – there are <u>12</u> others sitting around – 4 playing bridge – 1 playing the piano, 5 having an argument round the fire – I have been straining one ear to hear the Brains Trust but Giff – well he of course is taking my half the table with a mass of books – papers –envelopes, "Listeners" – "New Statesmans" and paintings, quite oblivious to the fact that he is not (quite) alone.

There is a rumour that our War Establishment is being increased by a further 15 cwt Truck in order that Giff can move his kit to our next location. Try and contact Buzzie if you can – she may be staying a couple of months in Sussex in the Spring which is an easy journey from Coulsdon – it is about 9 miles from E. Grinstead, so keep in touch.

Well Hazel – don't worry – why even old Giff does not know yet he is in the Army!   Be Good, Yours,   Ivor

---

... To-day it has been snowing as usual. On the radio they said cheerfully that "in the straits of Dover the temperature had gone up to freezing point" but apart from making us all laugh heartily, it didn't exactly Help.

... Mother said "I read in a book that for perfect love between two people the man must be father, brother, lover & child of the woman". I wonder where she read that, bless her. Oh, she had received the photo! and was exceedingly pleased with it. Darling, if and when I get leave, let's have a snap or photo of us to-gether taken, for her, shall we?

[9.2.45]

Hallo, you Thing, and many thanks for a nice letter yesterday – bless 'um, I wonder if you're feeling tired & quiet, like I am – I think it must be the time of the year – perhaps February is like that, like it is in bits of winter (mournful start for a letter: sorry, Bear!) – but I have been having my head banged about with artillery and blast and – had-a-puncture, and all-in-the-mud, and Spent all the day mending it – but I feel a bit better now... Oh dear... I'm tired, that's wot it is, & I didn't have (much) lunch. [2]

... Being abroad makes one's understanding so much broader, and helps like anything to help friendships between peoples – it makes everything broader and takes away pettiness of race and lots of narrow-minded-nesses and intolerance. But I must have said that lots of times, too – Dear Sweet – I should be saying exactly the same thing if I were in your place but, you Old Thing, you're being very – I just don't know the word (there's an air raid on at the present too, and my mind is a bit confused!)

... Mmm again – this Ack-ack is driving me daft (dafter).

---

[2] A major offensive took place, near Cuyk.

[*15.2.45*]

... What with Prisoners of war having to put things like knives, pens, scissors etc into a general lot, I collect a lot of them (if no one takes them they are buried or burned so I'm <u>not</u> stealing – just in case you imagine I'm a Looter!) – but I will try & be good & only have just three pannier bags & one rucksack – er one big & one small pack, & one blanket-roll and one other rucksack. There! Not very much, really.

[*16.2.45*]

... To-day I have been – er – maintaining my bike! Coo-er – I greased the nipples, tightened the nuts – took off the backstand, oiled the chain, greased the battery terminals, took off the top & looked inside, repaired the rear light, put metal padding under the clutch control, mended the High Tension Lead (or rather George the Sergeant-Major did), put petrol in the petrol tank (!), pumped air into the tyres – apart from cleaning the whole thing (helped by the kitchen bloke) – so There You Are, I am a very Conscientious Fellow, for to-day at least (er, inspection to-morrow). Oh, aren't I a low type of un-mechanical-minded specimen – the scum of motor-cyclists, a dreg of the DRs (Duty Riders)... alas (tears). But I'd do it again – he persisted through his sobs – I'd do it again – I'd grease my bike's nipples, tighten the nuts, take off the backstand, oil... he went on, but finally succumbed and threw himself on the floor in a paroxysm of desperation. Aaah... !

Cor, wot nonsense. One wod hardli think i was a clevver an' educeated purson, wod one. Hooray, here's another page – now I wonder what I'll say on it. My mouth tastes of petrol, my hands smell of petrol my ears are full of petrol, my face is covered in petrol, my gloves, clothes & boots reek of petrol – now guess what I cleaned my bike with? Well, fancy not knowing... Fluff, that's what it is... No brains at all.

... Ivor hasn't really got more <u>junk</u> than I – he just has more Property (spare pants, shirts, boots, civilian shoes), and Dignified

Objects – not clogs, books, chocolate, candles, candlesticks, boxes (empty), parachute silk, German torches, knives, ammunition, magazines, paintings, stamps – to quote one or two of them like I have... Well, well, how nice it will be for you to Look through It all (Pooh recoils in horror)......

[*18.2.45*]

At last we have left our beloved billet with the large family, the Manders in Cuyk, and moved to a place some seven miles away [*This was Gennep*] – and it's one of the most dreadful places I've ever been – sweet, it's awful; a dead and shattered place, and looted everywhere. I've never beheld such aimless and twerpish destruction. We got a billet – a shattered draper's shop, with no windows, dirt & filth everywhere. Collars, sheets – all lying about – at the back, plates & crockery smashed, chains, pumps, clocks – all without rhyme or reason. There are no civilians, and perhaps that is why there is such a Mess. Oh dear.

[*20.2.45*]

... For, as we get to know each other better, and the years go on, the spiritual takes the place of the material, ideas take the place of words, and the thoughts behind the words become more important than the words themselves. So it is that our language begins to mean less, for we have got very used to it, so that now we look for the ideas behind the language instead. That's why a good letter is so precious, for there are all sorts of exciting ideas & thoughts behind the same language. I wonder whether that is why some unions grow "bored" because they didn't realize that they would inevitably get used to the outward – & when they did, lo & behold, there was very little inward to subsist on, and so their partnership grew starving, and it's resistance to the petty temptations and quirks in life became weak, just as a run-down body is supposed to be more liable to ills etc.

[*21.2.45*]

... So she snuffs, does she? Well, perhaps it isn't really a snuffing matter, for it's quite open. A division, sweet, is really a formation, or number, of <u>men</u>, and consists of nine or so battalions. You have battalions of Black Watch, of Camerons, of Seaforths, Argyll & Sutherland Highlanders, Gordons (Middlesex, oddly enough). A battalion generally consists of men from the same regiment, therefore. Except for the Middlesex, <u>all</u> ours are Scottish, and don't include the others you mention. Then apart from all those, the fighting men, there are the services & support services, which go under the name of Divisional Troops (Artillery, supply, medical, 'n all that) – Hoke?

What about 21 Army <u>group</u> – well, as I've just put it, it's an army group – a group of armies (tiens!) and odds & ends of Independent brigades & divisions. 21 army groups badge was the one I wore on my little 4 day leave – oh no, <u>after</u> that leave. Just before I went away. Then the second army is a white shield with a blue cross & a yellow sword down the middle. But 21 Army Group is all British & Canadian etc. and doesn't concern all the American Armies, which come under SHAEF. (You remember the 14th Army <u>Group</u>, in Burma, yes?). So There You Are...

... I've been spending quite a lot this evening popping rapidly downstairs, for reasons of unheroic failings – i.e., there have been a lot of Noises above...

Last night was the night on which was celebrated the monthly whiskey issue, and an awful row went on downstairs. Snerges Jones & Gifford, however, crept up to a little room in the attic and wrote letters! Ivor said that we were unsociable etc, but I'm danged if I'm going to be sociable at a whiskey night! Rrrrr, no. Ivor is dreadful, he is growing another moustache! I shall have to write to Pamela about it – I promised I would! It's very Bad, nearly everyone is growing moustaches in the section now, and are turning from quite normal looking people into rather frightful-looking [ones]... ! Some, however, won't – our Captain because he says his face is bad enough without a moustache, let alone with one, one Bob

Cromberg who has just been on leave & therefore feeling very faithful to his wife – & D.J.G., who is just pig-headed (and conservative <u>and</u> faithful... !!).

[*23.2.45*]

... And do you know where I am just at present? In a cellar! Urrr! [*This was Goch.*] We moved to-day, and are sleeping underground, for rather obvious reasons! – Ron Jones, Ron Humphreys, Ivor & myself have made ourselves very comfortable in a <u>wee</u> little cellar! We all have mattresses, & a coal fire, a carpet, & a table, and three lamps – & are all now writing letters! I caused general havoc when I came down with my mattress, by knocking down the iron chimney so that all the smoke poured into the room... ! But we are all happy now, anyway. We spent most of the day clearing up a very battered house and getting dusty and dirty – sweet, it was a wonderful house, once – the bloke who had it was a wood-carver, and all over his house are the most marvellous carvings and books – he was very keen on photography, too. But now it has been put into better order, and apart from windows, electricity & the like, we are quite complete. We quite definitely "Roughing It", I consider!!

[*24.2.45*]

Here I am, as miserable as a squashed rat(!!) in a frightful cellar, with tons of high explosives going off & coming down all around – of all the browning off pursuits there are, making war is the worst (or rather, the most brown) – oh dear, and I shoving it all on to you to find comfort! Still, we <u>are</u> in a cellar, so that's something. Ivor is sitting here too, & bleats a sort of complaint every time one lands: "You never get any warning" or "This is hopeless" (though it isn't at all, really) – Poor old Ivor! We're all what the army calls "bomb happy" – i.e., dive under tables if we hear a whiz, etc.

... I have found three lovely books with hundreds of reproductions of paintings – gothic, pre-renaissance, renaissance, & Baroque – every reproduction in colour, and beautifully done, too. They are actually from packets of cigarettes (!), and stuck into a book with the text & spaces – but you'd never think they came from cigarette boxes, for they are very large, & the best reproductions I've ever seen. And after all that, I don't know whether I shall or should take it – for though the person who owned it will never see it again ('cos if I put it back someone else is bound to take it before the owner comes back – if he ever does), it still doesn't mean therefore that it's mine, by any means – in fact it isn't at all, and therefore what am I doing taking it. It's awfully difficult, all this, & one can go on arguing on it for hours within oneself — i.e., his house is half demolished & totally looted already – but all the same... Oh I don't know, I'll have to think about it. You see, the only thing that stops me from putting it back (apart from wanting it?! perhaps?) is that the rain and weather will soon reduce it to a sodden mass of paper or something if I do, so wouldn't it be better off if I did take it? But there's still something a bit un-honest about it all.

... Sweet, <u>please</u> (honestly & seriously), excuse this letter, but we're all on edge, and jump about five yards – there are bombs now – every time something lands. But I know it's awfully bitty and disconnected. Poor old Bear, I don't always do you proud, do I – always pushing & arguing (– I must get out of arguing – defensive arguing at least – I don't do it on you, but I always seem to have a lot of d.a. to do about my byke, and it's not good, really, 'cos once a d-arguer-self-excuser about bykes, always a d-a-s-e.). That's what I feel very much with regard to some people I see around me. The excuse they give for, say 'fornication', stealing, lying, drink etc – is generally "Oh the war makes us like that, we're quite normal people in civilian life, and don't do that." 'Cos whether war is here or not, the faults & vices are always, alas, in the mortal mind – war & the life we lead in wartime makes us show <u>all</u> our qualities & negative-nesses, and if people don't <u>show</u> the latter in peacetime, but practise them privately, that doesn't mean much, does it. It's just like a beach: in wartime, at low tide, the beach is visible, in peacetime at high tide, the beach with all its odds & ends & queer pebbles is covered up, and a smooth sheet of water is that which covers it.

[25.2.45]

... I've had all sorts of things to do to-day, and so feel quite happy – also, an anti-Typhoid inoculation this morning, but it's O.K. now. I had anti-Typhus & tetanus the other day too.

... Now what have I done to-day? Oh well, Ivor & Ron Jones & I have all come out on detachment with a 15 cwt truck, and are living in two rooms of an 'ouse, & are quite happy of course, being away again – but oh gosh, we've chosen an 'ot spot, for a few yards away, pointing over the roof, is a whacking great heavy gun, and pictures fall off the walls & plaster & windows too... when it goes off, which it does, often! – it's 'orrid. Even Ivor is a bit disturbed by it, & mumbles things at it when it bangs... I've never in all my life seen or heard such guns & noises as just lately. The barrages are terrific – that's no secret – I'm sure! And coming back Ron & I had a very long & exciting journey to-night – we had been in for the mail: 1st / when we tried to start, the 15cwt wouldn't, so we were towed, & it still wouldn't –so we pulled it backwards etc – & then finally switched the petrol to a full tank, & wheee, it went! All through this the guns all round us were clanging away furiously! – 2nd / Just as we were in the middle of a lot of other guns, we fell into a ditch! & had to be towed out – 3rd / we lost the way, 4th / had to smear mud all over the side-lights 'cos they were too bright – and 5th / Sent a lorry wot was passing us into a ditch (but since he had a 4-wheel drive, he emerged under his own steam!) – so that was quite an evening. And now I feel all Shattered & tired, & Ivor said I snapped at him (imagine me snapping! Mmm), but I don't think I did.

Yes, this is a lousy war, my sweet – I agree with you very very fully there. For the madness of a dozen or so politicians I have never dreamed that such horrible results could emerge. A Certain Town where I was up till to-day is an awful example of that. I saw Pamphlets about it (a pre-war one), and it showed a pleasant and beautiful little place, with Avenues of Trees and little castles & churches, but now... ! There's not one inhabitable house, and that's saying a very great deal indeed. Then more & more shells go every second onto other places, causing a mess in them – Oh isn't it absolutely bloody – in every sense! Ugh, it makes me very fed indeed – not for any effect it has directly on me, for I don't suffer anything compared to some blokes & people – but that such futile and aimless (yes, aimless) things should be started by such weaknesses in the human mind as Pride of Race, Pride of Empire, National feeling etc – three-score million weaknesses all bolstered up to support a damned crazy "scheme" – and it's all been started by that poisonous propaganda and "boosting-up". What's so extra-bad about it is the after-math isn't so pleasant, either. Oh zzzzz.

But that article about civilians that you saw – certainly sounds rather terrible. I don't know anything about the rationing system yet – though I know the actual place – it's a sanatorium, though, I think. We get plenty of orders and instructions about non-fraternization (but I can assure you Theory works out very differently to practice.). Mind you, re that article, there is one thing growing apparent (I've not been here long, so I can't say much), & that is that twerpish officers love to say How Sternly They Treated the Germans in Their Village, & How Hard They are Punishing Them etc – it's bluff, blah, a lot of it, because they think that that proves them to be Fine & Strong Pinions of The Empire (ho, getting a bit bitter aren't I). It's almost Victorian, their hypocrisy.

Still, that about the refugee camp may well be true – though I think the rations were probably small through necessity, and the Twerp-in-Chief turned that into An Example of His Excellent Methods With Germans. The ass. Still, I still think Firmness is a good thing, after all that – for They did allow a lot of bad things, &

They have a great deal to unlearn. But as you say, Justice and Fairness are very essential, and they are the best educators ever. For if we grind their noses etc, they will only come to look on the Occupation as a period of Horror and Misery, and long for the Good Old Times. The worst part is that there is such a feeling of "We must Punish the Swine" about everywhere – vengeance is another human weakness, & if only the French, Belgian & Dutch people thought of the religion they so devoutly practised on Sundays, they would remember one or two little sayings about vengeance.

... Oh well, more plaster falling down & windows blowing in & I think I'll go to Bed!

[*28.2.45*]

... And I've been pottering about the village too – you know, I'd love to be a Military Government Officer – it's really one of the most Constructive and far-reaching jobs there are. The one here is quite a good one, and is all out to get the community going well again – & is Organizing things so that life will return to normal soon. Jolly good, isn't it. I only hope there will be a lot of sensible people like that. You saw Churchill's speech, did you, re- the German people? Interesting work is starting for us now – I do wish I could tell you about it – but suffice it to say that it makes me quite hopeful about things, & that Germany may well not be such a terrible place after all. (I hope I am right when I say that.) Another thing I'd like to tell you about but can't is the place you mentioned in your letter (the evacuee camp article, remember?). I have been there in the course of my wanderings around, and am glad to say it's by no means as bad as it's painted – actual facts you mentioned are correct, but extra facts seem to be omitted in the article – for instance, a lot of them (the great majority, so it seems) have their own food and acquire food (goodness knows how!), so that they don't even take the soup & bread which is issued. I certainly saw very few undernourished & underfed people there. I do wish I could tell you more about it, though!

... 'Scoose if there are smudgy bits all over this – I'm awfully dirty, and can't get any water with which to wash! So I'm very Grimy. To-day we came back from detachment, to find nearly all the section had Breezed Off to Brussels for a spot of leave! I hope they'll let us go too, sometime soon.

[2.3.45]

... Oh sweet, I've been intending to ask you, <u>could</u> you send me my German Dictionary. I think it is in the "Gentry" kitbag (so my Efficient Diary says) – and – also a book called "Essentials of German Grammar Reviewed" please? Also in the same place. I must get my German to be quite fluent if I'm to be of any use in this 'ere place – and also I'd like to be good at it.

[4.3.45]

... By the time you receive this you will have heard that Mr. Churchill made a visit to these parts – I've been helping the security angle of his visit, & saw him & several other people, quite well. Ivor & I were standing on the pavement & saluted as he went past with F.M. Monty following. But no one else saluted at all!

... I long to "get moving" in life – ie, a job & start climbing up the ladder (or whatever it is), and find out whether I'm going to be much good in this 'ere world as far as earning a <u>good</u> living is concerned. (Now don't get 'het', you – I'm just thinking this, that's all) – 'cos in the Army I don't think I've done <u>particularly</u> well, principally 'cos I've been messed about & not allowed to stay on one job for long. But I <u>know</u> there's just <u>one</u> part of me that can do the job as well, or even better than anyone else in the whole section. I can't explain it quite – & I don't know whether to trust it 'cos I'm not sure that it isn't a thing which comes & goes with moods (& therefore is of not much value), but it's something to do with <u>energy</u>, and needs co-operation & can't work with antagonism, & is a magnificent help to speaking languages I know nothing about (ie. Dutch), and to being more-or-less efficient & conscientious. Its best promoter is an interest and knowledge of facts of the job, and its worst enemy laziness.

... Mmm, Ivor <u>is</u> a good companion a very good one, & very witty and right-minded. I'm very thankful for his company, indeed. He always sticks up for anything which is right and batters down arguments which are weak or without Righteous Foundation. <u>But</u> if ever there is a flap on (ie. we are both posted to live with a H.Q. formation which is on the move etc.), he gets <u>dreadful</u> & fusses about till midnight visiting people to see if they know anything about the next move – which is all very disturbing & annoying – and asks dippy questions, and says "what?" to everything everyone says... Still, that's not a very great fault, so he still remains an excellent fellow quand-même!

[8.3.45]

... Well, I'm writing from somewhere in Holland now – today we travelled 180 kilometres – through Germany, Holland, Belgium, & then back into Holland! What a long journey, egosh!... Ivor & I were on our bikes, & Ron in his Opel Truck. We have acquired billets in a café, and Ivor & I have two 'bunk'-beds built into the wall rather firm! But I must tell my news from the beginning. Firstly, we were given a sort of 36 hours off, & went to Eindhoven after all – with Ivor & Ron; it took us about 2½ hours only to get from Goch to Eindhoven, very good going indeed. We went straight to some friends of Ron's... Ivor & I went off to a cinema & saw a very Lighthearted & frivolous film called "Cover Girl", very smart & a bit glamorous & overwhelming, but nevertheless entertaining & did us good for we needed something rather escapist!

... The next day, in the morning, we did some shopping, & then had another egg-meal for lunch – we ate 18 eggs between us in the one whole <u>day</u> we were there!

... And so back to Goch – having had a very pleasant time. Honestly I've never known an occasion when I needed a break more (except when I wanted to come to see you!). Goch is <u>such</u> a ghastly place – not only the houses that are "down" – but the streets are all uneven & piled up with debris, and the air is thick & unhealthy with smells of death, decaying food, drains etc – a <u>terrible</u> place indeed – <u>and</u> most tragic – for only four or five weeks ago it was a beautiful little market town with avenues of trees and squares. Last night there was a fire there, so I went out to the market place to watch. Sweet, it was horribly eerie, climbing over the piles of wood & bricks along the street – everything was so dead silent – no troops, no sounds, no nothing – and lighting up the bare walls and heaps of masonry was the "artificial moonlight" – searchlights which shed everywhere a bright blue light, making it even more a Dead City. Then <u>opposite</u> all that was the bright vermilion of the fire, shedding a glow all round it – sparks shooting up into the air & forming a cloud, a golden cloud in the dark blue sky. The strange part was that there were no shouts, no noises – just silence and the spitting & hissing as the large building burnt. Then came some shells, so in I popped, after which I packed & then went to Bed.

But this morning we left Goch! Gosh were we happy. Yet for the countless souls that had to stay behind – in the town where their houses had been once, where they had led their quiet & contented & inoffensive lives (for the most part) – What of them? As you say, what have they to look forward to? It all depends on the good sense on our Military Government Officers – if they work hard things won't be so bad, and life will reshape itself and soon be as it was before – especially in the country. But it is up to the Big Chief in Germany if they would only <u>realize</u> that the best thing for the <u>people</u> would be to stop the war – life can re-start quite easily for those, say, who have homes left. But to the town-dwellers...

and as the tide of the front goes forward, so suffer the towns, and there are many towns to be reconstructed before material will be spared to go to German ones. It's hard, but there's a certain amount of justice in it all. Though the actual bombing I don't agree with.

[*12.3.45*]

... Today Ron & I came down here-where-we-were-at-Christmas which is only 80 km or so south of where we are, so we did it comfortably in the 15cwt in 2½hours. M. Mme Collas & daughter Arlette (15) gave us a terrific welcome!! and we've been living like emperors ever since we arrived at 5.0! A wonderul supper of soup, eggs & lobster mayonnaise, lovely wine, coffee – then I went on playing a simply stunning baby grand piano brand new yesterday – "Gaveau" – the most famous French make – a dark and light oak in colour; it's the loveliest piano I've touched since leaving home, honestly! Eee, but I had a good time, & Ron & M. Collas listened to me. Then a very good bath – gosh, the time I spent in scrubbing the bath afterwards!! I was so dirty! and washed my hair and all – now I am lying grandly in bed – of all the luxurious little suites of rooms I have ever been in. For leading in to my bedroom is the piano room, as you see! and it's all Pink (!!), and very nice. Oh sweet, I wish you were here too.

[*The next day*]

Oh sweet, what a perfect day I've had – very early this morning I woke up rather cold, so put the sheepskin rug on the floor on my bed! Got up at 8.0, feeling like twenty elephants in Springtime – had a lovely breakfast, & then went for a simply wonderful walk with M. Collas and Ron, up into the big hills behind – (the foothills of the Ardennes really), and Spring was everywhere & so exciting!! And came back through the village, stopping at the hotel where we were known & where we were plied with two sherries!

(The Hotel Casino of Tilff is supposed to be very famous.) Darling, that part of the world would be terrific for a honeymoon if we couldn't get to go as far away as the Pyrenees –eee?[3]

... After that, back to the house, anyway, & had our photos taken etc. Then coffee & tart – for gouté – and off we had to buzz, in the truck. But you know, I haven't had such a perfect two days (or one day, rather) since I left home & you, bless you. Everything seemed to come out so <u>well</u>, and it was the most perfect day from the point of view of the weather, too. Sunny, warm and breezy. Gosh, I am grateful for it.

... I have chosen 40 or so more books for the section library – which makes us 90 volumes in all. Actually, they're only Penguins, or their equivalent, but since they are new, they are quite worth having. Apart from rather a lot of Crime & Wild West, there are quite a few (about 50%) very much worth reading – Trollope, Eliot, Evelyn Waugh, Louis Golding, William Temple, J.B.S. Haldane, Somerset Maugham, etc etc. I can't remember half of them – oh, & Wendel Wilkie's "One World" – is that good, do you know?

[*16.3.45*]

... Ivor, Ron & I get on beautifully together; Ivor supplying the wit, Ron the Steady and Benevolent influence (& me – well I supply the target for all the kindly merriment that goes on!! "George's bike", "George's boots", "George's trousers", "George's hair" (hm!), "George's kit" – etc, etc). Oh, it's a great life in very many aspects which I am glad to have gone through!

---

[3] Douglas and Hazel went to Tilff and stayed with the Collas family for their honeymoon, and were richly 'wined and dined' in The Hotel Casino.

[*18.3.45*]

... Yesterday I toddled down to see Jo & Truce [Hendriks] again in the afternoon & found them playing tennis! lucky swigs... So I watched them, & then Jo sewed on some stripes to my greatcoat, and we all sat round the table and talked about Catholics & Protestants – they're terribly strict about that in Holland, & believe that Catholics should never marry Protestants & so on... and the priest of their village preaches against dancing every Sunday! Talk about narrow-mindedness... almost as bad as the Welsh Non-conformists! But Jo's argument about C.s & P.s. marrying was that if they were both idealists and sincere in their respective beliefs, a forced change (any Protestant in Holland must become Catholic if he wants to marry a Catholic) would do more harm than good. All this apropos of a soldier (English) who wants to marry a girl in the village, and the army padre has been getting Jo to be interpreter for him in talking to the girl's family.

... One thing I do know is that I love you terrifically much – I feel like a big 15 inch gun battleship pounding away at an island, and you're the island – only the gun is firing Loving Thoughts, not shells! Eeee, sweet – why am I such a pugnacious fellow!? Is it like that with all young and enthusiastic lovers? Or what?... Only I'd hate to hurt you in any way whatsoever, though I seem to be so full of pushfullness & energy sometimes that you do feel hurt (physically!!), and all I feel is loving and not at all cruel or evil!

[*20.3.45*]

... I took Tony to see the Hendricks the day before yesterday, and Ron (great achievement!!) yesterday evening. I've been going every evening lately: I do enjoy sitting there talking and being quietish & laughing etc – alas, we shan't be able to go there much longer. Sweet you must meet them, when we go on our Tour. (Tony, by the way – have I told you about him? Our Dutch interpreter, very quiet, with a charming family in Eindhoven – and an excellent fellow, very nice, & very unselfish and thoughtful.)

[*21.3.45*]

... So glad you may be seeing Mrs. Mason next Autumn again – that was a nice pair of rooms, wasn't it, and she's a very merry person. Is Owen still in England? Lucky fellow, if he is! I wonder too if many of the blokes in reserved occupations will get called up soon? I expect there's quite a lot of talk about it in England – it really isn't fair, though, that some of the Infantry lads out here will get shoved out to the East after this do, especially after what they've been Through – and really, they have done a lot. One feels sometimes that there is a danger of some people in England saying "Ah yes, the infantry" – rather vaguely, and not realizing quite what the word entails. But the difference in the life of an infantryman and an RASC clerk (or a Field Security N.C.O.!) is so tremendous – one is soul-destroying, the other maintains the balance quite steadily – one is a life of nerves and fear, the other – well not half as bad, anyway.

... Yesterday evening I had a really very happy time: I went to Heythuyzen to the Hendricks, & found them in the middle of a meal, so departed again, & went off by myself to a property called the Bedelaar – a large château with acres and acres of glorious woods – and a big lake. Do you remember my telling you that I went for a row on it with Truce, last November? Well, I wanted to see it in Spring again. So I asked the lady at the château if I could, & she remembered me from the last time and said yes, certainly! So I had a truly wonderful stroll through the woods, down to the lake, & then sat on a fence by the waters edge and looked at the twilight in the water & then stars appeared there, then the moon showed up in the reeds... and I had a lot of thoughts come to me – but I wanted so badly to tell them to someone – for little seedlings of thoughts when communicated to a companion spread & grow up and are helped an enormous lot by what the companion answers about them too – the value of communion with a fellow mind (& the value of religious Communion with God, too). And I thought how nice it was to make thoughts of one's own, and not ready-made ones from other mind-tailors. Though of course they're a very great help and guiding influence – but not the thing (just as one has to work out one's own salvation in life, and not trickle along paths hewn out by other Christians!). But oh it <u>was</u> a lovely evening, and the woods were full of life, of chirps of birds, rustlings, frogs, smells – gosh, the smells, they were just so filling and warm and informative... oh <u>sweet</u> – & I found a little shelter where I promised myself that we'd go one day – it has two little brick seats, and looks through the trees onto the lake... <u>mmm</u>.

And then I tootled back to the Hendricks, & they brought out some records – of Coppelia, & Orpheus, & Pagliacci etc – which we played – and <u>then</u> there was a lovely concert on the radio – of Beethoven's 4th and some Mid-Summer Night's Dream. <u>And</u> Jo & Truce are excellent listeners too, especially Truce. And all the time we were having tea and biscuits and chocolate – quite the most pleasant evening I've had there yet, and I have <u>always</u> spent quiet & happy hours there. Ron had given me a box of Belgian notepaper to give them, and I had one too, so when I went, & said goodbye, I gave one to J. & one to T. (for notepaper is quite unobtainable in Holland, whereas in Belgium one can get some quite nice boxes of it). They were as pleased as grigs with it, anyway, & so off I sailed back to my billet – then today off we moved again to pastures & fields anew, away from Jo's & Truce's and friends – alas [*Apeldorn*]. I became very dusty and acquired a black face – but that was a cheap price to pay for the glorious weather we've had today (the point being that if it had been raining, there would have been no dust to make my face dirty, see?)

Ron and I have a room with two beds and a table (& two paraffin lamps), so are quite happy & have been writing solidly all evening. Ivor is sleeping in another house, having arrived here yesterday and acquired a different place.

[*23.3.45*]

... I'm afraid I shan't be able to hear that radio programme there being no electricity or radio or anything. It has been lovely weather, & beautifully quiet, up till today, and now we can hardly sit still. Oh dear, to be back at Cuyk, or near Tilff, or with Jo & Truce, again! We're in the Wilderness far from home, temporary home or friends, zzzz.

[26.3.45][4]

Gosh, what a lot to talk about – for I haven't written for three days now – sorry, sweet, but a lot happened, as you have heard. First, though, thank you very muchly for a nice level-sort of letter, dated 21st March – I don't think very many men out here are marrying Dutch girls – but Belgian and French girls, Yes! Why, Ron is hoping to be married to one (Yvonne, at Paris Technical University), and Martin Levingston is actually engaged to another, in Havre. It's a worry for the English authorities, probably, as it will mean that so many more English girls might not be able to marry – there being not enough men (? – Tee Hee, aren't you glad you've got a 'man'! Bless you...). Still, there are quite a few English girls who have married Canadians and Yanks, so perhaps the balance goes down again. Certainly more English girls have got married to foreigners or Dominion men than English men have to Italian, French or Dutch. But that what the Chief Army chaplain wrote is utter trash – apart from being in appallingly bad taste it certainly won't have the desired effect. He doesn't know much about the psychology of his men; that sort of thing nauseates even the humblest private for he expects a higher standard of wisdom from any Padre.

... Wilhelmina isn't very popular in Brabant (the liberated part of Holland), for being Protestant, and they being Catholic, she hardly ever visits them – in fact, she never has, in peace-time – so they naturally feel rather neglected. But if anything, the Dutch would have a 'comfortable' affection for their Queen.

---

[4] The 6th Airborne Division dropped over the Rhine, during which event Major-General Rennie was killed.

... And as for my news – since the Radio has told the world all about our div: crossing the Rhine, I suppose I can say that I did too! All very interesting but noisy (though we didn't go over with the assault troops or anything) – crossing in Buffalos and feeling dreadfully cut off when we reached the other side – some of us spent the night in slit-trenches, but Ivor and I found a room in a house, and I a divan bed... ! Now we're in a house, too. Everything seems to be going very well. I wish we could hear the news from time to time, however. When we were being briefed for the crossing, Ivor got a bit browned off at the thought of it all, and complainingly came out with: "But dash it all, we can't cross, we won't have any billets across there" – !!! – a very classic remark, we thought! On crossing I was sitting on the opposite side of the Buffalo, and had a good view of him looking very solid and immovable, smoking his pipe, with the broad Rhine forming a background – a good advertisement. Good old Ivor.

[*27.3.45*]

... Ivor said "Ah you, Giff, with all your girlfriends – what a bloke" & so eventually I Attacked him & beat him up, too! Ho! So now he's very Docile, and daren't say a thing... ! And I haven't got <u>very</u> many female friends over here, what's more – Jo & Truce, Truus Telkamp, Jackie Manders, and someone called Julienne in Herenthals (the one who wrote those letters, to Ivor, me & Ron, do you remember?) – Oh, & Lenie Neuenhuisen, in the family at Eindhoven – so what is he talking about, anyway – He's just an Old Thing. But then of course he <u>was</u> joking, so what am I talking about anyway! But I dislike jokes like that <u>very</u> intensely. I rather think it's a failing of mine, too – for if I like having female friends I shouldn't mind – no why <u>should</u> I like jokes like that anyway – for they have a rather vinegary sort of way. Oh heck what am I bothering and flustering for anyway – but I do like to get things on a right footing and basis otherwise they're bound to work loose. (Darling I'm not talking at you, I'm talking at Ivor via you!!). Oh sweet, those things are so Complex – "Jokes" insinuating remarks – and so threadbare and worn – and I <u>don't</u> like getting involved in them, even if they are jokes. There! Now I've sounded like a dry & humourless old crank, full of self-righteousness and natterings – Darling Bear, I do love you, and I'm awfully concentrated on <u>You</u>, even though I like everybody else too and their company.

Today Ivor and I did some work in the morning, and in the afternoon I went round looking for the rest of the section, which got stranded somewhere – and saw some horrible things – there are <u>so</u> many dead cattle, and then even worse are the dead German soldiers – it just makes something grow sick and numb inside you – oh it's beastly – so far away from what I like to think is the real in life, yet so "real" in itself – then the eternal smells of burnt wood, mortar, and decaying flesh – over and over again. What extremes of life – and I expect there is even worse than this [in the] aftermath of conquest. Geee whiz! Aren't I being a mournful sort of bloke this evening! Sweet, I very rarely <u>talk</u> in this strain, so don't feel apprehensive!!

[*28.3.45*]

... Ron <u>has</u> given me a lesson – and I can drive a 15 cwt! Only the gears are awful, and they give an "electric" shock every time I try to change them (one has to double de-clutch, you see). But Jeeps, cars & P.U.'s (Personal Utility cars like this, that the army use) I can drive quite easily.

... I know when I see you again I shall be so excited that I'll be in a sort of Doze, or dope, like I was the evening we were engaged! I'll <u>never</u> never forget that, the starting point! Let's always try to live in the absolute, only relative in regard to each other. I say try, for however much we try there'll be the Relative dragging us down a bit (or not even a bit – a lot, maybe), but what I mean by the absolute (it always seems like a pure white flame, giving light and life to its surroundings) is what you and I feel <u>in ourselves</u>, with the Beauty and Spiritual side, including creed and belief in God, and ramblings in the forest of one's mind – and kindness and all the best things of life – all very badly explained, I'm afraid, but I think you understand; and then the relative pertains to the earthly, with its worries and seeming-drudgery sometimes. But that white flame in us is so strong, that it will cause the relative to fade and to take its proper place. And that is really the essence of Christian Science too.

Sweet, how I sympathise with your feelings about Reassuring of religion – how often ones goes on living, goes on praying, or being straight and honest and good – and then there are times when you feel "Oh gosh, what is being respectable and good anyway. I'm feeling bored with being like that stagnant and too placid" and that sort of feeling? I do – I feel like doing something unrespectable, ungood and unplacid, just to stir up the waters a bit. And though those feelings are very momentary and passing (for you stir up the waters of my soul far more than anything possibly could!! Bless your bones), the very thing which moves one to these moods might be eliminated with reassuring and encouragement in one's religion. Am I right, or have I been talking about something different, I wonder? Sweet, it's a very happy thought that our religion is bound up with ourselves, for that is the best cement for our union that there could be. Quite apart from the equally or more important fact that we can worship and serve God better that way. Oh, I do love you & the more I love you, the more I love the rest of the world, and life in general.

[*30.3.45*]

... I've found something absolutely Overwhelming in the last degree – it was a Nazi H.Q. – an enormous Nazi flag – a very nice red, and very light and nice material, too – just the thing for cutting up for blouses. I should think – so I'll send it, hein? You never could be a County-Gentry sort of girl if you tried, you're much too well-built and delightful for that.

I did tell you I never had that course in Brussels, didn't I! I crossed the Rhine a day and a half after the initial assault – about 36 hours.

... Today I have been searching a house which was all bashed about anyway, and consequently came back looking like a flour-man! – 'cos I had to Burrow and Scramble in all the plaster & bricks & wood to get at things. Thus drawing remarks upon my state at tea (or just before tea; I did wash etc!)

And I've looted something! Ain't that awful... Some sheets of stamps from the Post Office! (so it won't deprive anyone really, as they will never be used again). Oh, and a pair of sheets (from the Nazi place where I became all white & where I found the flag).

Isn't the news good – quite bewildering in places, what with Security Silences and vague rumours of Nüremberg being taken.

[2.4.45]

... Yesterday evening we entertained, in our little room, a Sgt (I. Corps) who has been all over the world and who even while in the Army went out to the West Indies! And also a French nurse from a nearby refugee camp that Martin brought along – we all sat round and chatted & gossiped, & had 2 bottles of champagne that we had in our NAAFI issue! There are quite a few women-in-uniform wandering around here: French nurses, U.N.R.R.A. etc. The organization of refugee camps is getting along quite well, though the soldiers are still thinking of the German citizen in terms of "Birds-of-a-feather-with-the-Nazis" which is utterly stupid – as stupid as the propaganda which bluffs them.

... I've really had quite a pleasant day, talking to pleasant Germans in the course of duty, and hob-nobbing with a Military Government Major about Oxford and Spain, and a Captain in M.G. (who thought I was an officer, I think) from the police in England, who thought he could do "a bit of good" by volunteering for this Military Government Job – & is getting rather discouraged by the hopeless way soldiers are messing up everything they're trying to construct – a kindly, Welsh-faced, ginger, heavy-jawed police officer.

Ivor and I eat at a refugee camp in a tent, together with the tall Sgt. we invited in last night (who was at Wentworth at the same time as us).

[*4.4.45*]

... Ivor is giving a Depressing Monologue to Arthur (Sgt) Lubbock, on Life Not Being Worth While – how wrong it is to have children and to bring them into this appalling world – (it's not affecting me, dear) – by the dreadful muddle in this world, the unhappiness of everyone's life – "chaos and misery of so many millions" – war was caused by the <u>escapism</u> of the millions of people. I've just called him a miserable old sod (now defying it with a gay laugh, of course), and giving out destructive criticism – and he says that I don't even give out that, I don't even think etc. etc – But I say I <u>do</u> think:

> [*Ivor inserts a response*] Don't believe this Hazel – You know me – I think – better than to believe Giff has expressed my remarks in a way which shows the real thoughts behind them. Anyway so far I have been trying to draw some <u>constructive</u> statements from the other two so far without result – We will now continue. [*Ivor*]

That's all wrong & ho, yes, he hasn't really at all, he's just been moaning and trying to make everybody black-biled (!) – (it's his stye, I think – he has a stye in his eye, and I've been dashing about all day getting boric acid and cotton wool from the Dressing Stations for him, and between Depressing Monologues has been bathing it, emitting grunts at the same time). Arthur Lubbock says Happiness depends on the person and a poor man living in hopeless material poverty can be happier than a rich man etc. Which is what <u>we</u> always have said – it seems funny that everyone doesn't think and practise that. Of course, Ivor didn't mean half he said, he just said it to stir up a conversation (as he said in his little paragraph!). Still, it was a jolly good argument.

[5.4.45]

... Now the papers have published it, it's all right to comment on the death of our General Rennie, I suppose. He was a terrifically decent bloke & exceedingly democratic etc – it seems an awful shame, for he was (apart from all that) a good tactician and military leader. Everyone was very depressed about it. The new general is called Macmillan and used to be a Brigadier in the 51st, very tall & oldish. All our brigadiers are enormous blokes! Over 6 ft 3, nearly every one!

... My gosh, do you remember my telling you our capt's jeep went up on a mine? Well, he's been to various places saying he has no jeep, and now has scrounged two 15 cwt trucks!!! So that makes us one 30cwt, 1 P.U., 4 × 15cwts & 5 motorbikes for 12 men!!

[7.4.45]

... No sweet, there is a 15th Scottish Div – a very good one, and they crossed below us on the Rhine, a bit later on. Then there is a 52nd Lowland Division, too. Just now we are in a very quaint little town, built on a hill ("somewhere in Germany" oh snout) with a lovely castle towering over it all – Tony and I went over it this evening – it's a very richly furnished place inside – looted, alas, till it's hardly recognizable (that's the most depressing thing over here after the bomb damage, i.e. the looting by our own troops, who empty every chest of drawers up-side-down, chuck plates, clothes etc out of the window, tear down curtains, smash windows – for the pleasure of destroying mostly), but it couldn't take away all the beauty of this place. We wandered through suites and galleries and chapels and quads, climbed towers, had a splendid view of the country for nearly twenty miles around (very flat country it is), in the glory of a spring sunset – and it has been a gorgeous day. The oldest part of the castle dates back to the 10th century. We went over the dungeon – a <u>dreadful</u> "hole" with only a small trap door 3 ft × 3 ft over the top – ugh! – then around the gardens – and there was all sorts of blossom there... In all, an excellent evening – and then had a glass of red wine – and now I am writing this with Ivor in our room. We have taken over a small hotel, and our room looks over the same plain as we saw from the towers of the castle – a lovely view, indeed. Oh <u>gosh,</u> it's beautiful. And the town has hardly been touched – no raids, no shells "just the job" as our section would say. [*This was Bentheim.*]

... Yesterday we spent in a wonderful town ("somewhere in Holland"), just free and hardly touched – a beautifully clean town, full of friendly people [*Enschede*]. You know, it makes <u>such</u> a difference to be in a place where there's no tension, or where one is "allowed" to be friendly; Tony & Ivor & I went for a walk in the evening & Tony got very moonstruck with all the nice-looking damsels fluttering eyelids at us, and wanted to go off for a walk with each one he saw!

... My Easter wasn't too bad – one hardly knew it was Easter day – but I worked hard all day, and that's one of the happiest ways of spending a day, isn't it!... How <u>exactly</u> right you are about it being hard to eradicate impressions – it's very much so with me – and especially yesterday, when I had a series of stupendous rows with half the section – including the Capt! All because they had an impression of me & Ivor they all nattered amongst themselves to create. As we went ahead, being on bikes, they all grumbled because they were sure we wanted to grab the best rooms – zzzz! Oh dear, I did let sparks off! Some little natter was immediately squished by a ton-of-bricks of Gifford-weight... There, I'm sure you don't believe me – but I <u>do</u> feel cross when I feel I've been wronged, I do! Rather like a clap of thunder I feel myself, preceded by lightning – and it's probably very wrong & unchristian (I'm <u>sure</u> it's wrong, for it's obviously a failure to keep control). Oh well...

... Do tell your Father that I'm awfully sorry about the chess but we've been so much either working hard, or moving lately –

that I just haven't had time to even unpack that-part-of-my-kit-where the chess-boards-are for I put them in a flat place so as to be safe – but I'll reply as soon as I possibly can!

Ho, I'd <u>love</u> a fountain pen – thank him <u>very</u> much indeed – it seems awfully greedy to say "yes-I'd-like-it-now-thank-you-very-much" – but what do you think? 'Cos I haven't got a pen now; have I? Actually I've hundreds of bits of fountain pens, but none fit well enough to make one working pen. So if he suggests that, I would! And thanks terrifically much for suggesting it yourself!

… But <u>don't</u> – <u>please</u> don't put off the idea of being a regular tutor just because we might get married that summer – I pray God it may be so, and that we shall; but it's an awful sort of Thing that I have that if you begin to bank on an uncertainty, it never comes off!

[*10.4.45*]

… Ivor & I had arrested a bloke, and requisitioned his car & camera (Leica) – it was a Nazi party rich bloke, so there wasn't much harm – for someone would have taken them later anyway. But I <u>knew</u> it was fundamentally wrong, though through human justice it was pretty well right. Well, voilà. Ivor with a car, & a Leica camera between Ivor & I. Hoke. Ivor doesn't know whether he wants a car or no, & dithers rather – still, he has it. Then tonight the trouble starts: he has also a motor bike, how's he going to ride both? So ask the Capt etc. – none of the rest of the section want the thing. Then someone has a bright idea: give the car to the Dutch Sgt. who had his car stolen last week! But Ivor doesn't like that. I, however, think it rather a good suggestion – and say so. Whereupon Ivor gets so dreadfully upset (for he really wanted the car dreadfully badly), and naturally feels I've let him down by saying such a thing – I quite understand how he feels, for I'm always his main support. Still he might have said so before. But for the life of me I can't understand whether this row has come up out of his having drunk too much (if he did?), or whether I've said something very unworthy and dreadful. I did think that the Dutch Sgt. (whose Field Security section – a Dutch one – has <u>no</u> transport whatsoever) could better have had it than us, who have no less than six trucks, and five motorbikes. Still, now he's come up to Bed, refused to speak a word, gone to Bed, and was promptly sick! (Poor old Ivor!) <u>One</u> thing I know, though (Gosh yes), is that Leica goes for ever out of my half-possession to-morrow – for I'm damned if I'm keeping it – things like that prove to be most hopeless bones of contention and sources of trouble and quarrels – and that's the lesson it's taught me. I'd love to have a Leica-camera, oh yes – better than any other <u>object</u> material that I can think of, but not this kind of Leica, which has a miniature devil inside it.

[*11.4.45*]

... Well, a bloke and I went on detachment today, with a Personal Utility car and a motor bike – and guess who drove the car?! Ho... <u>All</u> the way miles past the place, then <u>all</u> the way back again, all by myself? And nary a ditch or horse or cow (touch wood) – aren't I a clever boy!

I'm quite intoxicated with all the wonderful smells around here – honestly, you'd never think there was a war on just here – it's so quiet & untouched & lovely – and the <u>smells</u>... ! I just wander round & round under the tree just outside and sniff in blossom, blossom & more blossom – the air is <u>heavy</u>! It's <u>so</u> full of different sniffs – eee, but it's grand... It's been a marvellous day, too.

We went for a glorious drive this evening, too – back to the place where we were yesterday, and had a wonderful drink in the hotel – a sort of cherry drink, and beautifully sweet – and talked to the innkeeper. Then back here, and on the way I taught my companion how to drive (!) – he's a nice chap, awfully unassuming in a way – called 'Spike' Martin (rather a name-and-a-half!).

I think your Mother is a most terrific person (I've said that before!) – and I am just beginning to realize it more & more – she is so wise & sensible and exact (that's one of the best adjectives I can think for her), for she always does things so thoroughly and exactly – she's a very dear person, bless her for she does them in such a spirit of Love, too.

And Kanga-Mother is a terrific Mother too, though different in many ways & the thing about her is the overwhelming love she seems to have for everyone – she can just give out and give out – and loves me very much too! And it's just wonderful the way she's come to love you quite as much as if you were a sister of mine & her daughter. She is wonderful, and I have never met anyone quite like her. If ever she finds anyone who is at all needy, or poor, she befriends them in such a sincere and sweet way – and not at all "tough Red Cross Nurse type" who boss and appear fierce: – Oh she is a one. We have always had enough – in the way of food and supply – in Spain, even in the hardest of times, simply through her – for she never ceased to give away quite half our existing "stocks" to those of her friends that needed it, and we soon realized that the "more you give, the more you receive" – for for every amount she gave away, at least twice the amount would appear from various & most unexpected places! Oh, bless her heart – even now she spends a lot of time in the hospital, Doing things, and has made a lot of new friends. But it does seem so terribly unjust and wrong that she shouldn't have someone there to love her first-before-anyone-else.

... Yes, Bear, I quite agree with you about 'matter', but C.S. does too – you see, they believe (& I believe too) that matter in itself is Quite neutral, but is transformed by reflecting the image of God, & therefore possessing His qualities. Of course matter is not useless and despicable – otherwise why try & heal it and how can it be bad, which is such a lovely mirror of beauty and God? But, we say, when one day everyone has acquired the Kingdom of God within them, and have nothing else, then matter & things material won't be needed more for our expression – rather like the aeroplane, which does definitely need the ground to sit on before it gathers enough momentum, to make it unnecessary for it to have to be on the ground all the time going from one place to another!

But till that time, we find we can partly express God's creations through that which is called matter – like the trees & woods, & smells, & birds & things. Actually, matter & its reflection is very much bound up with the person contemplating it and his reflection – for what is his reflection will be the object's reflection.

... Have I made it sound frightfully obtuse and complicated – 'cos it isn't at all, really. I'd hate you to think that C.S. was incomprehensible and so utterly complex that it couldn't be true – for it is a Science, and quite a straightforward and direct science too – and as sure as mathematics. Oh, I think it was often the medieval Catholics who despised matter too much, somehow – "mortify the flesh", and make holes in yourself and twist your arm – despise everything you can touch or feel – etc. Of course every living thing in this world is God's creation, that's the beauty of it – his creation, & reflecting his spiritual image – how perfect that is! Still, to get back to the Relative & The Absolute (if I can!!). In our minds – which are the part of us which are the mirror wherein is the reflection of God – we must strive always for the Absolute – looking always up and getting more & more spiritual – gathering momentum, like the aeroplane – and that doesn't mean think nothing of eating & clothing, for we can't yet do without the relative & material.

The one thing that is Definitely Bad is what we call "mortal mind" (others call it the Devil, etc etc etc), which is essentially negative, caused by absence of good – which tries to instil beliefs into people.

[*14.4.45*]

... I don't think the troops act very differently to what you'd expect, over non-fraternization – they think it's a lousy business, quite sensible, very depressing and obey it when other people are looking! Especially officers. But one-or-two just don't non-fraternize at all. The general attitude is 'When you can't be seen by the police or high-ups, then go ahead' – which is very unsatisfactory indeed. But like a lot of things, it's changing, and relaxing very much. I think it's only meant to be a brake, anyway – which can be applied harder or lighter, according to circs.

[*15.4.45*]

... To-day we moved once more – we spent yesterday evening with our artist & teacher friends, talking – they were a very nice couple of sisters, and their house (or two floors of one) was one of the best examples of excellent taste I've seen. Here we're with very decent people too, who are spoiling us in nearly every possible way – they are kind. And I'm sure it's not because we are a "conquering army" or things like that – I'm sure I know a genuine person when I see one, or I pray God that I do. In a nearby town there was some trouble as the civilians said that some Polish workers got out of hand – but there I can't help feeling that the Poles were torn away from their homes to come and do forced labour in Germany – and anyway, who brought them here in the first place. Still, it is a pity, for disorder always causes discontent and evil.

[*17.5.45*]

I've apologized to Ivor, & he said it was quite O.K. – poor old Ivor, he's feeling dreadfully browned off, & having rows with all & sundry – when he sees evil he always rises up in arms against it, & argues and denounces – one has to have a sort of policy, though – really – either you have fruitless and depressing rows or you must go your way quietly & do the best you can, & not try to alter what is impossible to alter without about seventy steam-rollers. Which is what I try to do, actually – but can't help having a smallish row or two from time to time! (Or can help it, I just let myself have one!)

[19.4.45]

... What happened about Ivor's car was that the Captain pinched it, & then gave it to the Dutchman... ! What annoyed Ivor most was the sudden change of mind of mine though, from pro-car, to give-car-to-D—n, & I suppose he felt I was being dreadfully inconsistent, which I was rather, from his point of view, and now Ivor keeps on wanting me to have the Leica! Tee Hee. But I am going to get a good camera one day, yes, from Germany – but it'll be from a better source, I hope.

... I'm so sorry about your Mother feeling hurt over advising Pauline – but I'm sure it's a problem which must crop up very often – for the mother must get so confused, and also have a pathetic but inward determination to be her own counsel – 'it's-my-baby' – and to strike out for herself – it's always so: look at the boy of fourteen, who perseveres, by trial & error, to do something – quite against his parents' advice – they are hurt & anxious naturally for they know he's doing it wrong – but the experience gained by (unwitting) trial & error will be very valuable indeed – if you open a cocoon and let the chrysalis out without letting him fight (or bore) his way out, he just becomes a floppy moth & soon dies. If you leave him to bore through, thus gaining strength, he becomes a handsome fellow. But I still sympathise with your Mother's point of view, and know that even with her wise advice, she'd never let Pauline bring her infant up without thinking things out for herself.

[22.4.45]

Just a very short note to say hallo, and bless you very much and to tell you about yesterday. Well, 'twas thuswise. Spike Martin & I were travelling along in the P.U. over a frightful road when suddenly (yes, dear), clang!!! – and thump-thump-thump. So out we go, and looked, but nothing seemed to be very amiss, till we realized that one of the fins of the propeller-thing had broken in half! So: and the vibration was shaking the whole car about. So we tightened the dynamo up, & on we went.

Well, after a while the vibration stopped, & though there was a certain clanking we went on just the same. When we finally got to our destination I thought I'd just snoop a fatherly look at the engine to see if everything was fine – but imagine my confusion and shock when I saw the dynamo had fallen off! and was jolting about loosely, with the fins looking very drooping and wretched at the end of it. So we took it to a workshop, and of course they said "You've had it, mate" (as they invariably do), but finally found another dynamo and fixed it on. But they couldn't give us new blades for the propeller-thing. We went off blithely, but still with some vibration.

And swig me if just a few hundred yards down the road the dynamo didn't fall off again! This time one fin stuck itself right into the radiator, & broke it, so that the water came out. Since it was getting very late, & we were getting somewhat browned off, we got a tow back to a prison camp, where we knew some blokes and spent the night in the hay loft. This morning we found a 3 tonner, & then a tow-rope, & towed the P.U. back here! But what a succession of catastrophes. Oh, and on the journey back here whilst towing it, we suddenly (in front) felt something was wrong, stopped, & found we were just towing a tow rope & nothing else!

So we went back, & found the P.U. all by itself on the road miles back, the front buffer-thing (to which we attached the tow-rope), having fallen apart, & so it went off on its own. Gosh... Capt. Edwards thought we had been run over by a tank or something.

[*24.4.45*]

..D'you know, I had a letter from Mother to-day written June 7th 1940!! It was in France at the time of the fall and has "Detained in France during German Occupation" on it –! It was a rather sad letter, though. There are a lot of sad things in this world, aren't there. Mostly realizations emanating from a succession of happenings – also single happenings... comparing the past with the present, & realizing that so-&-so thing has gone, and how happy it was when it was here with us, and how happy it would have been still – all so very human, is sadness, all full of pathetic little faults & failings, which don't even want the strength to raise themselves out of their particular slough of Despond, and yet an unsympathetic mind won't have anything to do with them, or help them in any way. Mmmm – cos the uns. mind gets irate with them, & thinks: "Oh, the same thing over again" without realizing that even if it <u>is</u>, it still needs comfort & love. I must remember that.

[*26.4.45*]

... I've had a terrific purge in my kit, & got rid of tons of stuff & now only have <u>one</u> ammunition box (a new & larger one), and a pannier bag and a sort of haversack and a small pack! & that's all!!... eee. Oh & a blanket roll.

... We haven't done much to-day, moved in the P.U. yesterday – it's just like new; it really was getting a bit bad: to start it one would have to yank the starter right out so that all the wire came out. But now it's been decoked, etc. etc. – new radiator, new dynamo, new fan, a dip-stick, & everything! Just the job. But it has been raining, & my feet are wet through walking through slush.

[*28.4.45*]

... No it's wrong to say that "Germans are as a whole a frightful lot etc" for firstly it's an enormous country, and it's rather like saying the Americans are a bad people just because a crowd of

Idaho-ranchers lynch an innocent negro. But the main reason why I say it's wrong is this: I blame the system & the people who devised such a training and organization and propaganda that would bring out the worst in people as they have to the Germans. In the middle ages, the Scots were noted for their barbarity (and I'm afraid you could almost delete "middle ages" & put the present tense in), & cruelty – it's a deplorable part of the weakness called evil that besets everyone, or tries to.

And so out of the spot of evil has grown a greater evil. Watered and fostered by this insidious creed, which has played on their weaknesses so – "Germany has always been a warlike country" – "all Germans are blond & tall", "The Germans are a pure race", "master race" etc. etc. – and so it has become a sort of religion and people's actions have festered and turned other people's feelings to an awful hatred – the same system practised in any other country would have produced more or less similar results! (perhaps not quite as bad, for Germany was in just the right state for it). (But all this is great 'heresy' what I say, so you'd better not tell the world... !) Anyway, to continue – I've no doubt that a lot of these stories may well be true – in fact I know some are – a lot are exaggerated, but taking all the surplus newspaper drivel away, it still leaves a pretty black patch. (Of course there are many camps in Germany where prisoners have been well treated – don't forget that!) Still, all the same, some men & women have acted all most sadistically and it's only just that they get punished for it. Again, as with "the smoke & ruin of Germany" one forgets the untouched & peaceful villages, so with "The Black & Horrible Nazi" one forgets often the ordinary & quite normal people – "give a dog a bad name" – to put it rather feebly! Still, I don't think I'd trust anyone till I was quite sure of him, all the same – for they have, very many of them, been poisoned, and it's got to be worked out of their systems.

... Yes, we do sort out the goats & sheep here with the help of Black Lists, but also with our own questionnaires & experience – one of the best things, I find, is to ask a man his religion: if he says Catholic, he's generally O.K.; "Evangelisch" (Protestant), he probably is all right – but "Gott Glaub'ich" (Believe-in-God), he is pretty certain to be a National Socialist, for it is an entirely new religion (or denomination), which fits in conveniently with the Nazi creed! & so on. Still there are plenty of exceptions everywhere – of course.

[*29.4.45*]

... George is an old mug – I'd left my bike at H.Q. and hoped everybody had forgotten it was mine, and were carrying it on their trucks nicely, and I was driving the P.U. about merrily & peacefully, & now the rat has said I've got to ride my bike again! Isn't it awful, and it's such a horrible day – oh I do hate motor-bikes. Just like him to remember it was my bike, the old wretch... grrr!!!

Later – And we went & found the section, and my bike was on a truck! so I left it there!! Ho Ho, but I've got to collect it at the next location. And I had a letter from Truus Telkamp (of Cuyk – she helped me make that picture) – she is a dear sort of person, & always cheerful and I-won't-be-depressed, even though her fiancé was shot by the Germans (they were both in the underground).

... I expect everybody in England thinks the war is over; they've been thinking that for about 6 months now. Even the most confirmed pessimists at div. seem to think it "won't be so very long" – but I assure you the war hasn't stopped by any means!

[*1.5.45*]

... I've been keeping summat for you till to-day, & I marked a little "x" in my diary of when I could tell you (Ho), 'cos I didn't want you to have to wait too long, so I thought "three weeks – not too long & not too short" – 'cos it will be three weeks (he pottered on amiably). What is it? Oh ah... Oh bless you sweet – nowt much 'xcept my leave is due on the 27th May... ! So there You Are, I hope you're pleased. Oh <u>sweet</u>, I was extremely pleased to hear it, and wouldn't believe it till I saw it in print. So there... eeee!!!

I <u>do</u> love you! So it'll be about 3 weeks from when you receive this – oh darling <u>one</u>... still, it does give you something to chew on, doesn't it, sort of thing. You see, one of the blokes eligible went away from the section, so that made one before me, and we received two allocations! One thing, I must warn you that it may get postponed till the 28th or something if the weather stops one lot one day – but it won't be far off the 27th. If everything goes <u>normally</u> & as it is now, well, there you are.

[*3.5.45*]

... No, I don't think you'll get any more raids, but are you going to take those little wooden pillars down in the kitchen? Though of course Jerry might try & make one colossal & suicidal attempt – he generally steps up action if he thinks the end is near.

... I say, I have acquired a small portable typewriter! I shan't keep it or bring it home or anything – but it will be very useful indeed. I honestly don't think it would have stayed much longer where it was if I hadn't taken it: it was in a room of big & wrecked newspaper offices, from where the people had gone away – so it wasn't private property, then. I took it – Oh dear, I hope I'm not slowly slipping in this business of taking things – it's so hard to draw the line sometimes – I'd take things from a Nazi headquarters, and do – things like writing paper & pencils – but I think it's very wrong to do it from a private house & there is a difference twixt the two, I'm sure.

[4.5.45]

Ho, and greetings to Bear this evening, bless her. I have been allowed half an hour during the celebrations – we're having an omelette! – What good news it is, especially for the battalion lads – it must be a great relief for them... Wheee... everyone is letting off guns and sending up flares and lighting bonfires and blowing bagpipes! Eee, oh sweet, I wish I was in London with you now – I'd like to be sharing it all with you.

... We haven't been doing much to-day, it started off being a cloudless morning, & then became a pouring, hailing, drizzly downpour! We were with the police at their billet when "The News" came through – at once everyone went quite mad and began running round in circles! Gosh, what an evening.[5]

[6.5.45]

... Yes, I quite agree with your feelings about "cut & dried" regulations for VE day – "You will light a bonfire, blast you" kind of resentment, celebrations & all that should be spontaneous (ho, wrong word – joy should be sp.), and not planned – still people ought to be quite pleasedish!! But as you say, there's no earthly reason why everyone should get het-up and so mad.

... Yesterday Spike & I went up to one of the towns beyond the front line, where the Germans still are (?). They hadn't heard anything official about the surrender and weren't allowing anyone to go into the place (actually, shot two people who did try). We went up to the bridge and had quite a long chat with the soldiers there – they all seemed very happy that the war was over, and began bargaining for chocolate right away!! Unfortunately I hadn't

---

[5] Negotiations for Germany to surrender had now begun, and were completed by the end of 7 May 1945.

any, though. But it was an odd feeling, talking away amiably to a German soldier who was armed to the teeth! Then an Oberleutnant came up, saluted each one of us gravely & shook hands with us & had a short talk, to explain why he wasn't letting us in, & all that. A very nice bloke, and with a tremendously powerful but quiet dignity, and you could almost feel the respect that the men had for him. I wonder whether that is so with all their officers?

... It's hopelessly muddy around here now – what appalling weather it is, rain, rain rain, zzzz. And our P.U. gets thtuck every few yards, too, when we are going through the river of mud that leads from our billet. Ho, I have put my bike into workshop I have! It broke down, rather – for when I used to start it, it used to rev. up to an alarming rate and I could never close the throttle at all! And had to stop it by switching off the petrol and waiting till it stopped... Oh dear, I do think bikes are lousy things.

[7.5.45]

... Did I tell you Ron Jones has gone? He is going back to Holland, and left yesterday – I shall miss him very much indeed – He's a very good chap, too, as I've often said before!

Someone said VE Day was this week sometime, didn't they – I wonder what that means. I should think it will only take effect in England (Oh, & America & France etc.), er – but not here, as they seem to have had their celebrations already, by the looks of things.

It is funny, though – all over the place here one sees German officers driving about in cars, soldiers wandering about – in horse drawn carts or just wandering. Oh, but it is a nice day, & I do so want to snooze off into a dream... mmm.

Later / Oh we have had an interesting evening – (we're just outside Bremerhaven, by the way) – and after supper we took the P.U. & sailed into the town. First we paid a visit to the postmaster, & had a chat with him, very nice bloke I think, & then we wandered all over the port & town. It was just terrific, for being the first troops into the town (we arrived this afternoon), most of the people had never seen English soldiers before, and whenever we stopped a crowd surged round us, composed mostly of Belgians etc.! One woman wanted to "come home with us" to such an extent that she half climbed into the P.U. Upon which we earnestly advised her to go & see the Military Government Officer!! – being the only excuse we could think of to get rid of the poor creature. Still, she'll see some more Englishmen very soon no doubt. Then we went to the port, and guess what we saw? The "Europa"!! – <u>wonderfully</u> camouflaged, at 150 yards it looked like a burnt-out hulk of a wreck, really it did! It's a beautiful ship, though – 36,000 tons, I think? All over the place there were Wehrmacht, Kriegmarine, German equivalent of WRENS (looking rather glum, I thought), etc. etc. – and all the interesting docks characters – dockhands, loafers, prostitutes, natty officers, ratings, stevedores – everyone! Oh it was interesting. And then we came back, & found the war was over! Ho... oh sweet.

Oh and a very funny thing happened this afternoon – Spike and I, worn out by looking for billets and finding that the Signals blokes were in nearly every house, finally came to a Quiet spot. In the hall of one house (the door was open) stood a little fair-haired girl watching us intently. We thought we might be able to get a bed there, so turned in at the gate. Whereupon the little girl gave a piercing shriek and rushed in to her Mother! Oh it was funny, 'cos we felt such asses, causing such horror on the part of so innocent a little person... Still, soon after she was all smiles, and we laughed at her, & the whole family laughed at us, & the result is that we now have two beautiful beds with sheets and a nice little room – the bloke has just brought up a jug of warm milk and asked us if we wanted anything to eat! So all is well that ends well. Gosh, what a nice day – and the funny part is that the fact that least caught our notice is that the war is over!

[*9.5.45*]

... Darling, I've at last got a camera! I am so pleased, as I acquired it quite honestly; I bought it! Ask Gil whether he knows how to work a "Robot" – it's a Leica type of camera, but terribly wee, with an enormous lens! and takes 40 or 50 exposures!! I have a film in it, and a spare one too. We'll have to go to the shop in London to get the griff about it – it's awfully small & nice, though not outstandingly handsome, <u>and</u> I have no case for it. Still, I've got one, which is what I wanted very much indeed. Eeee, but I am pleased.

We have moved again, into the town, and have a lovely billet there – my bed is right under the window: do you like bags & bags of fresh air? I do! I sleep miles better if I have my head more or less out in the open... !

... You remember I put my bike into workshops? Well, they've again gone & evacuated it! and voilà Gifford-sans-bike. George was ever so pleased, too, as we have too many bikes and one bike less is a great help. Now I wondered why I was going about so lightheartedly to-day, that must be it, weight off me mind! Isn't it a scream, though – that's the second bike that's Gone Through My Hands! Ivor & I went for a walk through the docks & saw some Uboats!

[*10.5.45*]

... I've been gadding about all day with Ivor, enjoying myself very much – it's good to be with him again, though I'm glad I had a rest from his company by being away at Div. H.Q. – I don't know whether it's just a failing of mine (it is, but I mean I'm not sure whether it's shared by other people), but a rest from someone's company does do a certain amount of good, I think, no matter even if there is great friendship twixt the two... What do you think? (I think that it's hardly a failing, <u>really</u>, anymore than feeling thirsty is one. Mmm...)

... There's a big parade day-after to-morrow, I think – bags of smart & natty men, of whom (I hope) I am not a member. I shall watch, wiv' my camera. 100 men, though, from Div. H.!... I say, do you know how many pistols I have collected off officers (we're supposed to collect them, by the way) – well, Spike & I have now reached almost twenty, & I have 10 in my possession. I keep them not from love of pistols, but 'cos they are very useful for exchange purposes – I certainly don't want to keep any at all. Myself I carried (up till a few day ago) a Beretta Automatic, which I bought in France & now an old ancient Colt thing for which I have no ammunition & even if I had I couldn't load it – that and a wee automatic which goes in my little trouser pocket. So there are the arms of Gifford. It's amazing how many people have pistols in Germany. I don't think postmasters have them in England, do they? Here they seem to, also many business men.

... This Fraternization stupidity is fast becoming out of all proportion. A bloke I heard to-day got 15 years, it is really terrible – that was for sleeping with a German girl, yet for <u>rape</u> they only seem to get five years! Ugh, it's utterly mad, I fear. I quite understand we have to be firm and just and all that, but to sentence a man to life imprisonment – or what nearly amounts to it – for doing a thing which he might have done in every other country – it's very grim, decidedly. Still, Spike is of the opinion that he won't actually serve a tenth of the sentence; they never do. Oh well, I hope so, poor bloke. But our General is "allergic to Germans", as the saying goes, hence the heavy charges.

[*11.5.45*]

... I think it's a swizzle, that's what I think – we aren't to have (so the F.P.O. said) any mail for three days because of VE Day celebrations in England! Huh! And <u>we</u>, 'oo are the stallions of the Empire wot brot abaht this grite victory, thay forget us, they do, oh yus... Corblimey – Luvaduck, cripes, swish! But it doesn't seem quite right somehow! Oh well, three days isn't so long, anyway.

... Had a bath to-day!

To-morrow there is to be a big victory parade, or something –
all the participants have been cleaning their vehicles, painting
them, blancoing the white parts, boot-blacking the black parts – oh
gosh what a lot of spit-&-polish. Highly natty tanks keep going by,
with shining green paint, things that I've never seen before unless
they've been covered all over with mud and bits of trees! They will
be so anxious to clean their vehicles that they'll forget to put in
petrol, or something like that, & things will conk out in the middle
of the parade.

[12.5.45]

... Now what have I been doing to-day... well, this morning
there was a very Regimental Parade, with tons of troops & bags of
bagpipes; they looked very smart and it looked very nice – from a
fair distance (I was sitting in a room on the first floor of the house
opposite the stand on which the Big Wig stood to take the salute) –
masses of tanks & trucks rolled past, too. One thing I thought
awfully funny was a truck half-track affair, and it was all enclosed
except for one weeny little window, through which one could see if
one was <u>right above</u> it, like I was. And there inside I caught a
glimpse of Highly Polished Soldiers, sitting in a row!! Imagine, <u>no</u>
one could see them, hardly, neither the generals nor any spectators
on the pavement! – gosh, what a Do... The pipes & drums were
excellent, though.

And then this afternoon I didn't do anything in particular,
except for one small outing. Oh, & then I took the 15 cwt out, and
right in the worst part of town it stopped, and wouldn't start again

Gosh, it was awful. So, like the resourceful man I am (!), I went to a nearby Unit and asked if anyone knew anything about trucks.

(All right, I know that's feeble, but Jones & I just don't know a thing about 15 cwts!), and a bloke kindly took it all to pieces and in about ¾ hour it started again! Then I told George when I came back, and he said that he had that happen to him 8 times on the way to Rear Div.! Only being a practical fellow he fixed it in a tick or so. Trouble? It was a petrol stoppage somewhere... George was very fed this evening – we are having no cigarettes, no chocolate, no mail, etc etc, this week, because of celebrations in England – I don't mean that there shouldn't be any fêting & all that, but I don't see why supplies should be stopped. After all, we didn't have a day off on VE day or the next day, or any day at all... oh well, suppose that's a long enough grumble!!

[*13.5.45*]

This evening Tony and I went to the harbour, and slipped onto the "Europa", a lovely ship, & wandered around for a long time – spoke to the Captain, when we went up to the bridge; oh it is a lovely ship – 35 or 36,000 tons, I think Her sister ship, the "Bremen" was sabotaged and burnt out, as you probably remember, & lies out quite near here.

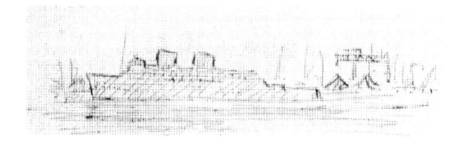

[*16.5.45*]

... This evening Ivor & a friend & I went for a row around the port! Great fun. Went alongside the "Europa" and took a few pictures & things with our cameras (my Robot & his Leica), & spent the evening very happily so... Now the electric light is off for some vague reason – but never mind, I've found a candle!

... Mmm, yes, & Ivor was remarking too: how different the atmosphere and everything is – with no guns and no shots and fear of being potted-at-if-one-gets-<u>too</u>-near... ! And all that, and mines and booby traps and dead cows and things by the road, and burnt-out vehicles, and mud... and planes, & flak, & steels helmets, & dirt – now it's smartness & cleanliness and calm and rather browned-offness on the whole. What blokes dislike most is that they just can't even speak to a German without getting shouted at or put on a charge. Of course all that kind of repression and squashing leads to evils like rape & thieving etc.

[*17.5.45*]

Just a little wee note to say I love you, afore I turn in... all sorts of nice things seem to be happening nowadays – censorship lifted, leave extension (to 11 days), and things like that.

... Ivor & his friend und ich have been for another row this evening – & saw what's left of the "Bremen"! We never knew it was in the harbour – but oh, it did look sad – just a big hulk, only a few feet above water in most places... & quite unrecognizable. And I got onto a 'U' boat (which had sunk anyway, but the conning tower was above water, so I got onto it!) – it <u>is</u> a nice port, to be sure, though – and it's such nice weather, too, now...

[*19.5.45*]

& how are you to-day? Getting excited as I am... I can hardly sit still! Oh gosh... Yesterday Spike & Derek Goodall & I came up to this place (Otterndorf, near Cuxhaven) in the P.U. – and have

been looking for a billet for the section all the time since. Now
we've found a lovely house, a gentleman-farmer's place – I <u>think</u>
they are people who haven't tasted the war at all yet, and when we
said that they must keep to one part of the house, they set up a
dreadful uproar & series of moans. (Actually I don't blame them –
but I <u>did</u> for suggesting that we go to their sister's house and put
<u>her</u> out!) Oh dear... anyway, it's all arranged now, and the section
will be trickling in to-morrow. I don't <u>like</u> disturbing people to all
that extent, at all – I have to unless the section goes under canvas
for the occupation, which it doesn't really want to do... ! Oh gosh,
One seems forever battling with words with people – no doubt it's
good training, but give me peace & quiet any day.

    ... Did you hear that censorship has been partially lifted? That
is, regimental censorship – the letters <u>may</u> get censored back at
base, I think – but not all.

[*20.5.45*]
    ... The "Europa"? Well, Germany had two really large luxury
liners before the war (Norddeutschen Lloyd Company), of 36,000
tons – the "Bremen" and the "Europa" – they were beautifully
streamlined, very fast and comfortable – and some say better than
any of the larger ships. During the war, the "Bremen" was
sabotaged, and its remains are also in Bremerhaven. The "Europa"
has been in the port for 5 years now.
    ... Sweet, how right you are about "chewing things up inside
one" – it's <u>so</u> unhealthy – I must have said masses of times, that
jealousy is a chewing-up feeling that tears one's insides to pieces
and turns everything sour too at the same time! And resentment
and 'I've-done-it-now-it's-his-turn', oh how I hate it. All bound up
with petty-small-hearted spite... oh sweet, how often we've
condemned that sort of thing – let us be forever sure that we never
fall prey to it... bless you.
    ... My Robot camera cost 160 marks, 300 cigarettes, 1 bar
chocolate, 1 packet chewing gum! – very cheap really. We must

give up the idea of that colour film – unless I can get another one, for I Don't Trust It At All, not being in the usual spool case – and I'm darned if I'm going to take any chances on our leave films. Never mind, I have 3 other films = 150 photos!!! And the Super XX for my Zeiss Ikonn for the larger pictures we might want to take. (No, I think it's bigger than your midget camera.) It's a funny little very scruffy camera, sort of, and very easy to work. You'll see it, as long as it isn't taken off me or anything!

... Our billet just now is just wonderful – the section moved in to-day, and we came here too – we are sort of off the main road: a beautiful red brick house, with a lot of ivy, in an excellent garden, & quite away from any other houses – the river is just 75 yards or so away, and the sea 15 minutes by foot or 5 by car – masses of trees all around

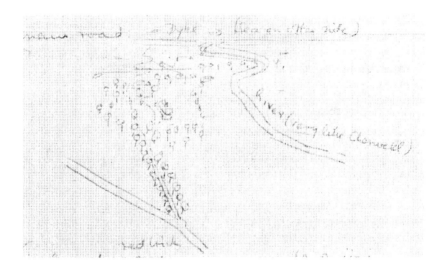

And the inside of the house... ! Just as spacious and magnificent as can be – really lovely. Tony and I went off this evening, borrowed a rowing boat from a fisherman, & rowed it from the sea to our house & moored it at the bottom of our garden. Then went to get some other & better oars from the Hitler Jugend boathouse. The evenings are so lovely now, too – the <u>most</u> terrific blues in the reflections of the river, too!

[23.5.45]

... Yes, I have a fine array of pistols. There are seven of them – all quite useless, of course but still, they are quite fun, as long as one keeps them unloaded. But I mustn't bring them home, though.

... Ivor and I went for a <u>glorious</u> row on the Meden (the river at the end of the garden) this evening – oh it <u>was</u> beautiful – so silent, with a symphony of birds singing; and the sun and the green of the banks, the lapping of the water & the delicacy of the sky. We rowed down to the sea, but found the lock was closed, so rowed back again... German soldiers peacefully fishing; we cheerily calling out and asking whether they had any luck – we chatted with one:

"Are you from the Highland Division?"

"Yes!"

"Ha, d'you remember in Normandy?"

"Oh yes, where you there too?"

"Yes, in the tank division! at Falaise!"

"Gosh Yes, – then did you come back by Belgium & Holland?"

"No, but I met more Scotsmen by Wesel & Bocholt."

"Oh yes?"

"Much more peaceful now, isn't it"

& so on – all while we were rowing along, & he, strolling by the bank – he, a Panzer Grenadier, and we of the Highland Div.! But it's much nicer so...   [*Douglas had leave from 28.5.45 to 8.6.45*]

[*8.6.45*]

Hallo My Darling,

I wonder what you're doing now, bless you – I'm being Eversobreezy on a pebbled beach sitting against a fishing boat in the sun. Being at the tail end of the queue, the boat was full up before we got on it, & so we have to wait for this afternoon's boat at 3.0 o'clock. And the sea looks very rough, too, oo er.

Oh Darling, what a terrific time that was – thanks <u>so</u> much for being so sweet & Doing Such A Lot of things for me – you darling thing – <u>And</u> for coming to see me off in the middle of the night – <u>Bless</u> you!... you are a dear one.

(As you see, this is written on Highly Respectable Notepaper, wot I bought in Folkestone as I wandered round. <u>And</u> I've bought two bars of chocolate, one of them milk, so you can set your mind at rest!) Oh you <u>are</u> a good person: you know, it keeps on coming over me, like waves from the sea – so active & conscientious, & not at <u>all</u> lazy or idle, & so wonderfully cheerful. Oh you one. Darling this is all very incoherent – but I just long to know what you're thinking now, & how you're feeling.

It was interesting watching other blokes on the train last night – even though I felt like a rather glum specimen myself – ! – they were all so different from each other, and some bolstering themselves up by telling tall stories to no one in particular, others quite calm but laughing a lot, a great many drunk, some asleep, others just listening or looking dreamy.

Eeee, I've gone & written 'Hazel' on top of pebbles... ! & 'Pooh' & 'Bear', too. Well, in a short time we shall be moving. I think – a small ship has just been tossed into the harbour and we shall no doubt be getting onto it – cheerioh my precious Bear. Hasta La Vista, & God Bless us both. Tons of Love to your Mother & Monique & Mr. C. – & mille remerciments again.

Later / Well, here I am! A nice crossing withal, and only a bit of rolling. I sat on a depth-charge or something at the back of the ship where no one is supposed to be, & read the paper & looked at the receding coast till it was almost invisible – & found we had arrived here. Mmm, quite a contrast, actually – mainly in that everything seemed <u>white</u>, in contrast to England's green, white or light brown. Lots of dust, and "weary" sort of smells – not energetic ones like coal-tar or trees as in England, but bricks & dust & drains – and of course, all the Frenchmen had berets on their heads, as usual! Then we ambled (or marched) off the ship & along a dusty road with "Mines in verge" along the side – and I got seized with panic & promised myself that when I brought you over I would guide you ever so carefully along the middle of the road!!

[10.6.45]

Here I am at Rear Div. & Ron Humphreys & I are waiting for the section to come along & pick us up (there being reports that they came up here this afternoon) – so this'll have to be very short.

... Anyway, it took me less than 48 hours to get from Folkestone to here. Which is excellent going, I think – don't you. Train from Calais to Osnabrück – then a <u>very</u> comfortable truck journey here, arriving about 2.50...

[11.6.45]

I wrote you a note yesterday to say that I had arrived at Rear Div. H.Q. – we missed George by a few minutes, actually – so waited till a Police Jeep went and got a lift – to Verden, where the section is (S.E. of Bremen). When we arrived there seemed to be an <u>enormous</u> crowd there – masses of old section members who had come over for the day. (I. Corps [field] being quite near nowadays, and most people drift back & stay there if they leave a section) – but the section billet is truly beautiful – an enormous house with balconies and ivy-clad walls and 3 drawing rooms (!!), not to mention masses of little subsidiary rooms as well. I slept on a couch in Ivor's room. He is very well, bless him, full of success with his camera – for he had <u>another</u> film developed, and they came out beautifully.

... Anyway, he asked approximately 1001 questions on how Pamela was & what she wore – & I gave him a long description and what we did etc. – very pleasant evening thus. Then to bed, & I lay thinking of my Bear, & there was an awful din going on downstairs so I couldn't get to sleep till about half past two or three – our O.C. rolling about the streets & firing his pistol, & people stumbling in, & opening the door and everything – & I felt you were so far away, & it <u>was</u> lonely without you close to me again.

... Anyway, I've now moved to Rotenberg, North of Verden, on a detachment with the two Scotsmen, Matheson, & Cromberg (it's only about 15 miles from Verden). We're in a very big & nice-looking house, and it looks as if we are to be here for some time.

[*15.6.45*]

And I <u>am</u> a clever Toad and no mistake! For wot 'ave I found? A <u>very</u> nice little room, where I have spread myself all over the place – books here, chess there, photo there, table just by the window – & also a very comfortable looking bed there which I long to sleep on, but since I already have a bed next door in the original billet I'd better stay there.

... To-day we have been dashing about arresting people & things like that. I <u>do</u> so hate that side of it all though – at the moment, you see, we're doing more Political Police work than security. Of course, in the long run it's the same thing, but one's much more interesting than the other, I feel. I did mention that I am now in Bremervörde, didn't I?

[*17.6.45*]

... Yes, companionship is wonderful when one sees it growing fuller & fuller & growing in all directions! I've never experienced it so full and happy as this last time – and I've never felt so much love for you, your mind, your sweet ways and all the happy chords that make up the one intricate & long symphony.

Yes, <u>indeed,</u> and it was so perfect to be together again after such a long time – & to find that we hadn't changed much – if at all! The same <u>friendly</u> sort of Bear... the sort that is nearly always in the same mood as you – not so much by an effort on her part, but by a naturally sympathetic bond with you, a sort of electric current which lights up both of you and keeps you burning with the same voltage. <u>That</u> sort of Bear...

... The Food (!) is really excellent here too – sorry, but I <u>must</u> tell you what we had for lunch – hot cherries in juice, then main dish of meat & mashed potatoes & spiced peas – then ice-cream and strawberries! And a big plate of cherries at tea, too..(and ham & potatoes & asparagus before that). The Germans often have the habit of having a <u>sweet</u> dish like fruit juice (to start off with), <u>then</u> the main dish, & then again a sweet one.

[*19.6.45*]

... The troops & the election? Well, since most of them read with first interest The Daily Mirror (which plays up to them), they all "talk" (when they do talk) Labour – but there seem to be an enormous amount not "bothering" to vote. Ivor is very fed 'cos he's lost his vote as Pamela will have moved. Not, he adds peevedly, that it matters, as Pamela would put his vote down for the conservative candidate whatever he said to the contrary! (& he wants to vote Labour).

[*21.6.45*]

... I <u>do</u> think a lot about teaching, sweet – really a lot. I feel, too, that I could do a consular job or teaching equally well, but that teaching is a wiser and healthier job. In a consular job we'd perhaps be different to lots of the kind of people around us, & build up something rather wonderful in an island-kind of way – <u>and</u> life abroad is definitely Fun. But teaching we'd be hard-worked, use our talents to the very full to the service of mankind (whereas in the first type of job they'd remain "interests" and go to the making of the home). Consular jobs would be keeping people <u>out</u> of fixes, giving them aid, etc. While teaching would be "learning 'em" not to get into fixes for one thing, & generally educating – a consul has much the same job as a Doctor, and we'd meet masses of <u>people</u> that way, rather than masses of <u>boys</u>. <u>Socially</u> it would be more attractive. Our children would grow up rather like I've done, schooled in different countries, & so on. But with teaching we'd both be in one place & able to build up very stolidly – a house instead of a flat, sort of thing – it's a <u>healthier</u> life, & not so cosmopolitan: – our music would be needed, so would our other things – to go to <u>educating</u> (and would we love our music & our books & our paintings as much, I wonder?). In other words, every ounce of use & our energy & our resources would be needed to help turn the Great Wheel. It's a more <u>Secure</u> & solid life – we would see our children (if God blesses us with them) much more & have more of a hand in their training – not leaving "things to chance" (though I don't believe there is such a thing – my education was mainly carried out away from my parents, & what guided me along was my beliefs & my religion). Still, it would be a happier life to train our children ourselves – or to a large extent, anyway.

[22.6.45]

Ho, I have got hold of (I hope) a civilian car! The Bürgermeister (= his car) doesn't seem to mind if we borrow it, and Mil Govt. don't mind either. At present it's being repaired, 'oweffer. Wouldn't it be fun if you were here too, oh gosh – the country <u>is</u> so lovely roundabout, what with the river & things. The Military Govt. people here are extremely good, too. The major is a Canadian, and a real character – <u>very</u> kindhearted and genuine, but a terror (in his bark) against wrong-doers. "If you come before me on this charge again, I'll give you five – no! – twenty years!!"

... One thing, touching wood & all that – I am beginning to feel very much on my feet with regard to this 'ere work, gaining self-confidence & so forth. I thought I would, once I had a chance to stay in a place for some time... it's 'cos I'm getting interested, really so, in it all. This morning I got quite worked up over the question of Nazi Bürgermeisters & rattled away on the typewriter at a report on them. The actual question in point was this: that as there are degrees of everything, so there are degrees of Nazis. And of course everyone who was in the party makes use of this fact. They say that they were forced into it, only joined up in '38 etc etc. And so a great number of Bürgermeisters have got away with it and are still in office. My whole contention is that the Bürgermeister is the man who matters in a community. He deals with them, lives with them, influences them, voices their feelings etc... he is the link, the vital link, between them and the higher-ups. It is therefore so important that this key man should be a non-Nazi. It doesn't matter a pin whether the old Bürgermeister had been forced (which is a very false excuse, by the way – considering that 33 out of our 99 Bürgermeisters had had the guts to refuse to be drawn into the "Party") or not, he must give place to another. Compromise is no good. Even if the new man be rather inexperienced at first, makes a bit of a hash the first month or so – what does that matter compared to the years in office he will have and the decades (we pray) of Security following?

I went & made a Mighty Speech to the Major & gave him a preliminary list of Bürgermeisters needing deposing – which he said he'd do: – I do hope it's possible to appoint a new one in every village & hamlet. As I said, the Kreis (or county) of Bremervörde has 99 villages, including Bremervörde and Zeven, the two towns.

[26.6.45]

... To-day I've been going about as usual (profound observation), and this morning we "did" an Ortsgruppe i.e. a group of villages. So, an Ortsgruppe is about 6 villages or so. The

Ortsgruppenleiter – the chief Nazi of the 6 villages, is supposed to be arrested, also the Financial leader, the propaganda leader, etc.

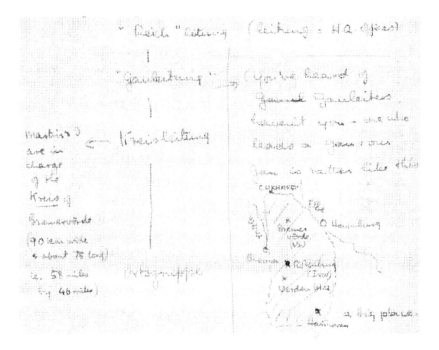

Well, along we breezed to one Heeslingen, near Zeven. We always go to the Parish clergyman, & ask him what the people around are like. Usually when we ask him what the Ortsgruppenleiter was like, he throws up his hands in despair & declares he won't have him near his church, no, not for a thousand marks, the big swine, etc. etc. Well, we went along here to the "Pastor's" & since he was out had a talk with his wife, a good old lady of great fortitude. Imagine our surprise when the Ortsgruppenleiter was found to be the church organist! And <u>such</u> a good man, she said... always being kind to little children etc. etc. Rather put out, we went to see the man himself, who seemed a benign old gent, the village schoolmaster. This was very different to what we're used to, the Ortsgruppenleiter generally is a big bold man with heavy jowls and piggy sort of eyes – very nervous and scared. But he was very different. Anyway, we went to see the Propaganda-leader next, feeling we couldn't very well arrest the Ortsgruppenleiter if he was such a good man. Well, anyway, we'd arrest the Propaganda-leader.

So there we went, looking very stern. In hobbled a rather ancient old fellow, who it appeared, had just had an operation on a rupture, & wasn't feeling at all well. Yes, he was prop. leader, yes – but of course, he had never made any speeches, as he was only deputy. Oh, ah – mm. Oh dear, we can't very well arrest him, he's not at all well. Well ANYWAY, we'd arrest the Finance Leader. Call him in. And in totters quite a young fellow, it's true, but he has an awful sort of deformity with a whole leg with the bone set, almost at right angles – quite impossible to arrest... So there we were, we couldn't arrest anyone! So after much argument & a bit of temper with Martin (who wanted to arrest the Ortsgruppenleiter), we decided to tell them all that they must all stay at home – & put on the report "under House Arrest"!!

Gosh, what a morning! – not that I particularly like arresting people – I hate it like poison. But one feels one is doing the neighbours a good turn if one takes away a particularly nasty & bossy specimen. Oh dear, how funny it was. Of course the Ortsgruppenleiter was to stay at home, but was allowed to go to church to play the organ!!

Then this afternoon our informers brought in an under-secretary of state to the Ministry of Education, or something like that! A big haul. The other day we got a Gestapo Police Inspector, too. Oh dear, I do Go On, don't I – about things one's not supposed to breathe about even!

There are a lot of members of the S.A. (Sturm-Abteilung – Storm-troopers dept.) around, but only a certain rank (& above) is arrestable – i.e. Captain. And then S.S. – a sergeant is arrestable in that they were rather a nasty lot, as you've perhaps heard. (!! Of course I am talking of the Allgemeine S.S. – not the Waffen S.S. – i.e. – the "general" (civilians too), as opposed to the weaponed – the military – S.S.)

I'm eating a boiled egg & bread & butter (lovely German bread), & chopped ham & fresh milk! And I've just had a big plate of blackcurrants & sugar... Ho! The Lady of this house is very kind, & feeds me with strawberries & sews my shirts and everything – & says that when you come we can have three rooms! She has just heard that her husband is alive & well in England – good news for her, as she thought he had been killed not having heard from him. She has three little girls, one only 3 months old.

... Oh and of course there's the Hitler Jugend, but that seems to have been a slight flop – we haven't found one "H.J." to arrest yet (the arrestable ones all being the older men who "scout-mastered" the lads). I thought we'd met one this afternoon, but found we hadn't.

The procedure (I say, I hope you're not getting bored!), (Whizz, as a book flies through the air...) is this – we get a party leader of something. We put him into our local jail & the next day I go along & find out his particulars – whether he's due to go the Internment Camp or no. If he is, I toddle back & type out an arrest report (in sex-teplet!!), and he goes in the afternoon in a truck to the Civilian Internment Camp at Westertimke (about 19 miles away), where he is deposited (it's a wee village with an enormous camp which had been used for British Merchant Seamen). There he waits until this War Crimes Commission thing comes out and he knows how long he'll be in for (if at all). My guess is that the lowest ranks (Ortsgruppenleiters etc.) will get 6 months to a year, perhaps, & the higher the rank, the longer the sentence. The big S.S. men will get quite a long sentence. There again I hope they'll be just, for there are a lot in the Waffen S.S. (no, that was voluntary, I remember) that were just drafted into it.

So... then there were other organizations, and the clever part was that whatever you were, teacher, lawyer, etc. there was a National Sozialistische Organization for it! You had to join it (in fact, I think you automatically went into it), and its demands were exceeding simple: "Pay your subscription to the Funds!" & that's all! Oh, what a racket these Nazi organizations have been! Still, I think the people realize how they were swindled.

[J/.6.45]

... What an excellent sermon that was you heard on what is Christianity – & how very true it is to get down to follow what Jesus followed, & not so much what people have built of their own. That's why one must always work out one's own salvation – & have the mind & thoughts that were also in Christ. He is an <u>example</u>, not a figure-head, a divine yet human being, not an idol or image. All his teachings go to show that. That is the lasting, eternal truth in Christianity, which was, is, & ever shall be. The Frankincense, Myrrh & Gold were things of the 1st century, just as the customs, clothes and food were.

... No, political police merely arrest people who have had positions or political careers in a big way. But security is to see that there are no people who intend to spy, commit sabotage, or injure the <u>army</u> in any way. Of course, as I said, they both come to the same thing in the very long run.

[29.6.45]

I've been reading a book about Doctors, & have decided that Field Security are themselves more like Doctors than anything else – they go their rounds, they are forever giving advice, & getting things done for people. This evening I've twice been interrupted – first to go and attend to a Polish Officer who said a Nazified American was to take his room & kick him out of it, & the next time a Sgt. Major came in to ask if I could get twenty football shirts made for him at a tailors... This morning I had to make out notices forbidding civilians to go into an Army kitchen – this afternoon to help someone from having their boat house pulled to pieces for firewood by soldiers... ! And every few hours along to the local prison to interview prisoners. Yesterday a very plump &

round gipsy-looking woman was shown in to me. She had no papers of any description, & wasn't in the least perturbed by it. She came in, greeted me gaily, & sat down on the sofa beside me! (I generally sit on the sofa while the person stands on the other side of the room, by the table). It transpired that she was half Mongolian, half Japanese – that she lived in Odessa, & had been coming to Bremervörde to get some papers, when she was arrested for having none! So I gave her a note to see her back to her Russian Camp, & told her to get something from the Bürgermeister, and off she ran, gaily and unperturbedly as ever!

... P.S. Darling, we've been able to get hold of a small RadioGram & have hopes of some records – could you let me have a packet of long playing needles. The records won't be new, I don't expect, & not used to thorn needles, so long playing steel ones will do...

[*3.7.45*]

... Then this afternoon we cleared up two more "Ortsgruppes" – one man to arrest, Propagandaleiter for 9 years... Martin & I went to the Civilian Internment Concentration Camp today, where all our arrests go, & saw several of the (95) blokes the detachment of this Kreis has arrested. Don't think they'll be there for long, though – a lot will be released. Yesterday we asked the Bürgermeister if we could have a carpet & table-cloth & chairs, to make our room look slightly more comfortable. The B., who hates Nazis like poison, grinned broadly & went off. In the afternoon, a requisitioned carpet came, a requisitioned table-cloth, & one or two other things. Then came four wives of arrested men, one after the other, asking whether they could send parcels etc. to their husbands etc. I took one or two, but by the time the fourth had arrived, was beginning to feel rather depressed & browned off – this last became very stormy all of a sudden – the carpet & table cloth seemed to have belonged to her! Oh gosh, I felt as red and blushing as anything! & really felt rather sorry, too! But the

Bürgermeister had certainly picked on a big Nazi to requisition things from!

... I <u>am</u> glad you went to that concert, but am upset to hear about "C.C." Meikle – he was up at Oxford (Magdalen) with me, as well as Wycliff, & a very brilliant brain too. Damned Bloody war that this is... That's Ian, David, & Colin gone! – there are just left the eldest daughter (who has become a nun), and Janice, aged seven, and, of course two very sad parents.

[*10.7.45*]

... I had three letters from other people yesterday – one from Mother, one from Victor, & one from Truus Telkamp (of Cuyk, who helped me over the wooden picture) – poor old thing, she has just heard that her fiancé "died" in Buchenwald Concentration Camp, on the 26th February! So is feeling rather lost & vacant now – isn't it sad? She is such a cheerful person, too – they were both in the Resistance Movement, & he was betrayed by someone and taken away by the Gestapo. Gosh, but there are a lot of sad things happening in this world. Nazism cheapened life to such a state, but that doesn't make it any easier for those to whom it wasn't so cheap.

... There are some <u>lovely</u> landscapes round here. I did a wee picture last night, actually – quite nice, of a village in snow & mountains – not very original, I'm afraid, but I felt absent-minded, & wanted to concentrate – then to-day my landlady was browned off because her husband was in a discharge camp near here, & his father was very ill & she wanted him to get to see him etc. & then said how nice my painting was, so I gave it to her, then wished I hadn't!

... How nice it must have been for Unk to have met you, & I wonder what he thought of you (!). He is bound to write an enthusiastic letter about it all – he always does. Poor old Unk – he must feel it hard – all the values conflicting, meeting the English you-&-me side of it, which must weigh the right way, and having under it all the love for someone which doesn't weaken by any means through absence, I'm sure.

[*12.7.45*]

... Yesterday evening I went riding! A friend & Martin & I took out three horses, ever such nice friendly ones, & trotted along sandy paths, & galloped through the woods! It was the first time in years that I had mounted an 'orse! (and even now my bottom is telling me how unused it is to being bumped around, also my shins). It's a grand feeling, whooshing through a pine wood on sand, isn't it.

Oh, & I had to be a witness in a court case to-day! A very sad case – a girl of 19 or so, terribly much a V.D. case, & 4 months gone with child. She had come in to us with a wild story of being Danish, gave us a false name & everything. We had a report that she wasn't well, so sent her to M.Govt. to be medically examined. There it was that the police said that she had been roped in, for prostitution, & that her name wasn't what she told us. H.Q. took up the case, & she got sentenced to 4 months, which is perhaps the best thing for her, as she will be in hospital all the time receiving treatment & getting special food, which is better than wandering about the countryside – and a soldier is reported to have been infected from her. It is all very very sad & wrong, for everyone. She said she had run away from home as she was always quarrelling with her mother.

[*18.7.45*]

... We went riding again yesterday evening – Martin's horse kept on wanting to go down every right-hand path he saw! Gosh, horses are intelligent too – they sort of gather round & talk to each other & you feel they are gossiping about you!

Oh, they <u>are</u> lovable creatures. I just sit on mine & talk away to it the whole evening, without stopping even to hear what it has to say! I love the pine woods, too, through which we go.

I went down to Verden to-day! & came back by Rotenburg & saw Ivor, still very serene. He has had an interview for a commission. Did I tell you there were civilian jobs going now for the likes of us – officer's status, but in civilian clothes. Sounds all right to me! And – oh well (he said, causing her to go green with tantalization), I'll tell you more about it when I hear how Ivor got on – but I'll finish the sentence: and they say that wives can be brought out with these blokes. Still, you ask Ivor what he thinks about it. You will be seeing him, won't you.

Yes the fraternization ban is lifted, & one does see odd couples walking about. I can at last breathe with relief that I shan't get imprisoned for having given my Landlady a painting. She must be about 35 – 40, I should think, very matronly, very Hausfrau. Beside her I have two other female friends here: one the Dutch interpreteress who is 18 to-morrow. I painted her a card from Martin-&-myself – & the other is a German Interpreteress of 24, who studied at Berlin – philology, English Literature & French – quite a nice cove, & is coming to inspect my books one evening. The first is called Peggy & the second Dorothy. I don't know them very well, so I can't say what they are like, really. I hope they can both play tennis, anyway, 'cos Martin won't, being too lazy – & there are some <u>very</u> good courts & racquets & balls to be had.

Peggy generally comes riding with us. So there you are, I hope you don't mind!

[*Douglas' twenty-first birthday – 21.7.45*]
Oh Darling,

Oh, people <u>are</u> nice & you especially!!! Sweet, I am terrifically thrilled with <u>everything</u>, & most of all with your <u>perfect</u> present – darling, you couldn't have timed or chosen a better – it is a masterpiece of <u>selection</u> even! Oh <u>Bear</u>, you clever <u>one</u>! Eee... ! Oh I <u>am</u> in a muddle, but such a glorious one too! And people here have been so kind too. Peggy went into my room when I was out & stuck flowers <u>all</u> over the place, in the frames of your photos, on the washstand, everywhere! Then our maid came in with two enormous bunches of flowers & handkerchiefs and a four-leaved-clover, and Dorothy was there too, looking at the books. I felt very overwhelmed with <u>three</u> ladies sitting amidst all my muddle! And all Mother's chocolate.

... Huh! Do you know the time? ¼ to two!! Dorothy & Karl came about ¼ to 10 & we had a longish meal – 2 fried eggs (D.J.G. = 4... !), ham, sausage, & pâté sandwiches, coffee, membrillo, apple-juice (called apfelmoss), & most important – your cake! It's a whopping one really it is, and has kept amazingly well & fresh, and as for the taste... thanks again, a hundred times, bless you.

We had the gramophone on for the last two hours – went through the Brahms 2nd Symphony again – I <u>do</u> love it, don't you – all beginning with an attempt to impress on Dorothy the superiority of a man like Brahms over Liszt, of whom she is very fond. We accused her of being a worldly person (which she is, rather!) – preferring horse-racing to riding, & so on. I told you Karl's father was a horse dealer, didn't I, & he is a wonderful rider. And so the evening passed, very pleasantly indeed, with people eating crumbs, almonds & bits of chocolate during the latter part! And finally I read some poetry which had been selected by the

Indigenous Toad –... Oh but I'm rather tired now, anyway! I shooshed them all out before Dorothy could find any more poetry – saw the two ladies to their respective billets, & now am sitting in the midst of the muddle, quiet again & very very happy! I <u>have</u> had a happy day, not that I've done anything in particular, but that I've done so many things!

[*25.7.45*]

Oh <u>sweet</u>,

Really you are a most terrific Bear! <u>All</u> at once I get three Overwhelmingly Loving & Sweet letters, alive as dynamite (so to speak), and that terrific photo. Oh darling, I'm absolutely <u>flat</u>!

 I really am! I chuckled with Fatness & Happiness <u>all</u> through each letter, & when I opened the photo... <u>eeee</u>! It's very <u>very</u> good, sweetheart, it is really,

– and ever so like you – my my, what a beautiful girl you are – fancy not ever noticing that before!

... *Later* / I've done such a lot to-day! First, I gave evidence in a court case – nothing so very sad – the postmaster has disposed of about £300 from the P.O. & had told the M.G. office it had been stolen by English troops! For which he got 1 year & a £250 fine.

But this afternoon – what fun! We bundled into the car (Karl has a new car, a really marvellous one – touch wood), & took Peggy as she wanted to come, & went to Hamburg! It's a <u>very very</u> pleasant place, & not nearly so bad as one might think: wide streets, lots of life, shops, cafés, theatres, trees, lakes, rivers, little white-sailing boats, more trees, nice bridges – everything! The damage <u>is</u> bad, especially in the port area & one or two others – but it is such a big place that there are other parts, which seem the best, quite untouched. Really, it <u>was</u> a pleasant surprise. Then we spent some time looking for the Field Security Office, found it, did the business in question there, & got invited to tea. So around to the billet, and played table-tennis for a time. They have a beautiful house by the lake for a billet, and all over the drawing room the Sergeant-Major has his trains! Winding in and out everywhere!

... We had a very nice tea there & then drove around the city looking at things – saw the Broadcasting House, & popped in there to find that The Hamburg Philharmonic Orchestra is giving a concert next Wednesday evening! Mmm, I would like to go, really I would. I think we'll try & get there if we can – though I don't see how Karl can get in, being a civilian. Still, we'll see. Maybe we'll go in Martin Levingston's truck!

Well, back we came from Hamburg, and at about 9.15 we went for a bathe, Peggy, Karl, & Karl's friend – a Fraulein Tiedemann – and myself. The water was quite warm and it was very agreeable splashing about aimlessly in the shallow water. Dorothy put herself into eternal disgrace by refusing to come because she thought it was too cold (an opinion held by myself privately, though it turned out to be quite warm after all). Then back to my room & talked & talked & talked & had coffee & finished your cake (Boo Hoo), but it was really a lovely one, sweet, & had kept very well – yes, I know that looks like a whacking great hint, but it ain't – it's just Pootly appreciation that's all!

[*31.7.45*]

... I've been all over the Kreis, chasing fictitious Gestapo men, & feel rather at a loose end.

... My room is choc-a-block full of flowers! A Polish interpreter staggered in with them to-day after lunch and said that Peggy had asked her to get them for me – isn't that nice of her? Gosh, they fill about 6 vases, Lupins, roses, pinks, carnations, & everything. They are nice – & she sent a very nice note with them which I'll show you when I come home.

... This evening I was going to listen to a Prom., but Slave No. 2 came in in rather a flap having told a friend of hers that curfew was at 10.30, and, since he had a long journey to ride (2 hours

147

long), dispatched him at 8.30. And of course curfew is now at
9.45! So as horrid visions rose up of him appearing before court on
a charge of curfew-breaking, we borrowed the Bürgermeister's car
(may his rabbits flourish), & dashed after him. But of course we
couldn't find him, so returned & out with the Bürgermeister sipping
cognac for politeness sake, & then home, & Slave No. 2 sewed on a
button & I read her some poetry as a reward. (!!What
condescension! No, but it all started as a joke of Peggy's that I was
always accompanied by my two "slaves" (herself & Dorothy), so I
called them No. 1 & No. 2 – hope you don't mind my keeping
slaves?!)

... *The next day* / Eee, sweet! Well, I've been to Hamburg to-
day! We left about 12.15, got there about 2.30. Got the tickets &
then wandered round the place – having a cup of tea at a canteen &
going to all the music shops we saw – "we" is a Sergeant Gubby
(the violinist) and myself. I bought some music & he some violin
strings. Hamburg is a really beautiful place – almost like Venice in
places with all its canals & rivers & lakes. There is a Woolworths
there! It <u>was</u> funny going in there – it's laid out exactly the same as
in England, but of course all the labels are "Pfgs" instead of
pence... got a terrific kick out of it all! We had a very good tea at
the Sergeant's Club (which is in a Ratskeller under the Rathaus), &
met two I. Corps people there I knew. Then to the Broadcasting
House. (And do you know who sits in the box office dishing out
tickets? An I. Corps Captain! Really, the duties some of them
have!) But the concert was grand, it really was: the orchestra, the
first German one I've heard, was <u>perfect</u> – really. The Germans
have <u>got</u> something we haven't got in music – they will have
nothing <u>but</u> perfection – even when they listen to music, they sit as
still as mice right through the whole work... and in their singing,
too there is something very subtle, yet strong.

... I want to talk & talk to you, & never stop. I want to go for
walks and rides and do with you all the friendly things one does
with a companion & friend. Sweet, may our emotions never be
permanently exhausted. I know a family is a wearing thing to bring

up – but I want you to be like your Mother, who is so full of everything & life – I love her even <u>for</u> her conservatism and won't-make-conserves-of-fruit, for she has worn through life with such a lot of character & liveliness. So may we always be careful not to wear ourselves out & become indifferent beings. I sometimes think that if Ignorance is the greatest sin, then Indifference is the greatest tragedy that can settle on to one of God's children. Even if you do suffer, never become too hard on the outside, for it may freeze you inside too – & then you are without life, & then only exist, as does a table or a chair...

[*2.8.45*]

... I've just been issued a special pass (he gabbled away unsecurity-like), with "Special Authorization" on it – Gifford-can-do-what-he-likes-sort of thing, & draw petrol & food if he feels like it, & use motor cars and not be interfered with. Isn't it fun! (Maj. General, general staff would have a fit if he read this!)

... Yes, I <u>did</u> ask for a pan of Neutral Tint, you are right, quite right! (and, er – coffee & gramophone needles). And I think it's time now I was reunited with my Wind in The Willows & Toad of Toad Hall – could I have them sent out too, please? (Unless you are reading them at the moment?) Thank you... I'd like to have them with me as I did when I first joined the army, & to read them to people – &, most important, too – my Hymn books – Wycliff Methodist (dark crimson purple), & C.S. one, please? That's seven things, oh dear... bless you, do you mind?

[*6.8.45*]

... Darling, Peggy seems to drift along a great deal with me, I do hope you don't mind. Dorothy does too, but not so much. I know you don't much mind, but then someone suddenly says "Ah, Gifford with all his women" and I suddenly realize what a lot of time I do spend in their company. I mean, much more than you ever seem to spend in men's company, bless you. But I like their characters, & they both like music, & literature, & Peggy is especially a good companion, & so cheerful. Oh sweet, it looks silly when I say that I know you don't mind, & then go away explaining & all — but I just wanted you to know everything!

[*10.8.45*]

... About music – I get so worked up over a passage from a symphony & people just nod their heads vaguely & say "very nice" or something utterly bloody like that! Grrrr! But it is so difficult for them to catch that particular phrase as you do, so they aren't to blame – and it isn't a type of thing one can talk about, either, very well. Oh dear, I do feel deeply about music & about the right listening.... I hope I'm not making too much of the word "listening", but music is one of the dearest things I have in our life – and listening is the reception of it into one's soul – the most important thing with composing, or rather, creating.

[*13.8.45*]

Here I am for the night in Verden – our C.O. is going to be demobilized this week, & this was (or is) a party which is the first of a farewell series, & the one to which the whole section had to come. There was dinner at 8.0, & then the drinking began, & Ivor & I sat on a couch watching it all – rather like being at the theatre! At a suitable hour (10.30), I slipped away, & found me a sofa to sleep on upstairs. When I think of my comfortable little bed in Bremervörde I bridle with resentment at the stupid and empty convention which demanded that I should be here.

[*15.8.45*]

Good Gracious, yes, the war is over! Tsk Tsk, had quite forgotten! Someone told me this morning, & I said "Oh yes" rather vaguely, & forgot about it! Isn't that awful! But now a party has just been laid on and we have to listen to the King's speech – after which I shall slip away – if I can, & play the gramophone – if I can borrow it!

... As far as I can see, AMG (= Allied Military Govt.) is now in force. This in time will hand over to a German administration, and an Allied Control Commission (A.C.C.) will be set up. Yes, there are masses & masses of policemen in Military Government. But everything will be going civilian in time. A.C.C. (of which there are a few now) wear battledress with "Civilian Mil Govt" on their shoulders.

Wilkie? Wilkie is: Sgt. Wilkinson of 1009 FSRD, whom I met in Goch – young ex-Scots guards fellow, but very gentle & quiet & terrifically humorous – albeit also very shy.

And Karl is just a bloke: his father is a horse-dealer, and the family has always been very anti-Nazi, & so has he. He is 21, and has been working for us since the beginning. A very honest & sincere chap, & gets very enthusiastic over things – & infuses spirit into everyone.

... The King's speech was indeed very good, or at least, well delivered, don't you think? Good Old King, bless his heart – I did like the way they wandered into the House of Lords hand-in-hand!

[*17.8.45*]

... It's so nice being quiet & writing & reading. We went for a walk in the Hönan again & sniffed the pines – it is a lovely wood. The pines so slim and smooth in their texture, going up & up & up, till they are lost in a dark green mass of pine needles... and the silence of a pine forest is <u>so</u> wonderful – such an electric silence, & you feel that it wants to burst into song and harmony at any moment.

... I've been working quite hard to-day – what with the weekly report. We arrested 9 people this week! Including one female. I have also divided all the teachers into 5 categories – ranking from non-party members to S.A. members & very undesirable people. Since you might be interested, I'll tell you the categories.

a) Non-party-members & nominal members of the Hitler Jugend (every boy & girl had to go into it).

b) Party members who joined 1 May 37 or later, & who have been proved to have not been interested in politics – or rather, the Nazi ideals.

c) Party members who joined earlier than 1933 – also Junior grades in other National Socialist organizations other than the party proper (=NSDAP = National-Socialist-Arbeit-Partei).

d) Party people who were also members of the S.A. (Storm troops of the party = SA = Sturm Abteilung = "Storm Dept"), or the S.S. (= Schutz Staffel, of ugly fame!) – and minor officials of the N.S.D.A.P.

e) Undesirables, Officials of the Party, arrested personnel, etc., suspected   people – these won't on any account become teachers again.

So there it is, did it all myself, I did! – I don't know what you think of it, but the use of it is when all the teachers in Category "A" are re-employed and there still aren't enough (which there won't be), and they relax the restriction a bit (as they will), I shall bring forward Category "B" for employment! And when they need even more, Category "C" will perhaps be 'released'! It's really all quite interesting, even though it's only constructive in a destructive kind of way.

... There are so many illicit ways of getting money now in Germany – selling cigarettes, coffee, Army rations – dreadful. So much of it is going on just now, too. What a peculiar thing money is – so sought after by many who have the least need of it...

[23.8.45]
... Mmm, what have I done to-day... well, spent this morning here and in the gaol, interrogating people, some of whom seem to

have been running an illicit mail service into an S.S. camp near here, called Sandbostel; all breaking the law, rather, & they will have to be prosecuted. Then this afternoon with Karl <u>to</u> Sandbostel S.S. Camp – it has about 5,000 S.S. men and officers, including also political prisoners. Then down to Zeven & collect a bloke, who wasn't there after all – a Count from Eastern Germany who was in the Gestapo (all this shockingly secret, by the way!)... The whole journey done with Karl in his "Wanderer" car.

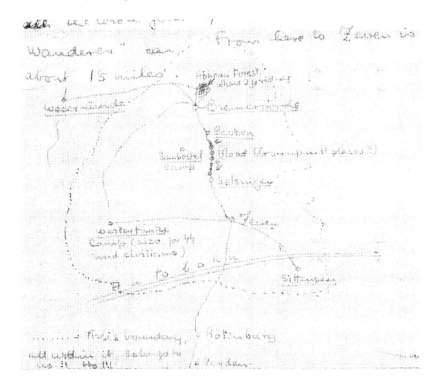

From here to Zeven is about 15 miles – all within it belongs to us!! Ho!! ... Then, after buying my NAAFI ration = 1 bottle of whiskey, ½ bottle of Gin, 65 cigarettes, soap, & 2 bars of chocolates – whiskey goes towards barter for Gil's Leica, cigarettes too. Gin to a bloke who's going on leave next week – chocolate if milk for me, if plain to Peggy (sounds horribly selfish, but anyway, she only likes plain, so that's useful!).

... To-morrow I'm going to Zeven for the day to operate on a Kreis Control point – I'm supposed to be there from 9 o'clock in the morning till 9.0 the next morning, but I shan't

[25.8.45]

... I think we must be awfully dopey out here, all back-waterish and all that, no one ever talks of the war, atomic bomb, Japan, or anything else of topical interest! Ivor talks of people at home that never knew there was a war on, but we certainly don't know it here, I must say – or didn't when there was one with Japan. You see, Woozel, people begin to forget so quickly. No, all we talk is on music, philosophy and art (if I am talking with Peggy) – music & photography (if with Sgt Gubby), 'shop', future jobs & section scandal (with Martin), Cameras, Loot & gossip (with everyone else!). The most important subjects like You and Religion and The Weather (!sorry, it isn't really important, but it just pushed itself in!) I speak about to everyone, but mostly to Ivor and Peggy, naturally. But we aren't really very world-conscience, I'm afraid, and we are in a continual doze – but it's very pleasant, and perhaps excusable after having done quite a lot to finishing it all off (?mm).

But people forget, oh how they forget! Woozel, if Justice isn't done soon about the goods Germany stole from Holland, France, Belgium, Czechoslovakia & Poland, it never will. Do you realize that before Germans left all those countries they took nearly all the horses, cows – everything, pigs, yes, even prams, bikes, cars – and it's still in Germany, it hasn't been returned at all yet! The farmers are laying in a huge stock for their winter needs by killing the foreign stock that came from the occupied countries. That's why now these nations are so poorly off for everything – everything has gone, and it hasn't been returned.

And why not? You see, unless there is issued a law or order about The Return of Foreign Stock, no Military Government of

Germany will do it of their own accord. It only means more trouble for them, taking goods away from the people under their administration, doesn't it? People aren't any different now to what they were before. Big business men are getting "Interested" in the fact that Germany's industries – or 80% of them – are in working order as you know – of course they are, they're no different either! And Military Government aren't interested in finding extra work. Of course, if the people starve they will no doubt say "Serve the bastards right" as so many seem to do out here, but it will mean an awful lot for them to do!!

... Perhaps all the stolen goods will go back to their rightful owners, I very much hope they do. But it's the people who <u>forget</u> that are going to be the obstacle. And the main obstacle consists of forgetting-people who never suffered a thing!

[28.8.45]

... Then I got back & found an <u>awful</u> shock, that one of the small party officials I had arrested last week had (a), been a very good & unpolitical member of his village, and the Bürgermeister and the whole village wrote a petition to say so, & that his past had only been purely nominal – not only that, but that he was a Christian Scientist! Oh, my <u>Gosh</u>, I've never yet felt so upset – I've always tried to be just – probably not always succeeded, but <u>tried</u>, and then comes this case and I do something horribly unjust like that. And now of course he's in the concentration camp and I can't do anything about it save write a report on him. Oh dear, I <u>am</u> fed & unhappy about it – I've been <u>longing</u> to meet a German C.S., and then the first I meet I go & put in prison!

Oh ... this is a lousy job, it really is, I can think of nothing lousier... <u>zzzzz</u> – and that bloody fool Martin must go & say perkily "Ah well, freemasonry again – you mustn't let sentiment come before your work!" – For which I could have cheerfully kicked him. By which time I was so fed, & I'd promised to take Sgt. Gubby to Cuxhaven, and wanted to write you instead – but thought perhaps the air would blow my gloom away, & if I wrote you I'd only brown you off, & anyway I'd promised, so we got into Karl's car, put Peggy in too, & drove off through a glorious evening...

They tried to cheer me up, & sang & talked (and looked at me to see if I was any happier, in such a sweet & naïve way, I just couldn't be gloomy any more, so talked & sang too!). Bless their hearts, Sgt. Gubby is a <u>most</u> kindly fellow, he really has an <u>enormous</u> heart! So we got into singing bits of Brahms' symphonies and guessing what they were, and had rather a wonderful evening.

... Ho, we caught a Kreisleiter to-day! I was browned off with arresting people, but he was so very much a Kreisleiter that I didn't mind so much. Oh but I am fed about the other chap... It's all <u>wrong</u>, and I've gone and been influenced by its wrongness. My work and my religion have been going closely parallel to each other for a long time, & now they've bumped, and it's a shock, a nasty one, too.

[2.9.45]

... You and your VJ day celebrations! What a gadabout old thing! Actually I secretly very much admired your campaign through London.

... To-day guess what I've been doing? I've been <u>sailing</u>, on the Elbe! George, Martin, Eric Baylis, Terry Clare, Tony Browers, the Landrat (Lord Lieutenant of the Kreis Bremervörde, more or less), and a nephew of his, on a little thirty-foot & one-cabined boat, which belongs to the Landrat. We started from Freiburg (N. of Stade), and went up the Elbe, towards Hamburg! Oh Darling, it was <u>such</u> fun, swishing along! The Elbe there is about 2 or 3 miles wide, so there was plenty of room, & it was rather like being on the sea. The cabin had fittings & two little bunks. The boat was like the ones that go about the Norfolk Broads, I should think.

Oh, but it was terrific and so lovely. In the afternoon the water became quite choppy and it was even more exciting. I took a turn at handling it, too... but isn't it terrific when the wind blows hard, & it slopes & races at such a speed through the water! Oh, it <u>was</u> an enjoyable day.

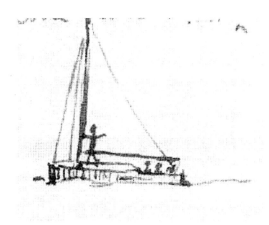

... Oh ha! I haven't told you! I've been promoted! (Everyone in Field Security has been.) All Full Corporals are to become Full Sergeants, all Lance-Corporals become Lance-Sergeants! So this is Lance-Sergeant Gifford speaking... and a Lance-Sergeant is an appointment which is just below a full Sgt. (6d a day less, that's all). I'll tell you how much I get now, soon!

[6.9.45]

... I don't think Life ever does line itself up into tidy rows & compartments, I agree with you there – but what I mean by the "Wrongness of it all" is that at times the <u>whole</u> thing seems so wrong to me. I know what it is to love a family & a home, & I am daily, on my own responsibility, taking away fathers & sons, & occasionally wives & daughters, from what they hold nearest & dearest. That is such a terrible thing to do <u>in itself</u>, that when I go and take a man who was really <u>innocent</u> away it is a <u>crime</u>, for which I am alone culpable. Innocent of what? Innocent of taking any part in the wrecking of Europe & the cause of the war. The C.S. I arrested <u>was</u> a man of this category – & I have got statements from the Bürgermeister of his village, the School superintendent of the Kreis, the chief clergyman of the Kreis, all to ask for his release & they all say he was an excellent fellow, & didn't even know he was a party official – so he couldn't have ever been very active. But anyway, I felt that I wasn't being careful enough in finding the just side to things & so being influenced by the tendency to do the job unconscientiously & without justice – for that <u>is</u> criminal – even if young-thoughtless-cum-careless. The arrest of that C.S. woke me up like a cold sponge and I saw then I wasn't going quite in the right direction – as I say, my religion & my job clashed, showing that my job had gone awry.

[8.9.45]

... And <u>very</u> many thanks for your letter of the 3rd Sept. My sweet, you've been feeling a bit muddled & depressed just lately, haven't you. Darling, I do understand <u>very</u> much and sympathise – work, or the failure to be able to rather, is quite the most frustrating of feelings, for it is energy turned aside. If that happens, the energy just walks gloomily round in circles inside you, its hands behind its back – and when you <u>are</u> able to work, it just turns its back and says "No, don't feel like it" – just to be cussed!

... I do feel this: that when I joined the Army I went somehow into another world – a world where men swore & said "bloody" & worse every other word, where drink and <u>shallowness</u> of character were not infrequent, where women served just one purpose & one topic of conversation, where music was a solo saxophone, where literature was the Daily Mirror, where food was often eaten with a knife... I met Bundle & lots of times with him slipped back into my old world again – where You were and where my real self was too. I met Ivor, & though much less, I still got glimpses of that world. Now I've met Peggy, I'm back in your & my world again, for she's one of us. And I've had depressed times as well as happy times with her – like when Stanley was neither here nor there, and it's been <u>very</u> good and happy.

... Yesterday & the day before we arrested quite a good lot – a Colonel in the S.A., a Colonel in the S.S. and a notorious sadist of an S.S. man to whom Bremervörde very much objected!

... & then off to see the C.I.C. (Counter Intelligence Corps), to enquire after a bloke (doctor) Peggy had worked for – we enquired there as he had also worked for the Gestapo (!nice friends she has!) – in a mild way. But we found he had been arrested – <u>and</u> released because he had done no evil or harm – so off we went to find him, & did – of course he was very pleased to see her & then we walked round the port a bit taking a photo. The Doctor bloke was <u>very</u> nice, & has some lovely children, one of which (aged 5) I was talking to whilst Peggy was in to visit him (I met him afterwards).

The journey back was terrific, as it was a glorious evening. In particular I noticed the <u>shadows</u> of the trees on the road were such a marked & beautiful blue, & purple...

[*10.9.45*]

... All day I was getting information on a bloke – rather an unsatisfactory business at the best.

[*11.9.45*]

... And tell Gil I've got his Leica! mmm! to-day... We went to Lüneburg to get a very big Nazi of evil repute round here & I asked him if he had a camera, & he produced a Leica! So I feel justified in taking it, as he said there wasn't a film in it when there was. So there you are. It's a F. 3:5 & up to 1/500th second, with a filter (detachable) – tell him I'm sorry it's not F1:2, but anyway it's quite good! I'll use it myself till I come home, & then he can have it, O.K? I hope he won't mind if we use it on our leave, too... I am glad I've got it at last, though – I've been trying for ages with no success. All I hope now is that it isn't taken off me by an enraged Military Govt.! I suppose it seems as if I am contradicting myself, for when Ivor & I got the other Leica I said it wasn't right, and I hope you don't think I am. I don't feel there is anything wrong in this case, for the person arrested was a very bad lot – has shot a French prisoner in the back & things like that.

[*17.9.45*]

... I obtained some NAAFI and one letter – from Truus Telkamp. Oh she <u>is</u> a sweet-natured person, she really is, and very fair & kind. While most continentals-other-than-Germans rave and swear and curse the Germans she, who has lost <u>far</u> more than most by their cruelty, never says a word against them unless it is "everywhere there are good people & bad". She had just been to the funeral service of yet another of her best friends who had died in Buchenwald camp, too. Yes, she is certainly an excellent person, and <u>so</u> cheerful.

[*22.9.45*]

... I've been to Verden to-day, to meet the new F.S.O., Captain Dyer – he's a very young chap, & about the exact opposite of the former C.O. – very enthusiastic & earnest, Catholic, 'sporty', used to be an actor before the war I think, has spent a long time in Greece training mountain troops. He had an "earnest talk" with me, and asked whether I was happy in everything. Whether I was intending to stay on and take a Control Commission post (to which I swiftly said Yes, <u>and</u> that I wanted to get married and have my wife out with me, as soon as I could), to which he said 'good' and he'd look out for opportunities etc. etc. I don't know that he knows an awful lot about it, but then I don't think anyone does, as it is still in the organizing stages. It is true that quite a few "A.C.C." officers have come out, but they seem to be mainly

Agricultural and Housing advisors. But I <u>am</u> going in front of the Colonel at 30 Corps, and find out what is what.

[*25.9.45*]

... And <u>my</u> motor bikes never went right again after they had once gone wrong! Even if – er – I did fondle them & clean them – & that's what made me suddenly feel, in my depression "The Human Mind <u>is</u> like a motor bike, and takes a mighty long time to heal – the adult one at any rate, for a certain type of mind, anyway" – but that was the result of the depression (the only good thing about depression is that you catch such interesting fish from the pool of your mind!), and your words of sense are very cool and refreshing on top of it all, Bless you.

[*26.9.45*]

And a very happy October 2nd to you! & here's something wot I drew & painted to show it... <u>Bless</u> you – it's been a very happy couple of years, thanks to your gentleness and understanding, quite the happiest I have ever spent! Oh sweet...

... But what I can't understand is, why on earth should any one <u>dream</u> of claiming to "possess" anyone else?! I think it's just either stupidity or downright paganism. – <u>no</u> one "belongs" to anyone else in this world – we belong to God, & Him only – I don't "belong" to you, & you don't to me, & never will! It's disgusting to say that someone "belongs" to me, just as if he were a stamp album or a Lost Soul or something! No human can possess another, <u>none</u>. And those verses in Romans were <u>very</u> exact, on actions towards your neighbours & very aptly quoted.

... Mmm, what happened to-day... Oh we had a <u>lovely</u> ride through the Höhne – there were thousands of frosted spiders' webs all over the little pine trees, making them look like Christmas trees... and one moment the trunks of the trees loomed purple &

everything was <u>bright blue</u>! Oh gosh, what beauty there is in this world.

[*30.9.45*]

... Saturday morning I spent Doing Things, mostly to do with a large S.S. Camp near here. Then Saturday afternoon I went with Mrs. Bloggs [Peggy][6] to Hamburg! And strolled into the concert hall & found to our delight that Beethoven's 9th was being played! it was <u>so</u> exciting a performance too – and <u>wonderfully</u> done – though as always, the soloists weren't too satisfactory – I think the soprano & alto parts are so difficult that it takes a superwoman to do justice to them, don't you?

... Went to the C.S. Rest Room in Hamburg, a lovely, typically clean and bright place, & met the two workers there – very nice people – ladies from Suffolk – I <u>am</u> so glad to know there is a C.S. centre in Hamburg. After chatting to them we went on to the Fair... a few things like Scenic railways & things, & at 10.0 it all closed down, so drove back to Bremervörde.

... Mme Bloggs & I went on to Wesermünde only about 9 or 10 miles away. There we visited the C.I.C. (American F.S.), to tell them that Martin couldn't go to a party there as he had gone on leave. And sat there talking quite a while, and had a glass of cognac – rather strong & tasting of soap. <u>How</u> people can drink that horrible stuff for pleasure, & lots of glasses at that, I just can't understand, really I can't

Then on to the American Red Cross Club, & ate doughnuts & coffee for a while & inspected the club's rooms – it's really <u>very</u> well organized, & all free. Music, writing, reading, drinking rooms – everything you could possibly want – even odd little rooms which don't seem to be for anything in particular, just with tables & chairs in them. We saw a Yank with a very fine American wind-jacket, over which Peggy got terrifically excited, & began coveting

---

[6] Bloggs was a name invented by the O.C. as a security alias for signing oneself out in one of the Sections.

it for all she was worth, as she had had one like it which was blown up when her house went. And of all lucky things the Yank came & sat at our table! & of course Peggy opened up a conversation on how desirable his jacket was (! – no, she led round to it, more or less – not quite so bad as it sounds), and I casually asked if he wanted to buy a pistol (I always bring one along in case I can get something useful in exchange), & in 10 minutes the jacket was mine! or rather Peggy's, as she wanted it in the first place, and I didn't really at all – still, it certainly was a good bargain, wasn't it.

[Douglas' second leave was from the 8th – 29th of October. A "12 days" leave extended to three weeks.]

[*29.10.45*]

It's an absolute scream, everyone has been looking furtively at their leave passes and asking other people what their Party Numbers are! It's terrific, really it is – there's <u>no one</u> who has the right one, I'm sure! The best <u>I</u> have encountered (or the worst, if you like!) is 56! Cor... and now in the train everybody is telling "How-I-reported-last-Tuesday" stories. I've never seen soldiers looking so coy before! All with whacking great consciences – I wonder... I certainly haven't!

Oh sweet, wasn't it a terrific three weeks – we've done <u>such</u> a lot, haven't we, & had such fun. I feel so full & happy, & not really very browned off – though of course I <u>might</u> well have done with another fortnight or so... ! Oh sweet, I do love you! There's <u>such</u> a lot to <u>digest</u>, isn't there, to be thankful for. I just can't <u>begin</u> to say how <u>very</u> <u>very</u> much I loved hearing you lecture and going round with you! It has filled up a big gap, I'm sure – I was always awfully misty & vague-feeling about your work, & rather lacking in interest because I knew so little about it – but now I feel I want a word for word report on each one! And it must be nice for you too for writing – miles happier & easier, as I know the people & everything.

[*30.10.45*]

Darling Bear,

Gosh what a train journey – but I managed very well (clever & astute Toad that I am). We were relegated to Wooden seats which was rather grim (at Calais), but I went off on my own and found a sort of throne in the guard's van where he looks out of the top of the train, to see what is going on (with a little table to write on in front of it). I clambered up & spent a very good night lying the whole length of them both! The guard sat down below on another seat. Then this morning I moved back into a wooden seated compartment, as the light wasn't too good in the guard's van, for reading. The journey only lasted 22 hours (instead of the previous 28 or 27), which was very good, really. The voyage across the channel was perfect – you could see the French cliffs <u>so</u> clearly from Dover!

[*31.10.45*]

... But here in Bremervörde the news is nothing short of terrible. (All this <u>very private</u> & <u>secret</u>, by the way.) Karl is in prison, Ella Bechmann is in prison, Spike Martin is under arrest, Terry Clare is half under arrest, oh dear... the worst is that Karl is in, for he is so honest. But there was a "do", where some bottles of drink were looted (by Spike – quite the natural thing for the section to do!) – or rather, dug up from a garden, and since Karl was driving the car which bore it away, he was arrested too. Oh dear me. Then Terry Clare is also a bit implicated in it. Spike will perhaps have to go up for Court Martial, to-morrow, poor chap. It is really awfully tough luck, and quite one of the <u>mildest</u> things the section has done (look at me & the Leica!), and they went & got caught. (The people complained to the C.M.P., took the number of Karl's car, & there it was, all done.) Oh gosh, what an awful mess. Ella Beckmann went into prison (for a year), for doing something in the Black Market, I think. Really, it is shocking. Karl is down at Div. H.Q. awaiting trial now.

I drove the Jeep quite a lot of the way up here, and have been talking over all this most of the time since with Martin & Terry, & then up to my room, after a long chat with the Schlichtings, who were very pleased to see me back. My room is much the same, & very cheering & friendly – some flowers left by Peggy about a week ago when I was expected back, and masses of tins of food in the drawer also left by her, I presume. (Things like tinned "Roast Lamb & peas" & tinned cheese & Spam!) I have put my photos (or rather, yours) & pictures up again, too.

[2.11.45]

... Well, the first day was spent ploughing through reams & reams of teachers which had piled up in my absence – last night Stanley & Peggy came in to listen to records & have coffee, which was quite nice, & cheered me up slightly. To-day we moved office to a larger place, & spent a lot of the day settling in. A row with Martin over office filing of information rounded off the day – & now I am waiting for Dorothy to come to coffee, with Terry.

... It's raining like nothing-on-earth & being foggy & misty here now – how is it by you? Oh Bear...

Sweet, could you send me a packet of saccharine tablets, please? 'Cos the rations here have now been cut down by a third & consequently there is not much sugar, & none extra for people like myself's use. Mmm, please?

[4.11.45]

And Hooray for the first letter! <u>Bless</u> you, and what a nice one, just what I wanted! <u>Eee</u>, my fat old woozle. Do you know, coming home last night in the truck by myself I sang songs praising you in four languages! About La Woozella, La Woozelle, Die Woochel, & just Woozel. It was <u>terrific</u>, and I enjoyed myself no end, & then I had four conversations (in Spanish, French, German, American, & English), bargaining for you! (!Yes, but I was quite alone, dear, so

no-one heard me!) Eee, but I did enjoy the drive! I had been to
Syke to get some more records – I got the 39 & 40th of Mozart
(40th minus the 1st movement, which they didn't have – grrr!), 4
symphonies by Haydn, Mozart's 32nd (all on one record – which I
bought – for 8 marks!), & Dvorak's Cello Concerto. Then went to
a place called Bassum where poor old Karl is languishing in prison
& got permission to see him after waiting for an hour – poor chap,
he is terribly browned off, & I don't blame him, either – having
suffered so much under the Nazis & now all this... but I managed
to cheer him up, & also cheered the prison up generally by ticking
the gaoler off, who is reputed to treat the prisoners very badly. Oh
dear, what a do. But Karl <u>should</u> have been out the day before
yesterday! Considering he's only a <u>witness</u>, really, anyway...

... Well, & this evening I spent writing my diary & listening to
all the new records with Peggy, who was in a Dreadful & Gloomy
Mood, which created rather a depressing atmosphere until she had
got it all off her chest. She was feeling she wasn't "getting
anywhere" – there are her parents & brothers who have lost their
house (blown up), & money, & she is doing nothing to help them.
So she intends to, at the first opportunity, & meantime study hard.
I quite expect she will, too.

... Yes, well, could you send the paper you-think-we-should-
do-Mr. Greystone's-card-on, and <u>also</u> (v. important) the green &
white <u>card</u> I bought in Oxford, eee? please sweet? And if I need the
rest I'll ask you to send it? Mmm, & most important too, could you
send me a pan of ultramarine & a pan of indigo?

[*6.11.45*]
... This afternoon I went to Zeven & did some sundry vetting &
met two members of the new Social-Democratic Party – one of
them was an old fellow with a <u>wonderful</u> white moustache!

He said that he swore he'd never touch politics & there now, there he was drawn into organizing the S.P.D. (Sozialdemokratische Partei Deutschlands).

Dr. von Heyman

[*10.11.45*]

Oh, I got Karl out of prison – or rather, I went along to Div. H.Q., & he was already being bailed out in court – he had to pay 250 mks bail (£6.5.0), & free he was! Another bloke was with him, who had also been mixed up in the affair, & he came out too. Karl was terribly depressed and thought it all a deep disgrace. Still, the town doesn't know anything about it, so his disgrace is only in his own eyes. It's rather a shame, though, to go & imprison witnesses like that. To-day he was his merry self again & went bustling around getting things. He has procured me a little electric cooker-ring, which isn't quite as good as a fire, but which will warm things quite a bit, & perhaps I'll be able to put my feet on it. Also, we'll all be able to make tea in the office in the mornings, & coffee at nights when Frau Schlichting isn't in.

And I had an <u>excellent</u> teachers' meeting yesterday afternoon, quite the best ever. We had a very good general discussion, & laid down some more definite rules about the reinstating of teachers, & then to business. Oh, a very cheering meeting altogether.

… And don't you go apologizing for wot you said to my driving, 'cos I won't 'ave it, see? Quite apart from that, though, & looking at it objectively, I do rather join with you in looking apprehensively at things like nervousness & narkiness, & I hope they don't worry you too much. With such responsibilities and in such circs. there is only one alternative to A Running Commentary (!<u>Bless</u> you!), & that is containing oneself & feeling rather het-up inside. Of the two yours is miles more honest & outspoken. I should <u>hate</u> you to become one of the Nervous-&-Sensitive-Elderly-Female types who store things up inside them and quiver silently at things. They have to break down to someone & to pour their troubles out & ask for sympathy. Poor Mother, she is prone to that quite a lot, and if she has become like that through all her sufferings, then the answer is simple. For rather than ever let other people suffer, she would take it all on herself in silence, & so store up a multitude of fears & worries while her neighbours would go on placidly, quite unaware of the storm that had been going on and from which they had been sheltered. I think that <u>pure</u> unselfishness is more saintly than human, but that <u>with</u> humans it just doesn't always work out to be common sense & practical, somehow.

[*12.11.45*]

Hallo & thanks very much for yours of the 7th, bless you. I feel all Flat & Exhausted, having been in a high state of excitement all day. Martin & I went to section H.Q. & found everyone terribly sour & browned off there – a horrid shock, rather. They are all at their wits' end over the O.C., who appears to be very queer. Poor George, how he stands it all, I don't know – what with the O.C. and us groaning away! Anyway, Ivor is Back! Sans moustache, again! Rather fed-up, poor fellow – it has been a terrific rush for him – he only saw Pamela twice I think & spent a week getting from England to here! And three days after Mr. Furst died, his sister had her baby (a daughter) – but all went well. I went with him to the photographers in Verden to give some films in, and then got some pay from George, and he typed out my official application for the commission. (He says the O.C. didn't do a thing abut it, and finally asked him to do it as he hadn't any idea how to!) So <u>that's</u> all right. Ivor says he's sure I'll get it all right – I have to serve a year's commissioned service, but that's pretty safe as I don't expect I'll be out under a year from now. Then just before that the O.C. had come in, and said we couldn't employ Karl any more, which got me very mad, so I went down and had A

Talk with him, pointing out the injustice of it. Actually, Martin was an ass to have brought up the question at all, but since he did, the O.C. thought he'd be officious just for officiousness sake. Anyway, in the end it became more or less all right – but I did get upset over it. I mean, if there was any <u>justice</u> in it I wouldn't mind, but Karl did <u>nothing at all</u> – he just did as he was told. And now the O.C. has gone and put Spike's case up for Court-Martial proper, when he needn't have done at all! My goodness, it's wicked, really it is – to do a thing like that. <u>Everybody</u> in the section has done something or other in their Army careers, and in all cases they're worse! I don't know exactly how much other people have taken, but I've had: <u>Two</u> Leicas, one typewriter, one pair of binoculars, one camera (folding), & goodness knows what else. Just imagine if I was charged with all that! I've taken part in the lifting of cases & <u>cases</u> of wines, spirits & what not (all this, of course, from Nazis, but still I have!). I don't say all this to shock you, but to show that Spike was just unfortunate. Bless you, I'm not saying it's <u>right</u>, in the very least, but you see Spike was taking (he thought) German Army property, and then of course it turned out to be private, by which time anyway he had returned most of it.

… Darling I <u>would</u> very much love some coffee if you can get it – I had half a packet (½ lb?) from your mother, but it's all gone now!

Terry? Is 38, a war-time policeman, a future farmer, but <u>very</u> dignified and quite sensible. He always has a pipe, moustache & often glasses. You'd expect to see him in a West End Club somehow. (How he was ever a policeman, I don't know!)

[*15.11.45*]

… Thanks for your letter of the 8th – after a good evening at Peterboro' – it made me very excited, especially when I could imagine it all – oh, it <u>does</u> help – with the vision of a Fatface sitting on a desk & Holding Forth, with Miss Stanyon bouncing up & down in her seat, the R.A.F. demobbed W.O.'s eyes glittering (!), the class representative (Mary?) getting excited, the funny old gardening woman in the front getting het-up, an elderly class secretary thumping his fist, the two cronies in the middle knitting furiously, & the pale-faced one at the back writing away at a great speed – of course, I don't enpoot they do all those things, but I can imagine them!! But Bless you, I am pleased you had such a good evening. And now it is 7.40, and you will be starting again at Peterboro' – on Huxley? I see you're lecturing some time on Osbert Sitwell, too.

... Ho, & I have a little radio! A little Phillips one & rather sweet, Got it to-day from the new Landrat. (Yes we instated a new Landrat the day-before-yesterday: put the Bürgermeister in his place, & put the Head Master of the Bremervörde schools in his place.) And also a new bulb (100 watt) to replace the old one, which was too dim (40 watt), in the centre of my room. And my little electric cooker is working very well, too, & I boil my shaving water on it every morning.

... I am doing quite a lot of interesting "research" on German politics just now – going through old election files & getting statistics & things. If I ever become an officer and can specialize, I would so like to do so in politics (internal), and/or education. The elections results of 1929 were rather amazing – the Nazi Coup d'Etat wasn't to come for another 4 years, and it was still in the money-collecting-boxes-in-the-streets-stage, and yet the largest party vote in this Kreis went to the Nazis! It's queer, isn't it. Then there was a party called the Black Front, which opposed the Nazis. One of the leaders lived in Bremervörde, and whenever a Nazi orator was laying down the law he would jump onto a table and contradict him! A very brave chap, and the amazing thing was that although he was persecuted for 12 years, he never was put into a concentration camp. He [Dr. Von Heyman] was a doctor, and went into the Army in 1939, where he was more or less safe for a while – till 1944, when he was put under house arrest, & then sent to Oldenburg to take charge of a hospital. He came to our office to-day, having been demobilized about 14 days ago. We talked away for hours, and he proved to be as interesting as one might expect. He looks rather like Sir Henry Wood, with his beard, only shorter & not so fat. His eyes are piercingly sharp, & his eyebrows turn upwards, like those of a demon!

[*19.11.45*]

... I went to church to a concert! The first amateur one yet in Germany I've heard. Oh sweet, it <u>was</u> nice. A choir, two violins, a cello & an organ – all up in the choir-&-organ loft. The Pastor espied me before, & came along with the music of "Unser Leben ist ein Schatten" and "Jesu meine Freude" for me to follow – wasn't that nice of him – I know him very well from the teachers' do's. Diedrich Buxtehude – could you look him up in the O.C.M.? – he's <u>very</u> like Rosenmüller, you'd love him. There were a great number of people in the church, which is very homely – reminds one rather of a drawing room. Pastor Schulz conducted the choir & trio & things. "Gemeinde" is where we all sang. ("Gemeinde" meaning community).

Then we fried things like spam & onions – honestly, the amount of food there is in my room. All stowed away in the night table! They come from Red Cross parcels the Yugoslavs had, & which Peggy collected, for the most part. (X'coose the list – now I remember what you said once about "lists of food"!)

Still, it's rather good because we can have something for supper about 10-ish every night.

[*23.11.45*]

... To-day I went to Stade to seek a War Criminal, but didn't find him – our transport situation is absolutely hopeless – H.Q. has pinched the P.U., and yesterday we spent trying to get the 15 cwt going – an enormous crowd of Mil Govt. people crowded round & we all pushed it, then an engineer truck pushed it, but all of no

171

avail, and the thing just stopped. So it was ignominiously towed back to REME, from whence it had just come, the petrol system having been renewed (or something) – now they're taking the petrol system down all over again – they don't seem to realize that it won't go because the batteries are flat. Mmm.

... Another thing about Release in Tuesday's Telegraph of the 20th – did you see it? "... a number of part-trained men teachers whose courses at university training departments & teachers training colleges who were interrupted by military service are to receive class "B" release from the Forces..." I would send you the cutting only I think I'll write to Tommy Wright and ask him whether there is any hope, showing him that. Oh, I do hope it comes, even if not in 1945, in 1946 some time...

[*29.11.45*]

Here I am, feeling utterly cheesed off, fed up & pipped... Goodness knows why, but we had a lot of orders up from the O.C. saying that we had to start nine extra card-indexes! And when I asked if I could go to Hamburg (to collect the Christmas Card blocks), he said I couldn't! What a bloke... It's so annoying – of course I shall go, and that side doesn't matter – but just the fact that he won't grant the permission, when every private gets at the very least one day a week there! (Generally one day in five), Oh zzzz. And Spike's case is coming off in a week's time, & he is going to plead guilty, as things look so bad... oh dear oh dear oh dear...

Later / And now I feel miles better! That was 7.30, that was, before Martin and I then went off to see Dr. von Heyman and his wife. They have a very nice house, & are well off. The wife is a painter, and the husband a doctor. He has a pointed beard & funny eyebrows that go upwards at the corners. He published an anti-Nazi newspaper in '32, part of the "Black Front!" – Goodness knows how he managed to keep alive till now! He was in the Army in Russia, as a medical officer. We talked all evening, about music, politics (!always!), and life in Russia – which was most interesting –

he had a very favourable impression of the Soviet System, and didn't seem to think that there was much evil – in the results, as far as he had personally seen. The means to those results were terrible, however. He had also lived in a Leper colony there, and praised the Russian doctors and the State system of schooling and medical aid etc. Apparently the Communist party there is about 2,000,000 strong – not very large. One can say what one thinks, and feels, and wishes, though, and the political set-up is in no way so petty & widespread as in Germany – one doesn't have to give a communist salute or say "Heil Stalin" for instance, as one did in Germany.

[*1.12.45*]

Eee! Here I am in Hamburg! Oh I have had a nice afternoon – Peggy & I got onto a R.E.M.E. truck and came down here – then collected my Christmas Card Blocks! Sweet, I do hope you like it – they enclosed examples of what it looked like, printed, and it is quite nice! Gosh I was excited! They've done it in red, blue, yellow, & black – the result looks quite like the original (!no, it really does! – I mean, even though it's only a ¼ as big, ever such a lot of details have come out). Oh Bear... our card!

[*3.12.45*]

... No, the Yugoslavs & Poles found (or looted!) a lot of Red X parcels themselves, & have been using them since, so there isn't really much wickedness in getting one from them – they have masses of them anyway. And I think they are going to be sent more from Canada, and they also get rations as well...

... Hmmm, I've been writing a report out on the political movements (results of three weeks work!). I'll send you a copy of it in my next letter – it may interest you – I'm afraid most of it is a list of names and addresses, but it'll show you what things we do (or I do, rather).

[*5.12.45*]

... I enclose that report I was talking about: "Niedersächische Landes-partei" is "Lower-Saxony-Lands party" – "Deutsche Arbeiter Partei" = German Labour Party (the bloke actually withdrew it two days ago, having realised that the S.P.D. & N.L.P. incorporated all his beliefs). The S.P.D. has long been Germany's main party up to 1933 – the N.L.P. (formerly the "Hannoversche" party) was very strong in Hannover, but not so much so in other parts (Bode is in the province of Hannover, as you probably know. The S.P.D. is Left wing, the N.L.P. right. The "Kampfgemeinschaft Gegen Fascismus" ("Fighting Union against Fascism") may be a Communist Party do – we're not sure yet.

Do show the report to Janet if she is at all interested won't you, but keep it Safely in your possession, as it's not supposed to have come out of Germany.

[*8.12.45*]

... About that release for teachers, darling, you <u>were</u> right, so many apologies – and anyway the scheme applies to groups 1 to 49 only, which counts me out. But I feel an opportunity <u>will</u> come along some day, so that I had far better have a go at everything that looks like one. I'll send on the commission thing now. I had a letter from Oxford dept. Ed. saying the application was in order, and they would be glad to see me when I get out, etc. – rather vague, I must say. Never mind, even if it was a path wot came to a stop, I'll still go up other paths, as I said!

... Dear me, I never knew I wrote breezy letters! Still, I'm glad it (they) cheered you up; Spike's Court Martial went quite well, actually. The prosecution only had about six words to say, no witnesses were called. He pleaded guilty to the charge of taking twenty bottles of liquor, but as it stands they belonged to the Nazi Kreisleiter of Wesermünde; the sentence has been promulgated, so we shall know in 16 days' time or so.

Your painting wot I gave you for your Birthday? Well, I got it from Alfred Wiegmann, a painter who lives near here in a place called Kuhstedt (on the map) and who periodically sends in rather

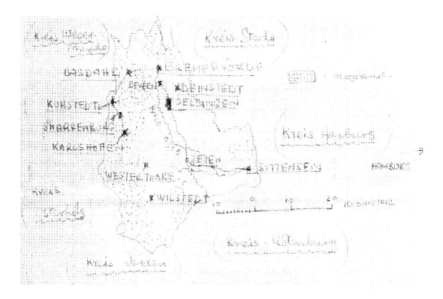

potty political denunciations, but who is one of the best artists I have ever met – a wonderful sense of shadow and light – surely I told you about him? Well, he does a lot like yours, and I especially liked that one, & asked the price – he said about 800 marks, if one paid for it (he is quite a famous painter), which comes to £20, which rather laid me out – but I managed in the end to get it for the sum of 250 cigarettes & chocolate & soap! There, I hope you aren't very cast down by the means by which your painting came into my hand! I also got a small one of his, which isn't so good actually, & doesn't have any trees. It's a flock of sheep, but I like it because of the sky. Oh, but I do love trees... I could go on painting them for ages & ages. Your painting, however, is of the moorland near Kuhstedt – it's typical of the roads or ways round here... It is really lovely country, in a flat sort of way.

... I say (he said, remembering his Gifford-self), can I have some coffee or Instant Postum, sometime, please sweet?

Later / and Stan came in and we had some cocoa made from chocolate, & some toast, which he made, and honey-in-the-comb. He has sold nearly a hundred of my Christmas cards – isn't he terrific!... then Peggy suddenly wanted to play poker! Drat the girl, I thought... and so we did, for an hour or so. I'm beginning to get horribly bored with the game – bad, isn't it. I don't know, I don't like any card games very much; they just seem a waste of time. A game of chess is different because there is skill in it – but games of chance & luck I dislike because you haven't achieved anything at all at the end. Or am I getting all grumpy & crabbed?! Oh um... I just wouldn't faint with grief if we didn't have a pack of cards in our home, that's all. It's not creative enough, though I suppose it does exercise the brain a bit. Oh well.

[*10.12.45*]

Gosh, I have been busy to-day Darling, here It is – I do hope you like it... ?!!!

I went to Bremen this morning and collected 800 more cards, this time well done, though smaller. I enclose too one of the former effort, wot made me so upset (now don't go & say you prefer it!) – the text is a bit nicer, & it's bigger – still the picture is the main thing – oh sweet... (he said, hopping about on one foot in anxiety). Well, it's done now. (Remember, it's a Christmas design, & not a

100% picture, won't you? I mean, in case you think it's too symmetrical...)

... But I've been feeling terrifically complacent this evening: for some reason I feel very pleased with my painted cards – your Mother's & Father's I am rather fond of – I say, I've sent Monica the boggy one – does it matter, do you think – oh it's rather a nice one anyway, & yours, & Gildas a rather small one, wot took hours to do – Deryck's is about the least good, but that took <u>ages</u> to do – I'm sending it to you to be redirected – have a look at it, eeee?

[*12.12.45*]

... I have got the bulk of the Christmas cards off – and as for the remainder of the 1800 printed George asked for 50 more to give to a padre, and himself ordered 12. Ivor wants some, I got the REME here to take 50, and I've sold about 100 to the Engineers, and 50 to Stanley, of course. I've received the money for the Engineers', Stanley's & George's dozen, coming to 97 marks (=£2.8.6d). I am getting a further 500 done with the text in German and will see how Karl can dispose of them in Hamburg. The rest Ludwig Meya has kept, to sell as he can (he has the queer ones). Oh dear, it's getting quite a big Concern – but I just want to get back the 273 marks, that's all = £6-16-6d, which was the total cost. (Blocks made 131 mks = £3-5-6d, bad print of Meya 50 mks = £1-5-0, & he kept 800 of the 1000 to sell himself, & 92 mks – £2-6-0 for the good print (8000 copies).) So there <u>is</u> quite a bit of work to be done yet not to lose on it. I'd feel a bit inefficient, somehow (I now feel), if we <u>did</u> come off very much the poorer because of it – though of course, what does it matter!

... You know, I'd rather get as much training and "paper" qualifications as possible when the opportunity is there, as later on in life it gets very difficult to be able to go back and do those things (like degrees, etc.). There is no doubt that they help enormously, too. And <u>if</u> grants are forthcoming, I don't see why we couldn't live in Oxford for a while. In a place like that, our sojourn there could be made into a dizzily happy time, you know – it <u>could</u> be just about perfect – providing you had something to do too, oh sweet, yes.

[*15.12.45*]

... I've written to Auntie Doris, & also to Uncle Sid – if you possibly can, could you go to Tottenham & see them there? – they would be <u>so</u> pleased & happy to see you, and it would be an awfully Good Thing... eee? They're not very grand people & all that, but <u>very</u> kindly and full of common sense, and – oh, I do hope you can manage it, sweet. Uh, I do ask a lot of you, though, don't I! "Meet this one & this one & this one, send this & this, & do this" etc. – and you never grumble or complain! But don't say that I was in London much on my leave – not that I was anyway – or they'll be very offended I didn't go to see them, I am afraid. I said in my letter that I was on leave in October and that I had only two leaves so far, but didn't mention the one in May, though it doesn't matter at all, really.

... I attended a German Vetting Committee the other night – that is, a group of about 17 anti-Nazis who want to clean out the local civil services and offices of Nazis who were in them before (It's amazing how many there are left – especially minor officials) – they had brought up a list of about 75 questionable civil servants in Bremervörde for us to vet & then at this committee meeting they would decide which people were to stay in or not. Out of the 75, do you know how many they wanted to sling out? About 72! Whew! They were "hotter!" than any Mil Govt. or F.S. meetings I've been to.

... I gather Dorothy is having rather a muddle, what with being fond of her fiancé and fonder still of her work – at present. But it was interesting, somehow, not because of Dorothy's case, but to hear her & Peggy expounding their views on the British after such a short acquaintance with them. They are both the same in that they know a lot about The British in general – (this came up because

Dorothy said she was sure the British families were happiest, having the best husbands) – and, of course, they (D&P) are a bit idealistic. Still, though it looks very muddled here, the discussion was quite logical in its course, though we did end up at the same point as where we started. Look, does this, do you think, ring true in England: "Men choose as a rule mates of a lower intellectual plane than themselves"? I <u>have</u> heard it said a lot, here and there, but I can't remember whether it was in England or in Germany. In any case, do you think that the <u>human</u> trend in a man is to Fall in love (or whatever you wish to call it) with a less intelligent person than himself? Mark the "human" (as distinct from the spiritual, or the animal as from the intellectual). You know, I've a feeling that is a very hackneyed subject, but I'm blowed if I can remember whether we talked about it before!

... But (he said, wandering off on his own track), I can't <u>quite</u> remember for what reason I did fall in love with you at first – I think it was because you were so <u>friendly</u>... mmm... <u>and</u> beautiful, of course – mmm, I'm not exactly sure, now I come to think of it... perhaps it was because you were so affectionate – yes that was it <u>definitely</u> – oh Bear, you <u>were</u> nice to me, & so-equal-and-not-haughty, or anything. Yes, <u>that</u> was it. But you were beautiful at the same time, and I liked you that way. <u>Mmm</u> eee, anyway, I've got you now (cries of "no you haven't!" from self-possessed and Independent Bear). No, well, I meant it metaphorically, so there!

I'm enclosing one of the Divisional cards for your interest – they're a bit like advertisements for something, but the idea is quite worthy – beating swords into ploughshares...

It's raining a lot, & snowing sometimes – dreadful weather – what is it like in England?

[*19.12.45*]

... I say, I've been listening to "Prince Igor", for the first time, really – isn't it great fun – I love it, and the whole opera was performed. Verdi's Requiem was lovely, too – but I told you about that, didn't I.

... Do you know what my NAAFI Issue for Christmas in sweets, chocolates etc is? <u>Seven</u> Toffees! Isn't it a swizz! And no chocolate or anything (tears). Cor, but there isn't 'arf a lot of liquor – though that isn't much help for me – still, I'll do quite well no doubt, on food (!), so perhaps won't need so much in the chocolate line. But it <u>is</u> rather a swizzle, isn't it. We got lots more last Christmas (sniff!!). Anyway, I was able to get a pot of Marmite.

[*24.12.45*]

... Ummm... well, I started off on Thursday morning in a Canadian Ford 15 cwt truck, sort of queer looking thing, & very wide one – with a Scotsman called Jock Cramb, a very nice fellow, quiet and gentle, as co-driver (though he didn't co-drive except once, for an hour) – and so by Bremen, Delmenhorst, Lingen, Nordhorn, Arnhem, Nijmegen and Eindhoven. We had to stop every 25 or so miles to put more oil in the engine (in 500 miles it used nearly 5 <u>gallons</u> of oil!), and I cut my finger on the oil drum, which was rather a nuisance. At Arnhem we ran into a thick fog, which made driving exceedingly difficult, and me even more exhausted & weary, having driven the whole way. Anyway, we got to Eindhoven and were warmly received by Tony and his family (the object of this journey being to pick Tony up off leave, as I think I told you).

... The next morning we started off at nine, called in at some friends of Tony's, and of course had to have a cup of chocolate there with them – then back to Tony's to collect something we'd forgotten (including my shaving brush and soap!) – and then down towards Roermond, me driving as usual. Tony began to feel a bit queer, and sat in the back of the truck. We stopped at Heythuisen, to see Jo & Truce, and poor Tony's <u>face</u> had swollen up to a tremendous size! Apparently it always does that when he has eaten red-currants. Anyway, we went in to see J. & T., and there they were, just the same, and of course very pleased to see me. Tony went off to see a doctor, who said that it was oversensitivity in his system that did it and that he should wait a few days before going on! Which of course he couldn't very well.

... Then off we went again, with Tony in the back of the truck, down through Roermond to Bünde, where Jock has friends, and Tony and he stopped there, T. not wanting to come to Tilff because of his face, so I went on, through Maastricht and Liege, and arrived at Tilff about 5.0. Received a <u>terrific</u> welcome from the Collas family, who were all 3 there – and had a wonderful evening, doing masses of things. M. Collas insisted on opening a Very Special Bottle of cognac for me – it was the same vintage and barrel that had been served to the King of England in 1936, and its age was unknown though estimated at the reign of Louis XV – all very exciting, though I suppose I couldn't appreciate it very much. Then we went shopping & visiting, and then played the piano, and M.Collas the violin, and Ho! do you know what I got him to play? The Chaconne! Very nicely indeed, though the fact that he had a bad G. string had to be taken into account – but gosh, did I enjoy hearing it. And, oh, <u>sweet</u> – we must spend our honeymoon there – I said we would! Quite apart from the people, it's <u>such</u> lovely country, and a river and all... eee? Do you mind? It would be wonderful, indeed it would.

... I had a lovely night's sleep, and then left the next morning at 9.0, laden with presents for the section, things to eat. etc. etc! They've also sent you something – I'm sending it to-day – The small ones are from <u>me</u>, by the way, when you get it.

Then back to Bünde, collected Tony and Jock and back via Venlo, Wesel, Münster, Bielefeld, Minden & Neinburg to Verden. Gosh was I tired after that! Jock took over for an hour twixt Wesel & Münster, but I found it even more exhausting when he was driving, so took over again myself. Then on to Bremervörde yesterday; Peggy hasn't received her leave pass yet, isn't it a shame? So she'll have to spend Christmas here. The detachment are going down to Verden for a few days. I very much wish I could stay here, but still... Then yesterday evening I feverishly did nine last minute Christmas cards, for the section, & Frau Schlichting etc., & so to Bed after taking Peggy home at 11.0.

[*24.12.45*]

... I wonder how you liked your Christmas card – sweet, you mustn't be too hard on it as it was the first one I have ever done, really, from actual life – I mean, sitting and painting what's before me, so you'll have to take all that into account.

... Some kind soul (Karl, I think) has brought me a Christmas tree, a wee one, but so very sweet, and now three or four Mysterious Little Parcels have appeared underneath it! And a bloke has given me a lovely propelling pencil – aren't people kind? I've been frantically busy all day, first writing to you, then dashing round with Christmas cards and little packets and things. I am giving Peggy that Bible and almost a whole bar of chocolate and my Christmas toffees (oh yes, terrific thing, I got 14 instead of seven in the end!), and a card. I ended up with no cigarettes at all and then suddenly realized that I had forgotten poor Dorothy! So I gave her a bottle of whiskey – not the best thing perhaps, but all I had left, I'm afraid.

... You know, I sometimes like to lean back and look at us both, to try and make head or tail of the many differences in us – I almost feel I'd like to write a book about us, using our two characters under the guise of two brothers – I think that people don't study (or realize that) the development and progress and difference between two married people as much as they tend to between two brothers or sisters, for example. You were so right when you spoke about that in your letter – that the individuality is <u>kept</u> in a successful marriage – you with your quick powers of reception and swift thinking, me with the urgent necessity always to <u>create</u>, and to go on creating; you with an earnest desire and ability to be conscientious, me with no particular master or authority in mind but myself; you sweet and bright to everyone all the time – me just pleasant enough when I feel like it, but with an <u>awful</u> tendency to become uncontrolled & grumpy if criticized justly – you thinking things, me talking things & going farther than my thoughts often; you sociable, me retiring and with a tendency to create my own circle rather than acquiesce to anyone else's. You with a definite & good taste in things, me not very knowing whether I like a thing or not, saying I don't, & then realizing I do; Eee Bear... but we are very alike in lots of ways, even then – but you know your Family had done a terrific lot of good to you, in building you up, I mean.

Oh sweet, we can be as hot as two white pokers, Calm as the height of summer, sleepy as two Bears in winter – yet we fit very happily, don't we? Both physically and mentally.

[26.12.45]

... Christmas Day was queer 'cos it started off – well – I went down to the section at Verden for lunch, and it was an awful nightmare, what with the horrible songs, bad food and hopelessly drunk people. It just seemed the very opposite of what Christmas should be, and the more I thought of you at home, the more upset I got. Ivor was fed up with it, too. So I decided the only thing was to get away from it all and go back to my room where I'd certainly find my other world – which I did; made some kind of excuse and drove back, getting there at 6.0 or so. Dorothy met me going along the street, and was very concerned at my browned-off appearance (bless her). Then I went to my room and had some coffee & cakes and felt <u>much</u> happier and quite cheerful, read Punch and things...

Then Dorothy rushed in and took me to the Mil Govt. Buffet supper, which was quiet and very agreeable – I <u>was</u> grateful to her for her kindness, 'cos she tried all the time to cheer me up, in lots of ways, and I think it was very sweet of her when she had so very little of her own. Anyway, after that I took her home, and we ate an orange by candlelight and talked for hours, about marriage, being sociable & not sociable, exams & how to pass them (!), life at the University and so on – <u>very</u> nice. Then at 1.0 I pushed off as she was looking sleepy, and so back to my room. Found Peggy had been there and also left me an orange (aren't people <u>kind</u> – they both were given an orange, and they both gave their oranges to me, or tried to!). So I went round to her room, saw the Polish people (Lucie & Co.), who were having a party, then went & saw Peggy & stayed talking to her & telling her what I had been talking about with Dorothy, and then left about 2.15 (!oh well, I was feeling quite happy by now, and anyway it was Christmas night). Then had a dreadful time getting into my house, as the house key was in the lock on the inside, and so I couldn't unlock it. Still the two Serbs on the Ground Floor let me in in the end.

Oh, and on Christmas morning, before I went to Verden I took Peggy a Christmas tree (which she had wanted to give to the Engineers) and all the presents we had got, and opened them – I gave her the Bible, a card, and some toffees & a bar of chocolate (I told you, didn't I?), and she gave me a packet of biscuits, some bits of cake, a bar of milk chocolate, and a <u>wonderful</u> ruler, just the sort I have always pined for, a metal one with inches & centimetres & all. Oh, and Lucie gave me a tin of peanut butter! and Dorothy some little bits of cake and chocolate.

… Oh sweet – there are some beastly businesses going on – it's awfully sad – two of the blokes splitting up at home with their families because of their "women" here – it is so tragic & one of them is Eric Baylis, too. And sad to see that his wife's photo by his bed has been replaced by that of the German female, who looks an awful specimen, to say the least of it (very uncharitable of me, but that's what she looks like) – oh <u>zzzz</u>. It all makes me feel that there is somehow a <u>secure</u> side to being "unsociable" – one doesn't run into squalls and unworthwhile actions.

[*28.12.45*]

What did I do yesterday? Oh painted all afternoon – there is a mythical man in the section called Bloggs (no, really! the O.C. put him forward as being a good name to sign oneself as, for security's sake). So we have made lots of jokes about Bloggs and now I've painted his family's coat of arms and nine family portraits (4"x3"), ranging from Blog the caveman, Athalstan the Blog, etc. to Sgt. Bloggs. I'll bring it on leave with me for you to see – it's an example of 13 F.S.S. humour, such as it is!

[*30.12.45*]

<u>What</u> a nice letter from you, indeed, made me feel Ever-So-Proud! Ho... I am <u>so</u> pleased you liked your Christmas card... 'cos you said, some time ago, about painting the real thing (no, <u>I didn't</u> get offended and moody!), and I said to myself, I said, "She's plumb right, and she shall have the real thing, bless her bones" – and what I am so happy about is that you like it even though it's a first effort of its kind. When was it done? On the Saturday & Sunday afternoons of the 8th & 9th of December. Coo-er & was it cold! But the sun on the snow was <u>so</u> lovely, and the sky glorious. I managed to get what I wanted on Saturday, which was lucky, as Sunday it was a bit cloudy. Finished at 4.0 or so, went back to my room and added the last twigs to the tops of the trees wot were too hard to do out there with me pore cold 'ands. Ho, but it was great fun. I didn't sit on the ground, though – I took Karl's car & sat in that, not that it was much warmer. And then it wouldn't go, having got frozen up, & had to be pushed by four Stout & Hefty Farmhands!

... Oh (to change the subject), could you send me two packets of saccharines again, please, sweet? As Dorothy's mother, who is in Berlin, wanted to know if she could get some... so could you, do you think?

1946

[*3.1.46*]

... Mmm, yes, Christmas day was a bit mixed over here. I just felt rather panicky half-way through, thinking how terrible it would be to spend the whole day like that – but Dorothy was sweet, she really was, & brightened the whole thing up, by Firmly Taking Me In Hand. Poor one, she has (they think) got diphtheria to-day, & as gone into one of the hospitals here – it is bad luck, really it is. And I don't know how Mil Govt. will run without her, as she ran the Public Safety Office pretty well (the officer there being on leave!) and being the head interpreter.

... And then on New Year's night a Sergeant from the Engineers fell into the river here and was drowned. His body wasn't found till to-day. Terry and I spent part of last evening going round houses and interrogating people who had heard him singing on the wharf and getting statements from them – a beastly business, he was only 30, married and due to go out of the army next month, and a very decent fellow. He had been a bit drunk, and gone from the Sgt's mess party to the Dance hall, & on the way back went on to the wharf like that. Oh dear, isn't it sad...

zzz...

Isn't life queer – it isn't any use saying that it's <u>easy</u>, or that it's funny, or that it can be taken lightly. Yet without an ability to see humour in nearly everything, and to have a good sense of it, everything is hopeless, literally hopeless. But fundamentally it <u>is</u> serious, and a thing you just can't work out so very mathematically – a small fault which you indulge often without harm comes and snaps back at you, causing untold unhappiness amongst the people left behind. It's hard always to see where the justice lies in so many of life's happenings – and then moods, like the weather, are so mixed and variable – with such a lot hanging on each one – such responsibilities.

[6.1.46]

... I first went to see the director of schools for the Kreis, and had coffee & cakes with him – very nice, but sad couple – the wife very intelligent & obviously well-educated (both about 55) – their only son was drowned whilst sailing, at the age of 22, about a year and a-half-ago – very sad indeed. And of course they told me all about it, poor things. Oh dear. And he gave me as a present a short history of German Literature, and a book of "philosophical reflections", which was very decent of him. And the Superintendent of churches here that afternoon gave me a small book on Christmas – with pictures, poems etc. in it. So I now have three more books! But aren't people kind...

... What a sweet letter you wrote to Peggy, bless you – you <u>are</u> wonderful, you have such a fund of love for your fellow beings. I think that to write like that to someone you haven't met is a thing not one person in a thousand could do. (Of course, I greedily read anything you have sent, whomever it is to – I could with equal greed read three letters a day from you!) Mozart is rather unusual in a minor key, isn't he, like in No 40.

... Yes, and can one get zip-fasteners in England now? If you see one about 5 or six inches long, could you get one of them too?

Frau Schlichting's daughter Margaret (aged 11) has a pair of ski trousers which she wears all the time, and two of the little jiggers in the zip have gone (the teeth), so she asked me.

... Sweetheart, re-leave in February – I have got myself mixed up in a War Crime, and have to attend the trial. It's so stupid, as all I did was to witness a bloke's statement and sign it as witness. The trial is due to come off at the end of January – and ought to be interesting – but when it will finish I am not sure, so it might be March before I get leave. On the other hand I think I might apply for compassionate leave instead, because I would like to see Auntie Doris before she goes back. Mmm, well, I just thought I'd tell you – don't worry or be browned off about it, sweet, will you? I'll be there sometime, never worry!! Ho Yes... ! You see, War Crimes Commission can't stop compassionate leaves, and it seems they can the others... Oh, I'll see what happens.

[*8.1.46*]

... I thought you were going to see the Kinghams this last Friday? Glad you had a nice time with Dusty. I just don't know much about his emotional side – that is to say, how it stands now – he is actually dreadfully shy, or was – and had a rather bad inferiority complex at school etc. Mmm, he was rather a "good" boy, and Fred and I used to get rather exasperated by his arguments forever defending Authority, when we liked being mildly bad, or felt like it!

... Oh I have had such a beautiful Christmas card from Mother!!! – Sweet, I've gone cuckoo (more or less) over it – it is of some steps up into a Spanish village... Mmm. I do love it!

I have received about 25 Christmas cards this year – how many did you?

Oh Bear I do want to marry you. I feel Ever So Pure and don't "want" you like that (er – not so much as other times, anyway), but just long for your companionship, and how perfect if we were four here – I long to get to know you in one way; that is, what you're like when there are just two or three friends with us, every evening, quietly, – what you are like then – I don't mean just-one-evening-and-then-I-have-to-dash-off-again-to-morrow, but the sort of quietness and happiness that is the natural development of lots of similar quiet times. It is sad in a way that you aren't here, and probably won't be, for up to now I think this "set-up" of Stan's-&-Peggy's-& mine has been so happy and deep and quiet – such as I have never really known before with a pair of friends... if only you were here too – you'd love it, you know – it's a very happy life indeed.

[*10.1.46*]

I'm rather drooping at present having done rather more work to-day than I am accustomed to (sounds bad!)... .Hmm. Well, there was a gathering of all the Landrats, Schulrats (head school directors of the various Kreise), and Youth Movement leaders, of the region "Stade", presided over by the Regierungs president, a man nearly 7 foot tall! I took it into my head to write down what they were saying, and having begun, I decided to finish it. It began at 10.0, went on till 1.0, began again at 2.0 or so & went on till a ¼ to 7.0. It was all right at first, being nimble at and putting down in English what they said at the same time in German, but I got rather tired after four or five hours of it, and so Drooped.

[*13.1.46*]

... Bless you, & did you think I'd be all spotty (or whatever one is with Diphtheria) and wuzzy? Darling I should have told you that we were all given an "eight-day protection" injection against it the very same day that Dorothy went into hospital. All three of us, that is – I had it too (as it doesn't do really to have thoughts of other people thinking against one if it's just easy not to – perhaps it's lazy, I don't know). But I thought I told you – poor old sweet.

... Poor Janet, I am so sorry to hear that about her – aren't people thoughtless – I always think it's so cowardly, in a way, to write things like that – it is sort of feeling Brave and Firm when the other person's back is turned, and there is no opposition whatsoever. Such letters are so cold, too, with no reason there being a thousand and one things the person wants to ask... oh dear, poor Old J. – it is a shame, and as you say, over a more or less unworthy object, too. Oh Bear, Life is so like a road which is humped – for going alone in a car there is always the pull on the

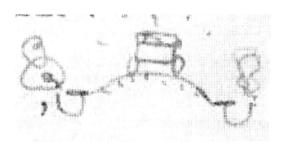

steering wheel, tending to make it go off to the right, or to the left, and so into a ditch – one has to keep firm hold and steer carefully all the time; with marriage the ditch on one side seems to be Infidelity, and on the other, boredom. Eee, we'll both hold the wheel, won't we, very firmly, always keeping in the middle, more or less. For being humans, it is never quite perfect, but we will nevertheless, with God's help, keep on the road. No, they don't mean anything in particular, I just thought I'd draw them... Just the idea of steering, some boats being easier than others.

... Then went to look for the University in Hamburg, and found it – very bombed, alas. It's quite a small building, though – I was very amazed. I had to find out for Dorothy whether the English Library was open or not (as she wants to get on with her thesis for her D.Litt, or whatever it's called in German). I found the place where most of the seminars had moved to, and learnt that it was open, & that she must write, etc. So back to Bremervörde, and in the evening I went with Karl (he had come with me to

Hamburg, too) to Zeven, where we attended a de-nazification committee, which was interesting, and I told them what was wanted for village de-nazification committees, which was also good.

[*15.1.46*]

... Oh dear, our work is horribly scratchy-on-the-surface, you know – the more one does, the more apparent it is. It's not really depressing but just slightly futile – yet without us (with all due –ah – modesty), it would be rather a mess. There's enough grumbling now over the incompleteness of de-nazification – yet one sometimes feels one does more harm than good. I feel that people in England rather take it all a bit for granted – "Ah, de-nazification – yes – all going well? Good, well, all be done quite soon I expect – all it remains now is – ah – to re-educate the lot, which of course may take quite a time". My dear, to 're-educate' the Germans ourselves is quite impossible, for the Germans to be re-educated by their own people is only a little less so. The only thing that may happen is this. Certain forces and organizations will be encouraged in the next few years, which must bring about a change of heart. (Forgetfulness will be one of the chief ones!) Then if the Church can get going, the Youth organizations, and so on, and get a hold on the population... and if at the same time they can begin their re-construction of cities, roads, etc (& that will be the time when an Allied Control Commission will be needed most). But it will always be a case of winning over the majority, and the Nazi minority will have to be always the underdog. It sounds very unsatisfying, but it is so. At present the state of mind of some Germans is extremely inconsistent. They do their daily jobs, discuss the English all day long – are exceedingly anxious to please them, are intolerable to their fellow Germans sometimes and very helpful and friendly at others. Their main concern is now to live, and they are anxious that they should survive, that they should get homes, furniture, food. This is the first stage, and the most natural.

Their concentration is on the everyday things of life, which have taken on an enormous value. The next phase will be when they feel secure, and begin to look around them, try to reaffirm their rights, go all political and vote for a hundred different parties, shake their heads with sadness over the last war, point out the obvious mistakes Hitler made, etc. Then it will be that these forces will have to be very strong; their minds, ready for something, will have to be put onto a new track. Mind you, some Germans are already entering on the second phase, but most are still in the first.

... Ho, Mother's sending me some Turrón (honey & nuts), too. Bless her, & she was asking me if I wanted anything. Is there anything you want, sweet? Apart from most impossible things, I can't think of anything! Unk told her that you told him you couldn't agree with C.S., though you'd tried, & he seemed rather pleased – goodness knows why, I don't see much point in trying to be malicious like that – perhaps he wanted to score off Mother, or something – oh isn't it horrid, all of it.

... Darling, could you send me a couple of packets of gramophone needles, please? And the saccharines?

[*17.1.46*]

... To-day I had an afternoon to do three or four days work in, and working till 9.0 tonight managed it. "Who are the political leaders of the future in your Kreis? What young members have you?" Gosh, what a tall order that was!! But I did a very fine effort, I hope, if rather irrelevant in points!

[*19.1.46*]

... Bear, I'm very glad you go non-talkative and quiet – so do I, and don't let's ever have the word "sulky" in our home – it's one of the most hopeless and unpleasant terms I know – people always are mistaken when they apply it to someone's mood – and it is really horrible if you're feeling thoughtful & quiet to be called that. And even if one has had an argument, & feels quiet after it that isn't sulking. To sulk is when, after a row, one person insists on being grumpy and not say a word. But we will never do that, please God, so don't let's ever let the word in, I hate it, don't you?

[*24.1.46*]

... I've got a wonderful new armchair in my room – big thing, & very deep and cosy, but modern: and Stanley has gone to-day – came last night and stayed quite late; he gave me about twenty of the official war photographs taken during the last campaign – mostly of the Rhine Crossing, the capitulation & the victory parade – all of which I took part in, so that they are very interesting indeed. He seemed very browned off, and even more so when it was time for him to go. I don't know quite how he is to be promoted. He didn't want to stop being a captain whilst in Bremervörde, yet had to arrive at his new unit as a major! So will have to get out of the jeep half-way there and sew a crown on, or something!

... 'Twas a nice letter of yours sweet. I do love the way we say things, & at the end of the thing put another sentence to smooth, plane, & round it off so that it won't hurt, offend, or shock the other one!

... Oh, and, quite important, I was called to Div. H.Q. yesterday about this War Crime... A very Penetrating and Serious Captain Who Was Obviously A Lawyer asked me some penetrating and serious questions, which of course got me into a hopeless muddle, as I couldn't remember for the life of me what I'd said to the bloke – it was a case of a German guard shooting a Polish major in a PW camp before we came. The Poles arrested him & took him to Mil Govt. The Legal Officer more or less asked me to get some statements off the German, which I did. Now the Captain wants to know, did I ask the bloke or order him to make out a statement? Well! I just haven't the vaguest idea! Oh well... anyway, the trial should be coming off on approx 7th February, and won't take more than half a day, the officer says – so after that I shall be free to come on leave.

... Yes, you betcher, they all regard dancing around here as a very Evil Pastime, away from which youth must be drawn, etc. But that is because this is a Kreis of farmers, & hardly anything else in the towns it is very different. Bremervörde is not really a town, either – it is just an overgrown village, and all the houses are farm or village houses only in long rows, and some are shops.

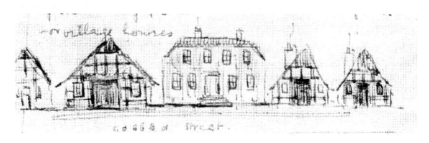

[26.1.46]

... I went skating yesterday and to-day with Martin, Terry & Karl – oh it was lovely yesterday – such perfect greens in the ice, and exciting purples in the snow on it – so much so that I took out my sketching things to-day. Karl took his car onto the ice, and I sketched from it, but as it was cloudy there weren't any of the colours of before. Still, I began, and have painted the ice part of it (horribly difficult to paint, is ice!!). The skating itself is progressing in leaps & bounds. I can go quite zippily, & Martin falls down much less. As for Terry, his thoughts & ambitions are turning to "Kunst-laufen" "art-skating", i.e. doing figures of eight, or about to attempt to.

[28.1.46]

Thanks for your letter of the 24th. Eee, we've both been a bit muddled lately – not feeling bad or anything, but just not so inspired as usual... mmm? Not that your letters are any the less lovable, for goodness don't think that – but – oh well, it's a January feeling, I expect, and the less said about it the better anyway.

I'm sending you an interrogation report I made some time ago – it's of an SS man, who was more or less everywhere during his Army Career – also for a time at Dachau, though he says he didn't have much to do with it – they all say that actually, so it's rather hard to tell whether he was or not. Anyway, it's more of an example than anything else. A "Junker" is a cadet-officer. Sweet, don't show it round, please?

... To-day we went on a visit to Sandbostel camp (internment for SS), just to see what was doing in that part of the world, & this afternoon to Stade by myself, to see the education officer (a Capt.), with whom I had had a lot to do, but had never met. He turned out to be a very nice chap, a teacher before the war (Biology), who went into REME & then transferred to Mil Govt. – very gentle & mild, & intelligent – we chatted for quite a while about teaching, & how much they were needed in England. He isn't sure whether he wants to take Class "B".

... Yes, but he is so happy in his job here he feels he doesn't want to, very much. He thinks I ought to be able to get a Class "B" quite easily.

Then to another bloke, who was Public Safety Officer in Bremervörde at one time, & eagerly exchanged scandal & gossip for a while with him (all this at the Regional Military Government in Stade). Finally to the Field Security Section there & had tea with them, left at 6.0 and got back here in time for another one!

... Yes, don't let's make any more comparisons between ourselves – it's a very bad thing to begin doing, as (a), it narks the other one either way – or will do (b), it unconsciously creates a feeling that there are two markedly different human beings instead of two working as one, & (c), it's wrong anyway. So no more about it, Gifford.

[*31.1.46*]

... What else did I think of, now – something very clever I'm sure. Oh yes, another painting I'm bringing, bargained for it this afternoon – 210 cigarettes & 100 marks, from the same painter as your birthday one only it isn't about hers, it's a river. (I didn't really bargain for it at all, actually – they told me to give what I could.) Dreadful job there was in getting transport to arrive here (Kuhstedt) – Karl came & said his car was in the garage, having a hole mended somewhere – so we tried to get the Landrat's car, and that was having the carburettor seen to. So we went back to Karl's car, but the 'ole was still there, so back again to the Landrat's, stood Fiercely over the mechanic as he blew through the carburettor & finally it went. To Gnarrenburg, & attempted to inspire a bloke with enthusiasm to found a S.P.D. group there, but failed, and only got him to head a de-nazification committee, which is something, I suppose. He doesn't seem very keen on anything. It is said that he drinks rather a lot. Gnarrenburg is in the manufacturing area (Ha Ha, one glass factory), & consequently has masses of S.P.D. people, also unfortunately just as many Nazi Party members. (185 members out of a population of 500 or so!!)

Sweet, I sent you a "British Zone Review" – very interesting we find them. The article on Political parties is good; "Lower Saxony Party" being The Thing around here (Nieder-sächsische Landespartei, or Hannovensche Partei), wot I told you about on my last leave.

... To be serious however, humans are often lazy and they drift – and this is what happens. (a), They take their home for granted, and in leisure hours get bored, now knowing what to do (b), Turn for amusement in leisure to their work-companions, & spend their leisure with them, or (c), Turn for amusement in leisure to their neighbours – but in any case, they have two kingdoms still (maybe three), to the wife's one. Well, that inequality leads to different states of mind & so on to discord. Now, what is ideal is that he I.B. wise fellow will, while working from one kingdom, the same as his wife's (thus both have a common footing), share the interests outside the home also with his wife, even if he doesn't always feel like it – thus the more they have in common, the happier they'll be. Quod fuit dictum an awfully long time ago anyway. Eee, I do wonder how much we'll chuckle on re-reading these letters one day! and an intelligent person is one who can, in his mind, break away from habit at will. mmm?

[*1.2.46*]

Eee, darling!

And a very happy month to you! <u>And</u> that you have some nice people visiting you (Ho!) and... oh <u>sweet</u>... EEE! I feel ever so Ho-Ho-ish (what started all was the wedding March by Mendelssohn, too!) and I thought how exciting yet odd it would be – you coming along up to the altar... and the organ, & Deryck looking ever so kind. Oh Bear... and feeling terrifically queer yet happy, & entering-on- a- new-existence.

... We're having a busy spate in the office – quite interesting, but mainly concerned with hauling in 44 men who have been guards at concentration camps. To-day we had a Captain of the SS who was a doctor, in charge of gas chambers and such-like at Neuengamme camp.

... It's raining here, now pouring in fact, so I can't paint & am going off working instead – try & find an SS "Totenkopf" (Death's head) concentration camp guard, & take him to Verden. Have I ever explained you all that, I wonder? About the SS? That they were primarily the "General SS" (allgemeine SS), which was a para-military organization, to which civilians belonged. There were also "Duty troops", however, who were professional SS men, & did raids, "kept order" etc. these were called "Verfügungstruppen", and later on merged into the Waffen, or armed SS, which were Commando-like soldiers. One special branch, however, even before the war made the Waffen SS necessary, was the "Totenkopf" troops, who provided guards for the concentration camps. They were formerly also a separate group, like the

"Verfügungstruppen", but unlike them, did not get swallowed up into the Waffen SS but stayed in the camps. Though they were greatly depleted by having their younger members drawn into the fighting units, a hard core remained of toughs & thugs, who were directly responsible for all the business.

This bloke is an Unterscharführer. A "schar" is a squad, & the rank is equivalent to Sergeant. There are unter, ober, & Haupt Scharführers, which are all N.C.O.S. & then the officer's ranks begin with a "sturm" between a platoon & a company thus Untersturmfüerer, Sturmführer, Obersturmfürer and Hauptsturmführer (Kramer of Belsen was a Hauptsturmführer), ranging in equivalent rank from 2nd Lieutenant to Captain, with one extra, and the rank of Sturmführer is obsolete anyway. After that comes a band of sturms, a Sturmbannführer (Major), Ober-ditto-, then an Oberführer (I think Ribbentrop was an Oberführer – it was an honorary rank – Colonel), Standartenführer (Colonel, or Lt. Colonel – sorry, it comes under "Oberführer" – yes, it's Lt. Colonel), then Brigadedführer, Ober-ditto, etc. At the very top was Himmler, the Reichsführer. They all wore their ranks on their collars and from Sergeant to Major there were silver pips and silver strips on a black background. After the rank of major they had oak leaves on instead of pips & stripes, one oak leaf Lt. Colonel, two Oberführer, etc. etc. – again on a black background. Himmler had oak leaves in gold with a laurel wreath around it. The uniform was black, too. I expect you know – and they all wore skull & crossbones on their caps.

[6.2.46]

... The picture arrived from Wiegmann! It's a lovely painting – I do hope you like it; but sweet, I won't bring it with me this time though, as it is being framed, and won't be ready, and also the present weather wouldn't do much good to it in transit even if I could get it in time – so you won't mind, eee? (All those aren't just excuses to keep it adorning the wall of my room!!). I'm having a thick frame made, which will come apart so that I can bring it home easily. The size of the actual painting is 1 yard × 2 ft, & it's of a stream in Thuringia.

[*Douglas was home on leave from 15th to the 28th of February.*]

[*4.3.46*]

… But I'd better stop grumbling & telling you how browned off I feel, it doesn't help at all… I sailed on Saturday afternoon, on the "Rapier", which was indeed rather a dreadful affair. 240 men all sleeping in one hold 8 foot high, which grew so hot & stuffy that I just didn't know what to do. Then the journey was pretty awful – squalls etc. and the sea very rough indeed, so that the boat was pitched all over the place, with enormous seas breaking over the decks. I <u>quite</u> lost my appetite! And landed, feeling extremely dead, at Cuxhaven last night. Whereupon we were put into barracks, where we slept till this morning. Then in the back of a truck to Bremervörde. Went along to the office and Terry was there. Martin arrived back Saturday morning, only having sailed on Thursday as he overslept on the Wednesday morning! A <u>wonderful</u> bath in the afternoon made a new man of me, in body if not in spirit, so here I am…

… Ivor, Bob & George are all being demobbed on Wednesday, so there is a farewell party to-morrow in Verden. I rang up Ivor this morning. Peggy is still here – Stan came over this weekend (they waited till 2.15 in the morning for me to arrive last night! bless them), and she is going over to him again this weekend.

Oh yes, herewith please find £1.10.0 – perhaps it will help make up the £10 to go in our savings? – or at any rate make it £9 instead of £8. After having been sternly warned that bringing English currency into Germany was a heinous crime, to be dealt with by court-martials etc. – we changed our money into German notes in fear & trembling. Afterwards I put my hand into my pocket for one 'anky, & there I found a 10/- note! Whereupon I hastily hid it in a secret recess of my wallet, where I found a £1 note deposited there in a like manner when I had come off leave in October & since forgotten! Oh lawks... so here you are, if you'll acccpt such criminal money... ?

[*8.3.46*]

... I got very fed up at the thought of slowly but inevitably changing back from a live Pootle (you a personal Pooh) to a correspondential one – it's like going under an anaesthetic – a sort of dulling & forgetting, somehow... mmm? A sharp edge becoming dull... the desire and love is still there, but – oh dear, I suppose I am too materialist & depend too much on personal contact.

... It's beastly to have two worlds – or rather, to have to get re-used to them time and time again after having tasted a bit of life wherein everything is coherent and one. The first few days after this leave I just ached and ached, cursed the army (& only thought of one thing, & that was to get out of it!). Then, as I said, the pain grew duller, & now I am just dreamy, & live for the evenings.

[*10.3.46*]

And it's Sunday evening again – a bare week since I have been back, and I'm sitting by the stove waiting for it to warm up. We (Martin & I) have been with the American Field Security (called the Counter-Intelligence by them) for lunch to-day, and spent quite an agreeable afternoon exchanging views on things. It was a wonderful lunch – roast lamb, asparagus, a lovely kind of salty butter, peaches & cake afterwards. One of the chaps there had a "Minox" camera, do you remember having seen the advertisement? They are about three inches long by the ¾ inch wide by one inch broad, take a 10 millimetre film, and are made in Latvia – take 50 exposures on one film, with quite good results. The bloke who owns it has it in a little bag attached to his key-ring! And exposure-time from ½ second up to a 1/1000 second! 3.5 lens, too, mmm. I was offered a Rolleichord for my Robot, too, but it's not worth it. <u>Please would you ask Gil:</u> what are the cameras that are about equivalent in exchange value to my Robot? Would a Kodak Retina f3.5, or Baldina f3.5 ? – I would just like to know, as I <u>might</u> [exchange it], though I'd much rather get another decent lens for it. A photographer I was speaking to to-day said that it would be very hard to get a 3.75 cm lens. For one thing, the Robot factory had been <u>completely</u> bombed out of existence! An American said that the best place for things like odd lenses were second-hand shops in England or America. Oh well.

... Oh yes, I asked Martin what "frigging about" was, and you were quite right! Ooo-er, and the times I've gone around saying that (in <u>complete</u> innocence, of course!). That's what Martin says, at any rate, and he knows. (?!) He is getting very perturbed at the thought that your opinion of him must be that he is a sort of "Encyclopaedia Sexualis" – as I generally say "we thought we'd ask you what that meant", and he hastens always to assure me that it isn't true that he is like that – but I think he's rather pleased, underneath it all, somehow!

[*11.3.46*]

... I quite agree about writing things in letters – I suppose it looks so <u>permanent</u>, but one shouldn't mind really – they're not going to be published (?!), and the more like ordinary conversation letters can get, the better it is.

[*14.3.46*]

... You know, that letter of the 8th of yours was extremely good in a quiet sort of fat way – all about feeling calm & then getting quirked at things. I know that so well – proceeding down the Neuestrasse (main street) feeling Calm & a Sailing boat proceeding along at a steady pace – then when I get to the office someone dashes in with some silly flap, at which we all get het up, and fly off in different directions. And as I fly off, I suddenly realize, & think: "Umm, was I feeling calm and content before? Well, well!" And thus it goes on, up & down & down and up, or perhaps sideways & then forwards...

Yesterday we had a flap like that, & were dashing about for the rest of the day. I do dislike upheavals. "Ah yes, this area will be combed", "How many men to search this town – a battalion? Certainly, certainly" or, worst of all "Ah well, you can do that Saturday or Sunday" – and ever since that I've been feeling unsettled, & wondering about trying feebly to find something to do. At last to-day I found someone in Zeven who wants to start an organization of the Communist Party, so I almost fell on his neck.

... Then to-day, flap still on, and going out just to get away from the office: down to Zeven to see the Communist chap. He is about 27, and an interior decorator, with a wife who helps him in his Party work. He sounds very much of an idealist, & said very firmly that the perfect Christian was a Communist, & that they accepted & believed in the faith, but not in the churches and their conventions & doctrines. It is curious that the Right Wing Party, composed of all the richest farmers & merchants are the most "earthy", then the Democrats, with a membership amongst the professional classes, then the S.P.D., amongst the middle & lower classes, with rather more ideals – then the Communists, amongst the working classes, with an enormous amount of ideals & no money to back themselves & their organization! it's funny how one line in the graph goes up (Ideals), and another goes down (class distinction, education & financial backing). For instance, it was nothing short of revolting to hear the Right Wing (The Lower-Saxony Party) having a meeting – the main points that seemed to concern them was that there shouldn't be any splitting up of estates here as there was in the Russian Zone. The whole tone about Russia was fearful all through – borders of Europe now being along the East side of the British zone, etc. Umm. s'queer. Oh I do think politics are lousy. If the houses of Parliament work in at all the same way as our Kreis Parliament do, then Goodness help us.

The only trustworthy man in Bremervörde is one who belongs to no political party at all, a teacher and a Headmaster & that is our Bürgermeister. In the Kreistag he is the only man who isn't weak-kneed and doesn't allow himself to be speechified out of his opinion.

[*16.3.46*]

... To-day has been absolutely wonderful weather – sun and warmth, and we actually felt hot in the office! This morning I went out with Karl to one of our SS internment camps. It actually was pleasant to be out there, which it never has been before. Oh sweet, the suffering that these people have to go through – no communication with their relatives, etc. I have least pity for the SS, but whatever they have done, they are paying so hard for it now, innocent & guilty alike. Do you remember the War Crime trial I attended? The man got a life sentence, which I think was <u>horribly</u> hard, and quite out of proportion to his offence. I don't know, perhaps it was my recommendation for him that modified the death sentence to one of life, but the poor chap probably feels just as fed up if not more. (He had shot a Polish Major, in self-defence.) Oh it is hard for him, and even worse for his wife. What a topsy turvy world this is.

... There are a lot of rumours going about wives being allowed to come over – I should say this will happen during the summer. The only thing is that only officers & men who have signed on for regular engagements have been allowed to apply for their wives to come out! 810 Mil Govt., with characteristic infidelity, don't seem to want any of their wives to join them! Dorothy was saying last night how terrible it must be for British women who feel that their husbands are falling in love with German girls, & signing on for longer and longer periods of service in Germany. 19 out of 20 of these girls do it purely out of greed and for what they can get. The helpless worry and anguish the wives at home must feel must be a sad affair, not that I know any, do you? But just to look at the state of affairs here is enough to make me realize that there are such women. The Public Safety Officer and The Sergeant-Major share a flat with two women (widows) – both are married. The Major also married has his flat & woman. The 2nd i/command has his interpreter, but I don't know if anything goes on which shouldn't – and I also don't know whether he is married. That's just the officers in Mil Govt. Several abortions have had to be carried out, the last one to the Sgt. Major's female. A previous officer in charge of Administration fell very much in love with an interpreter, but being happily married too he finished it when he was demobilized and hasn't written or sent word since – so he has been graced with escape, presumably.

[*17.3.46*]

... I got up quite late this morning, posted my letters and then went to a church service taken by a Padre – only a few of us there, though. Then lunch, after which I tried to start the 15 cwt truck that had been lent us by H.Q. – that failed, so Peggy (who had arrived), & I went & listened to Brahms 4th on my gramophone. Then to an S.P.D. meeting (Sozialdemokratische Partei Deutschlands) – a very intellectual looking person made a long speech about capitalism and the right of the small-holder – quite good on the whole. The hall was very crowded at the back, but hardly anyone sat in front! Perhaps they feared his wrath... He delivered some attacking points against the Lower Saxony Party, and more or less said that they were a lot of isolationist twerps with no thought for anyone but themselves, and that Germany must become one unity again, with a central government. Also that 90% of the refugees would have to remain where they were now, and so on. At least it was much more interesting and laudable than the speech made by the Lower Saxony Party speaker at a meeting last week. ... *Later* / Oh, I am to be a full Sergeant! No Lance/S. anymore! I shall get rather more pay, I suppose if it isn't all taken off in Income tax.

... The Padre's sermon this morning was on the struggle in life
– that God fully intended that we should meet evils & suffering, &
also implied that he created them too. I don't know that I agree
with that, but it opens up an interesting line of thought: It is
certain that one's character is purified and developed through
contending with evil and fighting the good fight. But is that in the
same category as work? For through hard work we develop just as
much, surely – or if not as much, than in a degree. If, then, we can
class work and suffering together, is it also right to say that it is not
the actual suffering, struggling or work that develops us, but the
concentration & application that results from the training of our
<u>minds</u> during the period of work or struggle? (I do mean <u>hard</u> work
when I say that, not routine jobs that are taken up in the daily
round.)

[20.3.46]
    ... Talking about "The Merchant of Venice", there was a
passage that rather clicked somewhere as being akin to something
one of us said once:
    Salarino: "Oh ten times faster Venus' pigeons fly
    To seal love's bonds new-made, than they are wont
    to keep obliged faith unforfeited."
    Gratiano: "That ever holds: who riseth from a feast
    With that keen appetite that he sits down?
    Where is the horse that doth untread again
    his tedious measures with the unbated fire
    That he did pace them first: all things that are,
    Are with more spirit chased than enjoy'd."
... and on... I'm not sure that it's wrong or right – there seem to be
lots of examples to prove it, but I haven't noticed it with us (but
then of course, I'm still chasing you, aren't I!!). Martin, notre sage
professeur, says that sexual intercourse is not at all satisfying, it is
only the breaking down the girl's morale that he enjoys (!!), so he
seems to be of the same opinion (hm!). But I quite see the point of

view expressed by Gratiano, though it isn't true for everyone, I should think – anticipation <u>tends</u> not only to be better than realization, but much worse too (if you think too much about drills before you go to the dentists, for instance!), so it cuts either way.

But when I am anticipating a leave, it <u>always</u> turns out better than I thought it would be, even!

[*24.3.46*]

... But depressions <u>do</u> come along, to everyone, sweet – it's rather like having a sniffle: a combination of events that tend to get you down and nothing on the other side to counteract them, no antidote; Having to deal with all your burdens yourself, and no one else nearby with whom one can make jokes about them, or get sympathy. Depressions come to any normal intelligent person who does a lot of things with many irons in the fire. And again, it isn't so much just <u>happenings,</u> little Herbert hitting you over the head with a spoon whilst the milk is boiling over and you are on your hands and knees picking up all the raisins which have just broken forth from the china (Royal Doulton) dish which is also scattered in pieces over the floor. No, it's rather that, afterwards you get a depression because little Herbert is plainly heading for a career of crime, you have no more points to buy raisins, and what are you to say to Mrs. Bloggs, from whom you borrowed the china dish? All those being worries and anticipations of future happenings, just as I worry before I go to the dentist. Everything is tied up with consequences.

... Mmm, yes, war does let loose the worst side of man, i.e., his animal side, but it oh gosh how it lets the good side loose too – or did. I suppose they must have been the good natural instincts. It's sadly noticeable when people are <u>so</u> rude, and unhelpful & selfish. During the whole campaign it was a very rare exception to come across someone who was selfish & non-helpful – funnily enough, most people were polite, too – mainly because they were friendly, I suppose. Yes, men got drunk & profligate, and women the same, but at least their hearts were not stony. Frankly, if there be two states of social behaviour and conduct, I prefer the former to the latter, attended as it is by selfishness, unkindness and cold-heartedness – which are <u>100</u> times more unchristian than immorality. <u>Oh</u> yus. Morals are a code on which we lead an orderly and balanced life, but Love is life itself and without love there <u>is</u> no life to be balanced or planned.

... Actually what I meant by Hard work, suffering & struggle was confirmed by what you said – but I <u>do</u> think that they are linked together and are of the same <u>kind</u>. And the distance between Passive and Active is about as small as between Love and Hate – in fact, there is scarcely a dividing line between them – so whilst suffering can be on one side of the border, struggle can be just on the other. Mmm?

... (This pen is being a bit odd – scratchy, and not holding much ink. I must have dropped it on its noddle, or something. Still, it has its moods too, I think.)

... After dinner, Martin and I went up to Wesermünde, to the American Counter-Intelligence people there...

Well, sat there talking and had a bite or two in the kitchen, & did all sorts of deals in swapping tea for coffee, & marmalade for plum jam...

Then some of them began to get pickled, Martin included, and at 2.0 or so I laid a firm hand on his shoulder and said we must go home, so into the truck we got, and thinking he was steady enough, I didn't shove him out when he got into the driver's seat, but I very soon regretted not having done so, as he wasn't steady after all! My suggesting he let me drive only made him very obstinate, as he didn't want anyone else to say that he couldn't get home all right! Lor, what a bloke. And when I got out & said I would walk, he said he'd go to sleep by the side of the road, then kept on starting & catching me up & pleading with me to get back – really all extremely funny & after a period of this sort of thing he became more or less sobered up, though still refusing to let go of the wheel, so as I hadn't the slightest intention of walking 25 kilometres I (rather feebly I fear) said 'all right' and got back in on condition that at the slightest swerve he should go into my seat & I into his. Still, he <u>was</u> O.K. by then, & we got home quite all right. But my goodness – drunken people <u>are</u> obstinate – never argue with one!

... Letter from Mother to day more or less the same, except that it was longer. Apparently Unk slips away from the Woman in the evenings to come to Mother & have a meal, telling her (The W.) that he is working late!! Honestly, it's just like a novel, isn't it, in some ways.

[*26.3.46*]

... This afternoon we were going through Kuhstedt when we espied a crowd of people outside Wiegmann's (bloke who painted our pictures), and found they were more or less forcing people into his house, with their furniture & all – all of it arising because the Billeting Officer who leads the Nazi clique there, doesn't like Wiegmann, who is a rabid anti-Nazi. So we arrested the Billeting Officer & Town Clerk and made off with them.

... Sorry, I just can't write, I have a horrid notion that there is a storm brewing over this afternoon's do with Wiegmann – the Military Governor was personally touched, & got very angry. These storms only arise every six months or so, I suppose, so one must be thankful really.

[*27.3.46*]

... To-day we have been hanging about for Fishface [Douglas' C.O.] to come, which he did finally – then I had a Teacher's Appeal Committee (Teachers who have been dismissed by us appealing against our decision), and out of 17 we passed one. That's rather severe, I suppose.

... *The next day* / to-day <u>has</u> been lovely weather, though – I went out to Kuhstedt again, and arrested someone else, also saw Wiegmann.

... Oh, masses of flies have come into my room – it sounds Bad, but unless I have some fly-paper, it will get so full of them that the ceiling will be like a spotted dog; I don't think fly-paper is obtainable anyway. I don't like it, but it is better than going about swatting them with a slipper, and there come so many.

... Have you settled down from our leave yet? I think I have, just about, and am not aching & longing to get out of the Army all the time. Aren't human beings changeable, though! Not so much underneath as by their moods. The important thing is that most results, action etc. emanate from this moods-state of mind, and that the "upper" and surface-like part of man's mind, being the first to hand, speaks & does. That is so with everything here, practically. Only too often is it so that the Administration is run like that.

So it is, the moods in man. Of course, I'd shoot out of the Army this minute if I got the chance, but with other things I <u>haven't</u> been so very consistent – whether to be a teacher or not, whether to go into the Army, Navy or Air Force (as I did in 1943). I do feel consistent in wanting to marry you but at times I get doubts & fears when I take Frank Looks At Myself (figuratively speaking), and think I give an impression of shallowness just because I'm feeling Vague... and oh, so on & so on, till one gets muddled & sleepy over it.

[29.3.46]

You <u>did</u> write a good letter on the 26th! Did you know that? And though you said it was scrappy, it wasn't at all... that was so wise & loving, that which you said about home, & <u>so</u> much more wise then my feeble & petty suggestions. That "setting up of barriers", however, isn't quite unknown in Mother's family – and she herself is very adept at it! One more or less has to guess what she'd like to do and then make out as if your whole day would be spoilt unless she goes with you too; even then it isn't easy – unselfishness almost hardens like a shell.

... Oh, <u>very</u> many thanks for the magazines (Studio, Artist & New Statesman.), which arrived to-day...

This afternoon I went on a fruitless errand but a lovely ride, down to a little village down in the bottom of the Kreis – then to Stade, to see the Education Officer there. A problem was before us: what would you do: Four boys had each been sent to one or more of the Adolf Hitler Schools ("National Socialist educational political establishments"), where they were being drilled into being good Nazis. Well, what with the war, they didn't finish there, & are now trying to finish their education at the High School in Wesermünde. The question is, though, should they be allowed to continue there or not? Since they were sent to the A. Hitler School by their parents when they were 12, they are hardly to be held responsible for going there, are they? And to stop their education now, you will perhaps sour them for life. So it's rather difficult. I rather favour their finishing off myself, but of course the anti-Nazi element don't agree there.

[*1.4.46*]

... Stanley went off quite early this morning, & then about 7.30 a maid came over from the hotel & called up to my window & said that there were two officers wanting to see me, & were waiting at the hotel. I almost got up, but suddenly realized it was April 1st, so I went back to bed!

... This evening both Dorothy & Peggy have been in. You know, as time goes on, those two seem to be resolving themselves into two different categories – Dorothy into a purely intellectual one, and I just seem to be always discussing things with her, or reading poetry – and Peggy seems to be in a personal & somehow non-intellectual sphere – do you remember my telling you that subjects for discussion had run rather dry with her? Well, that is what is happening now, & she remains a friend with whom one spends most evenings, does things, cooks things, eats & sits & writes letters, whereas with Dorothy one spends perhaps one or two evenings a week, & gets into deep discussions, etc. What I would like to know is, are they constituting a difference in quantity or in kind? Is D. a less developed P. in relation to me? Or couldn't D. ever become a P.? I wonder... I often notice a contrast if, for instance, I have been visiting Peggy, & then come to my room & find Dorothy there – & the contrast isn't generally agreeable – I feel a certain artificiality in going from P. to D. Oh well, it's not the slightest bit important, really, except they neither feel each other's presence a good thing – Peggy's happiest state is when Stanley, she & I are together (after being alone with him, of course), & Dorothy's is discussing with me alone (after being with Terry alone I presume!)

[3.4.46]

I wonder whether this lovely weather is making you feel less fed? Is it like August in London? It is here!

We've been having energetic flaps & raids on, & searching houses, for the last two days – so I feel rather sleepy. That "Operation Nursery" of which you have probably read was mostly to do with us (F.S.) – only we didn't do any midnight raids! We just arrested people quietly, beginning last September on till the middle of March or so, when the higher ups were sounding very urgent about it – I had just come back from leave when it was at its climax, and having forgotten most of it, got rather browned off with it.

... Then this morning I waited in the office, & this afternoon went off with a bunch of CMP's and searched a lot of farmhouses on the moors. I don't know of any country in England to compare with the type just near Bremervörde – picture to yourself that moorland, criss-crossed with lots of very deep canals (with deep banks, rather), very straight roads, and farmhouses surrounded with pine trees set well-back from the road. The air there is very healthy, all piney and dry. The earth which isn't peat is composed purely of sand, too. The houses are built on the peat, and each piece of ground had its owners digging for their fuel out of the garden!

I have got to be up at 5.0 to-morrow morning which is a bit of a do & very energetic of someone. More raids & whatnot. Then, we hope, they will be finished... .!

[*5.4.46*]

    ... Um yes, when I get enough cigarettes again, I'll go to Wiegmann's & try for a picture. Unless you'd like to contribute by sending 100 or so by post? Otherwise it will take a month or so. But it's not much use paying for his pictures – they are priced at £20–£50, and rather out of one's reach. It would help if you sent some cigarettes though. I have just finished getting 500 for Frau Schlichting to get a wireless, and now they are able to get a really good one for 600, so it means 100 more, and though I get 130 a week, there are people to give lots to, like Karl & Dorothy & Lucy, who like them so much that it seems mean to hoard them.

    ... Mmm, I wonder if having many facets of personality is like being a many sided prism, reflecting one thing at many different angles...

... A lot has happened here since I last wrote, too. Early Thursday morning (at 6.0), we rushed into a village called Selsingen, near here (10 miles), and made raids on several houses which were suspected to have illicit mail to be passed in to the big SS camp (Sandbostel) – in we went with two companies of Gordon Highlanders, in Scout cars, Bren Carriers, jeeps, everything! Terrific din and what not, a command post established in the main square... It ended about 7.30, with all targets raided & shaken up. Then the section went to some Good Contact in Selsingen who made us some tea!

Then back, and we felt so relieved that the Sandbostel Do was over (it had been going on for a month), we took the day off. First, to Freiburg where the sailing boat is wot we sailed in last summer, saw the people, & gave them some white paint which they needed to paint the boat. The two boys there are learning to be dentists, & we watched them taking casts of teeth, making crowns, etc. Then went and looked at the boat, which is laid up. It should be ready by Easter!

And Martin found a detachable petrol tank off a 'plane, and is making it into a little canoe-cum-sailing-boat! Or is having it made, rather.

... Oh, and this morning I was very pleased with myself: Martin & I had gone to the Engineers to see if there was any pay going, & a mobile library bowled up. So I went and asked, as I always do, and they said they were giving them out on the exchange system! So I bethought me of the lots of awful trash I had collected in my room, through welfare and normal scrounging, went and got an armful of them (all rather tattered and if not that quite unreadable detective stories – and I got three good books in return – one large one "British Painting", one called "Book-collecting as a Hobby", which looks rather fun, and a albatross edition of "Women in Love" by D.H. Lawrence.

I don't know of the book at all, do you?

[*9.4.46*]

... Oh but what a Do these last two days: did I tell you Karl had his tyres slashed on Saturday evening? Well, he did, and not wanting to show that it made any difference to him, he borrowed some tyres off a bloke in a village near here, for two days. That meant we had those two days to find three tyres in, in a land where there just aren't any! So we zoomed round yesterday & ended up in a jealously guarded civilian car dump, where we were told to apply to the chief Transport Officer of the region, a Major. So off to Stade, saw the Major, & were told that there were only two tyres in the whole region, and that they wouldn't fit!! We trailed back to Bremervörde, our tails in the dust (or between our legs, or what you will).

Nothing daunted by this, however, we went down to Kreis Rotenburg, to try our luck there. Jock Cramb, the Scots fellow, came with us to an Army R.A.O.C. dump, and by gosh we got four new tyres and four new inner tubes!! Wasn't that great! So we're more or less O.K. now – that tyre-slashing business is stupid – they did it to our truck four or five months ago, the front-off wheel was punctured.

Then from Rotenburg down to Verden, to ask Fishface if he minded Karl using British tyres on his car, which he didn't.

[*11.4.46*]

... As we were sitting in the office with not much to do (Terry writing to his mama, Martin thinking about his boat, me looking through things like General Routine Orders, etc), came Bombshell No 1, a Gestapo man who had been wanted for ages – spotted by the Landrat's son and brought in by Martin in the space of two minutes or so. Well, that was all right, though staggering enough. The second was absolutely awful. The Major came in to say that the Landrat (a very good bloke, & friend of ours) had been discovered to have bought on the Black Market 27 pounds of butter, and that the order had come down for his arrest! Cor...

Some German Investigation team had found it out and reported it, the B——, (Bastards, dear), and so the order had come down from Stade. Of course, it's such a stupid charge, as all of Bremervörde have done that, and worse, and as for the Governor himself... But the Landrat was unlucky enough to have some enemies, and they more or less framed him. The Major refused to arrest him, but had to put him and the Food Board Officer out of office. Oh dear... and now the charge will come up. It's such a shock to everyone, you've no idea. Then of course there is the problem of where to get another Landrat, another Food Control Officer, etc. Oh Wah!

That's what's making me feel so fed.

Then this afternoon flapped about vaguely & sadly & interrogated the Gestapo man (a doctor, & when he was in Zeven Peggy used to be his assistant, and he was in the habit of beating her, or hitting her! Nice type!)

[*13.4.46*]

... On Friday I went to Zeven to see a merchant who is more or less the best-trusted man there, and had it out over a teacher who wanted to get back to teaching, & who had been dismissed for being a leader in the Hitler youth. Then to the Communist Leader in Kreis, B——, and only found his wife (they've been married 4 months), & so back...

Then yesterday I went up to Wesermünde in the morning, to check up on the Gestapo Doctor we arrested on Thursday – nothing to be found, however – it seems he would never tell the truth, and consequently the whole thing is rather difficult. Did I tell you, his wife and four children were all killed by one bomb, which fell in Bremervörde a year ago?

Then all afternoon clearing out my drawers again, & going out to watch Martin launch his canoe made out of a petrol tank (off an aeroplane!). He got in, wobbled along into the middle of the creek, paddled unsteadily about for a few minutes, & then quietly turned over! And swam back to the shore midst great laughter &

merriment from the bank of the river...! He went off to change, and afterwards a lot of people got in and paddled around, & no one fell in! But I think it was because the seal he used in it was too high, and consequently made it top heavy. They're going to have another go at it this afternoon...

[*15.4.46*]

... I feel a bit perturbed about Winnie [Hazel's 1934 Morris car] being patched up – don't you feel that no matter how much an ancient thing is patched up, it'll go wrong anyway, if everything is on the verge of breaking down?

... Oh won't I do anything naggable-at, uh?! You wait, you've never seen me tidying up my room, have yer? It takes me <u>quite</u> two weekends! Well, two days, anyway – it's not that I'm untidy (he said hastily), it's that the drawers seem to get so.

... But it would be the most <u>awful</u> thing I can think of, if you were to enjoy being worried! For it would be a beastly form of hypocrisy. I know what it's like, though I don't ever feel it – I can imagine it: I'm-Worried-therefore-I'm-in-a-higher-grade-of-human-beings-because-of-my-responsibilities (either a Martyr or a saint!)? or something: but you won't, never fear, not while I'm around!!

[*17.4.46*]

Yet another flap is on – this time perhaps with permanent effects: the section is to move down to the south of the British Zone, with effect from next Saturday. It seems pretty definite, as we rang up the H.Q. of I. Corps this morning, & they confirmed it. All blokes over Group 40, that is, and the rest get posted to odd postings all over the place. Will you send letters to "13 F.S.S., BAOR" from now on, Sweet? Till I find a convenient Mil Govt. to attach myself to! At first we thought it meant The Far East, but is isn't apparently. Still, we'll see how it ends up – it might be fun (he said, hopelessly vaguely, not knowing anything whatsoever). It's quite a business preventing oneself getting very browned off indeed about it, too.

Dearest, I'm sending some parcels home, of my books, and whatnot. Up till now there are six, but a seventh is hovering in the background. They also include Punches, Studios, Artists, Letters, & odds & ends. Oh, & one is coming with lots of photos... The Robot photos are great fun! Nothing particularly brilliant in the way of technical prowess (though better than last time, much), but some fun, & two lovely ones of Peggy & Stanley. Well, you'll see them, bless you, very shortly – as soon as they have been printed (I want to keep the first set as it has reference numbers & whatnot on the back) – but oh, they are a nice set.

To-day I went to Div. H.Q. in the 15 cwt with Peggy, and took all the 50 odd gramophone records back. Then speeded back here right away, to dinner. Then sorted things out again. Oh I feel all Upside Down – not exactly miserable, or happy or pleased or anything, just Queer, & hopelessly unsettled. There's such a lot of work to do, to hand over Politics & Teachers & whatnot, and Terry & Martin refuse to do any more work! Oh zzz. everything is in a state of flux and what have you. As it is, I shall have twice as much kit as I can even hope to carry, too. Then I want to take my little radio, and cooker. I suppose I can't take my plants. And I should go to Hamburg too. And I'm stone broke too, & haven't the money to pay for postage for the parcels. Mmm. Well, that's a long list of troubles, but they needn't be very overpowering!

... It is silly not to be able to force oneself to be mentally calm & settled, but I'm just not!

[19.4.46]

How are you this sunny and goodly day, I wonder? It is lovely weather, and no mistake – I'm feeling a bit more settled and & less flustered & fed up with things, which is very good! Also, this whole business (of going away) seems to have been put off for ten days, so keep on writing to 810 Mil Govt. for the time being, will you sweet, please?

[*21.4.46*]

There I was, all fed and needing watering, so to speak, and now I've <u>three</u> letters from you, of the 15th, 17th, and 18th! And that <u>lovely</u> book! Eee, <u>sweet</u>, very <u>very</u> many thanks for it, it's one I've been wanting ever <u>so</u> much, since I saw it when on leave! Ho, now I'll draw yer trees! Oh and <u>such</u> nice letters too! Wheee, I am a lucky fellow, and no mistake.

And I'm not as angelic as to have sent you <u>all</u> the quince jelly – I'm too fond of it myself! Sent you 'arf, see? Mmm, glad you like the chocolate.

... Oh <u>sweet</u>... I've been thinking a lot lately about us too, and, just wondering how to get through three more leaves and? year? two years? without overflowing, but I have <u>too</u> come to the conclusion that we're being <u>much</u> too serious & strike-me-pink about it, as if it was the Last Word, The End, etc. – but it <u>isn't</u>, at all.

... I feel quite sure that the key to the problem (no, that sounds too glum), is that we ought to aim at <u>Control</u> rather than self-denial. Complete self-denial isn't control at all, just as letting everything have its way isn't. Real control, <u>I</u> think, consists in knowing how much or how little to pass through, like an 'ole in a lock-gate... Complete self-denial <u>is</u> just bottling everything up & keeping it back, which certainly looks very good to the outside (?), but which doesn't do any good whatsoever to the bottler-upper, eee? And human emotions <u>don't</u> keep, they go stale or sour with <u>unuse</u> as much as they go weak and flabby with <u>misuse</u>. Look at a piano which is never played. And it isn't right to say Ah, all human emotions of that sort aren't good, so bottle 'em, & put them away, as I rather feel was the way of the Early Victorians (I wonder?) – for everything that has been given us by God is of use. And as thoughts control emotions which control actions, it all comes down to right thinking, if I must go on analysing it!

[24.4.46]

... My next destination, when I move from here, will be to OLDENBURG, not the Rhineland as we had feared at first (general rush of Bears to get at an atlas). Oldenburg... .Oldenburg, ah yes, Oldenburg – mmm., on the other side of Bremen. W.N.W. of it about 60 miles away, not bad at all, is it! it's supposed to be quite a large place, too. At present we are awaiting our movement orders – I don't know how long they'll be in coming.

[26.4.46]

... Oh <u>Bear</u>, I've been wondering what you'll look like when you wake up in the mornings! 'Cos Peggy was saying that females look <u>awful</u>, what with curling things and creamed–faces & so on...

oh dear, do you look like that?!! or are you bedworthy & beautiful?!
Eee, not that I <u>mind</u>, of course, I just wondered... !
I got into a fearful state this evening, having to endure 2 hours sitting with a drinking party. My Hat, I've never known anything so utterly boring, piffling and enraging than having to talk with people who are drinking themselves silly. Golly, was I mad. Then

back to the cool quiet of my room, where Peggy was sitting coolly & quietly – a very striking contrast to the Schlichte & Cognac in the office! Before, earlier on this evening, I went for a truly lovely walk with Dorothy, out 2 miles to an old mill at the edge of a large forest N. of Bremervörde. Ho, & heard the cuckoo, and Oh it was lovely, & we sat on a tree trunk & waited for the cuckoo, & listened to birds & looked out for squirrels, and talked a lot – & <u>then</u> heard the cuckoo & felt <u>so</u> pleased!

Eee, I acquired a stop-watch to-day! A most cunning & wicked move. Do you remember that flap we had at the beginning of April, when we raided masses of houses for illicit mail? Well, I was going through one house, which belonged to a bloke who had been in the S.A., & who had a lot of odds & ends belonging to it. I was going through his desk, when I came across a strong-box with two stop-watches in it! Apparently they belonged to the SA too! So a day or two ago I sent round a note to him saying that all SA property in his possession must be given up! (Which is quite a proper order, as Party property <u>is</u> to be handed in), and in he came this morning with tons of junk <u>and</u> the two stop-watches! One I gave to Terry, & the other I kept!

[*28.4.46*]

... In the evening I went to a meeting of the Christian Democratic Party of Germany, at which was said exactly the same as any other party in Germany to-day. I went to another, the Free Democratic Party, to-night, & that was the same too! Except that they slung mud at the Christian Democrats! Oh dear, what a queer business it is! They're not <u>ready</u> for Party politics yet.

[*30.4.46*]

... I am off to-morrow morning at 9.0, to Verden, & the day after (or Friday, perhaps) to Oldenburg. We heard it this morning, & Martin had to go off this afternoon, poor fellow. Really, it is a bit thick – <u>all</u> the administration of the section has devolved on him, as the senior Sergeant of the section: The poor bloke has been up in Bremervörde all the time, too – & hasn't the faintest idea how it has been going on at Section H.Q., for we had nothing much to do with them, being on detachment here... I managed to stay till to-morrow morning on the plea that there was a lot more work to do, reports on political meetings etc. Oh I <u>shall</u> be fed up if I can't snoop around with politics in the new area! Oh dear, the horrible spectre of Military Security Looms ahead of us – lecturing troops on How to Be Secure, testing sentries.

... I paid a last flying visit, this evening, to Wiegmann, & have two more paintings, one for Deryck & Dilys & one for Pooh & Piglet (Ho... .).

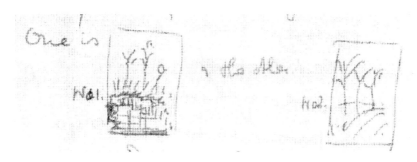

No 1. is for Deryck & D, no 2. for us. I am sending D.& D.'s off now, in case you want it soon – it's painted on wood & a <u>very</u> typical scene of Kreis Bremervörde (oh zzz, I want to keep it as well as the other!!!). No, & anyway, it'll stay in the family – they can have it as a present from us – I gave 300 odd cigs & soap for them both.

... Oh yes, I've been made up to Staff. Sgt., i.e. have crowns above my stripes – could you get hold of two pairs of brass crowns such as Staff-Sgts. (or quarter-master Sgts) wear, please if you can? 'Cos there are only horrid printed things here! It's only a local rank.

[*2.5.46*]

Sorry I didn't write yesterday as I said I would, but things are still rather a mess, & very unsettled. I am in Verden now, & am leaving for Oldenburg to-morrow – wearing <u>the</u> most Obvious & Hideous crowns over my striped — the only ones we could scrounge! When they should be discreet little ones, ah me!

Oh dear, what a muddle everything is in. I don't know whether I shall be able to keep it or not, but I have acquired a Volkswagen – a little German car wot has its engine at the back – you may have seen articles on it somewhere, & is emerald green, it's quite fun. Martin has likewise acquired a Mercedes-Benz, a very superior car, which runs beautifully!

[*4.5.46*]

Enfin, after three days, I can again find a moment to spare, & write. Oh <u>what</u> a lot has happened, I almost feel a new man! (or a different one, at any rate!)... Well, what has happened...

We left Verden Friday morning, & swished along in convoy, till Oldenburg, which is a <u>lovely</u> town, & ever so big, with masses of clubs, coffee shops & entertainment, opera house, theatre, etc. And the section billet is an <u>enormous</u> hotel with a whacking great yard, stables, dancing hall (grand piano!), dining hall, bar, lounges, etc. etc. Absolutely full, too, of Canadian Field Security who are moving out soon. And I was told I could do Political Intelligence for the area, too – at which I was extremely pleased. <u>THEN</u>... someone else cropped up, & they needed a man out on detachment with a certain amount of experience, & so here I am, out at a place called <u>Cloppenburg</u> which is here.

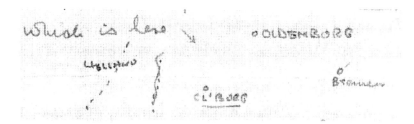

It's a place very much like Bremervörde & about as big (perhaps a bit bigger), & with about the same kind of area. I still feel it's a sort of nightmare, & that I'll suddenly find myself walking down the main street in Bremervörde again soon! Oh <u>dear</u>... .And if you were here it would be so different... zzz. Oh Bear, I <u>do</u> hate moving.

Still, the Canadian F.S. Detachment from whom I am taking over is a very nice trio of blokes – two C'dns & one Dutch interpreter – but they are moving out on the 8th of May or so...

And of course, I now have a car! I told you, didn't I – the Volkswagen, so if ever you come out here, we'll have grand fun!

So here I am on detachment (by myself, Staff Sgt. Gifford... Coo, it does feel odd to be called "Staff"! Martin has got off less lightly than I, perhaps, as the poor chap is doing Office Administration! Though of course he is staying at Oldenburg.

... What I miss an awful lot are my daily two pints of fresh milk! Have to lay that on, somewhere – only it's now forbidden to buy milk from Germans!

[6.5.46]

I'm still in a flattish sort of spin, & awfully unsettled & floating around, have been to Oldenburg goodness knows how many times during the last few days; so forgive vague & floating writing – <u>bless</u> you!

Oh well, I'm getting to know the detachment, finding out exactly how big the Kreis is, & how awful the roads are up North, which seems to be a boggy desert (will appear different when I go out there, no doubt!). I have received one bloke, a Corporal, as a help – but as he knows nothing whatsoever about the job he'll need some instructing, which won't be so helpful for a while at least. Still, he's Quiet, & is studying how to speak German, which is a Very Good Thing.

I went round to various people this afternoon, with Sgt. Archer (the Canadian Detachment Commander), & met the Polish

Armoured Brigade Intelligence Officer, with whom we talked cameras the whole time – another officer came in with a Robot like mine, only with just the lens I want! A Biotar 4 cm f:2! Gosh, I went green with envy! Oh well, I'll get something some day! (he said tearfully)

[*11.5.46*]
Just a very short note, as I am hopelessly sleepy – but I've some rather disappointing news – & that is that I'm pretty definitely not coming on leave in June – the Colonel in charge won't let anyone go on leave this month, and since there are now 7 to go before me, it won't be till July at least that I'll be able to come – I feel so fed-up about it, but it's just no good & no use letting it get us down.

... Don't be too fed up, darling – the Army does stupid senseless things like that from time to time, & there's nothing one can do to alter it. Stan says I should write out an official complaint, but... .Oh dear.

[*13.5.46*]
... Colonel wot stopped our leave came in to-day to visit my detachment, and was quite pleased with it. There is a conference on Thursday, so that we may hear something about it. Oh isn't it maddening.

... To-day the Canadians left, thank Goodness – they were a bit of a handful: & always giving away things, & then taking them back – they got rid of all the curtains just before we came, & the carpet in Ron's room has disappeared since we came... and the boxes & boxes of milk chocolate bars they had, & thousands of cigarettes – they all took it with them, and goodness knows where they'll all go.

[*15.5.46*]

... The work isn't at all bad, actually – great fun reorganizing it all and getting cracking on Political Intelligence etc – and since the Canadians haven't done any work for a month or so, we aren't exactly kicking our heels... !

... And no, young lady o'mine, I hain't crashed no Volkswagen yet, see? I take it into workshops every week, & it is fussed over by mechanics who take it to bits, polish it, screw it up, clean it, breathe on it, wash it & every conceivable thing they can they do! Thus the V'wagen is exceedingly natty in every respect, touch wood, so stop yer nasty remarks & cast no more nastershums, see?

... The other fellow here is called Ronald too, & I am getting to like him very much – he's quiet, studies hard, likes music, and isn't a know-all as so many Security Recruits are. In some ways he reminds me of Fred.

This evening we have both been guilty of getting three other Sergeants most fearfully drunk! Really, it wasn't exactly intentional – but they dropped in to see us (the Sgt. from the Town Major, the Sgt.-Major from Mil Govt., & a Dutch interpreter Sgt.), as we had asked them, in an effort to be sociable, to visit us when they liked. Well, we took out a bottle of German gin & one of orange juice & gave them a "Gin & Orange" each, taking plain orange juice for ourselves – and they stayed on & on, & drank more & more, till one was in an awful state, reeling all over the place and smashing glasses etc. So we took him back (this was the Town Major Sgt.), and Ron & the Sgt. Major (also very pickled) put him to bed, & then we took the other two home. But isn't it dreadful, getting them drunk like that! The first part of the evening nearly bored me to tears, but it got so amusing later on that I forgot it all. They had drunk three bottles of gin & one of orange juice by the end.

Oh gosh. What a dreadful responsibility it is to have to be sociable here – I do hope such a thing won't occur often!

We discovered a library in the YMCA to-day, and some records, and two English women! who were working there as helpers.

[*18.5.46*]

Again many apologies for not having written for such ages – I can only attribute it all to this business of settling down – only I thought I'd already done so.

... Where shall I start?! Well, to start at last Thursday there was a Conference at the Area Intelligence Office, & they have gone & put me in charge of an Intelligence Team, covering two Kreise! And one of them is the biggest Kreis in Germany, so they say! I'm going to have a loverly time organising them as far as Political Intelligence is concerned, anyway!

... Well, on Friday we spent most of the day getting rations & pay & whatnot. Then to-day we went out to a farmer & bought a chicken off him (or bartered it, rather), after having dealt with the business in hand. They were kindly people, though, & insisted that we should sit down to a cup of coffee & ham & bread, & when we went to collect the chicken this evening, all trussed & ready, & gave them a lot of soap & chocolate & cigars & Schnapps etc, they gave us some hot milk soup (which is milk & oats – very filling!). In this neighbourhood they are much more kindly than they were in B'vde., I must say.

[*24.5.46*]

I'm in a very queer state, all mixed up, sort of – somebody just stole all our NAAFI from the Volkswagen, & then there was a lovely letter from you to counteract all that... so there are two opposite camps glaring rather at each other... !

... I wonder if we realize exactly how much a part of each other we have grown – how most of our faith & hopes rest in each other's hearts, and how much we lean against each other... I get mad at myself for doing pushful things & making you say "shut up" or something & then feel upset for hours, cursing myself & then say stupid things too, & think you don't ponder over things deeply enough, & get into muddles with myself; but – you are my all, & centre point, & nothing can change it very easily, even if I wanted it to, which I don't. And I often feel that about Can-any-people-live-happily-together, & then generally amble along to the decision that of course I can live with you, & what's more I can, I'm going to make it our business that we do it happily. Which we shall, if we give it thought & take notice of each other's thoughts. Oh Darling don't let's get into muddles on our own in separate corners – let's go into the same corner & share them. I say that, not because you are in the habit of doing that, but because I do it awfully easily... You're very practical, Pooh, & do the right thing by instinct rather than by puzzling it out, and I'm a dreamer, rather, & get to an opinion by dreaming over it, then go & do exactly the opposite. Which is quite unreasonable...

Anyway, Bear – do believe me, I do like to look at us from different angles, & whichever angle I look from, it still looks good, like a Christmas pudding, only tons nicer!

[30.5.46]

... These last two days we've been moving the Vechta detachment into Cloppenburg office, with masses of this & that to look after, & desks to shift & shove. So now there are five Sergeants here, or they have moved their kit in, at any rate. And have been for a walk with Ron this evening.

Do you know, I think that one of the ways to success in marriage is the gift of not keeping on thinking of what one has already done for the other person – "Cor, I polished his boots yesterday, & now he says I'm a bad cook" – but to appreciate one's duty to the other, & not count past dues paid when asked to do something. Oh I don't know what made me blurt out with that, I feel fed up with myself this evening, rather, & feel I've been doing it – not with you so much as with friends.

... Mmm, Do write to [Peggy], as she'll be feeling ever so fed up, perhaps – Poor Peggy – she was worrying about a lot of things. I feel I did wrong not to see more of her during the last days here –

as I spent all the office hours in the office working, & she was alone in the billet...

... No, I don't think I'll go <u>particularly</u> skew-whiff, with regard to married life & life in general – but I do think there's a danger of getting too reserved & selfish seeming & narrow really being ten times worse than wot the Cynical People say a man lowers himself to. I'd hate to be a humourless stodgy old imbecile with no kindliness or warmth in him – oh isn't life difficult – one either swings the one way or the other if enough care isn't taken. Though I'd consider myself far less evil if I did go immoral in the conventional idea – for at least I wouldn't have lost the warmth in my soul. I'd <u>far</u> rather you be unfaithful with twenty men (no, that <u>is</u> a bit too strong!!) than you lose your personality & cheerfulness & love & become selfish, reserved & cold. I really would.

[2.6.46]

... The next thing is that I have Obtained a very good camera, will you tell Gildas? A Kodak "Retina I", with 3.5 lens etc. I also got 30 metres of 35 mm film at the same time, so we shan't be too badly off, <u>dear</u>! And two exposure meters, etc. All this for 500 marks (£12.10.0), and 1000 cigarettes, plus an odd few bars of soap etc. It's a lovely little camera, & has an ever-ready leather case like Gildas's Leica,. It isn't as good as his, as it hasn't the range finder, or high speeds (goes up to 1/300), but even then, it's very good. Takes 36 exposures, & all that.

... The next thing is that I went to Bremervörde for the weekend, mainly to see Dorothy – got there about 6.0 & we went to a dance in a neighbouring village (British unit dance), & did all sorts of weird & wonderful inventions of dances as we always do, & then talked for ages in her room till I dropped off to sleep, so woke & went back to my room. This morning I went riding on a very energetic horse, with Karl – really a wonderful ride – except that while we were miles out it started pouring with rain so that we got drenched to the skin! Came back, then went to Dorothy's for the afternoon, & helped her make out an application & life story (she wants to change her nationality). Then came back after taking her to dinner. Terry Clare is leaving Bvde, which is rather a blow for her, poor soul.

... When I got back here I found that one of my sergeants had (a), got bashed on the head with a bottle and (b), got drawn into HQ to do the section administration work – which makes us one less... He got bashed on the head by a very drunken Canadian, who smashed the bottle first on a CMP's head, & then hit him with the broken end!

[*3.6.46*]

... Gosh, what a lot of work there is to be done – Political Intelligence report to-morrow, oh cor... much as I love doing it, & what would you say if I was offered a job at £650 – £700 a year plus keep plus having you out here, in Political Intelligence?!! NO, I haven't been, 'cos I didn't apply, but I would get it, if I did – that's been making me feel rather muddled, lately, 'cos I am very keen on Pol. Int. as work, & mmm,, oh I don't know, we must talk about it.

[*5.6.46*]

... I had a perfectly awful time trying to make out a Work Ticket for my Volkswagen. We have to make one out each month – or rather, fill out a line for each day's trip – how much petrol drawn, how much remained after the trip, how much used, etc. with what the mileage jigger said before & after, & where I went. And the awful part is that all the petrol has to be totalled up, and the "start" + "drawn" must equal the "end" + "used" part. So that when yesterday I blithely handed in a work ticket I thought was all right, Bernard Eaton asked me things like: how I made out that here & there I had 4 gallons at the start, drew 2 more, used one and had three left at the end! And made me sit down & write a new one out, of which the totals didn't agree at all – so I had to spend ages this afternoon writing a Good One out with totals wot agreed... phew! Anyway, before that I wrote a whacking great Political Intelligence Report, so I've done something at any rate. Then sped into Oldenburg and handed in the results of my labours, had tea there, & then came back.

... Well, so you don't think I'll be Hen-pecked, do you? Ho!! No, I don't think I shall either, neither will you ever be cock-pecked, or whatever it is called, for we're both, well, "monstrous clever", as Dorothy would put it!

... Yes, well, most sin <u>is</u> a result of other things, isn't it – the easiest way along after bad things have happened in or to you (that's why there is no great virtue in being "good" when it's the easiest thing to be – it <u>is</u> right, of course, but one shouldn't pretend it has been a struggle, & demand great credit for it). In a way, I rather think of it as a mirror, and that analogy tallies with my belief, in that any sin in a person is a reflected thing – a mirror in which are reflected many evil happenings & doings, which, crowded together, give the impression of being something else – just as when you look at purple, you are really seeing red & blue spots. That helps me to realize, too, that <u>any</u> person's sin is really a combination of spots of different basic colours, and that some of the spots aren't his fault at all, & others are just his having been weak, or not properly educated or brought up. Mmm?

[*12.6.46*]

<u>Still</u> no news of anything, and I keep on saying to myself: "won't write again till I do know so as not to get you all Anticipating at the sight of masses of letters, & after having read them all, feeling depressed & I-don't-know-what, but I just feel so much like writing... .Oh I've done it all badly, getting you expectant (or rather, expecting!) like that & then lingering a long time about it. You see, wot 'appened was this: We got all the allocations for leave that we needed, & having too many at the

same time, we sent some of these away (including mine), & asked whether we could have some allocations in place of them for later in the month. And these we are waiting for now... So any day they might come (and of course there is always the possibility that we shan't be able to get them anyway), and there are now three more people to go (incl. me).

... I've been thinking a lot about us & Later on, & what problems would crop up (! 'orrid couple we are, aren't we), & all... great fun, that, actually – why I've thought out all the answers (from my side!) to any possible problem, dear! So You Need Have No Worries At All! (except think out all the answers from your side!) Ho!

Sweet, we must go to Oxford this leave sometime... mmm? eee? Apparently all Groups up to 55 of students are to get Class "B" release – rather maddening to be one above it. Gosh, I shall be 22 next month, too! Cor... Most people here in Cloppb'g won't believe I am that young! Hm! I was thinking it all out in my barf' – if I am 23 when we get married, you'll be nearly 26, then when I am 26 you'll be 28 & 29, & when I'm 37 you'll be 40. Good Gracious... Then when I am 67 you'll be 70. Between 26 & 40 how many children can you have? 14?! I mean, without rush – 4 easily, couldn't you?... Oh well, we'll see. (No, dear, don't let's publish all our letters!)

[*16.6.46*]

... Thanks very much for yours of the 12th, sweetheart – it was good to get it, oh sweet, you have a very nice personality – did you know that?

I do feel envious of your sailing! I know just what fun it is, to be swishing along, & then tacking, & ducking as the boom thing whooshes over your head... You lucky one! you know. I'm awfully pleased you are having a good time, & Plenty of Variety & All, 'cos if it was raining all the time you might get time to feel fed up because I wasn't coming – I know I would, & am not just being hopefully vain or anything!

[20.6.46]

Bless you for a lovely long letter, full of everything, & dated the 24th – I did enjoy it, it was so alive & feeling. You are a feeling sort of Bear, you know, & that's one of the things I prize most highly in you, that quickness & warmth of spirit which you have, responding to things. Mmm, you are responsive – oh dear, I almost weep when I suddenly realize what ages it is since I've seen you, & that some of my memories have grown dim & not so sharply edged... mmm. Which brings me to my news; leave. I got an allocation for the 23rd July (yes, all right dear, & don't knock the teapot over!), but have arranged to come on the 16th instead, so as to get everything in. And I get 19 days, so I'm told, so Be Prepared!! Which would bring us to Saturday 3rd August, eee? With Birthday & Rape of L. – aren't I a clever Pootle? (under his breath), "say yes!" Woozles: (terrified) "Ye-e-ss!" So there you are!

[1.7.46]

... You know, I treasure those early letters an awful lot, don't you... I do think we're a Couple of Ones, too – and ever so well-knit. Darling, I do hope you never become a nagging sort, & I hope I don't either. I often find here that I tell Ron or someone off, & find later it could have been left unsaid & was really not all that necessary. So do let's try, won't we? And I think we'll be very happy, if we do, 'cos we're not all that bad-tempered, or selfish, or greedy... really I think we aren't. I often train (or try to) myself, & when I think "Cor, can't give that away to the woman who washes our things or something, it's my last bar of milk chocolate" – I clamp myself fiercely on the shoulder & say "Oh is that so, well away you give it then" – I'm not saying this to show how good I am – for Heaven's sake don't think that, it was just the thought of you making yourself go into the part of a railway train which might get the worst if it crashed – just to overcome the fear – that's what put it in my mind.

Dunno' why I thought of <u>that</u>, really, except that when I think of us I realize deeper & deeper that without control & self-discipline we won't be anything – just two silly moths flapping up against a lighted window, or two piles of brick & mortar, waiting to be built into something, & never getting anywhere. Just the raw material & nought else. That's partly (though it's rather a long jump from that point to this) why I think long engagements like ours <u>aren't</u> a thing to be desired in normal times, as something which is in itself fine & natural has to be repressed (rather than controlled), which in God's eyes <u>isn't</u> a good thing, I'm sure. And the harm done <u>is</u> in the repression, while on the other hand one becomes a hypocrite being a Christian & not repressing it, so where-are-you. But if a couple aren't Christian I really don't see <u>how</u> they can be "bad", do you... oh I hate the terms "bad" & "good" in those ways, anyway – a thing is either intelligent or non-intelligent, full of character or empty, truthful or not truthful. We wouldn't be "bad" if we lived a colourless, blameless & church-going life together for all our married lives, if we gave away that which we never needed, if we helped at social functions, if we ran bazaars & things... but we wouldn't be much good, either, for that's no <u>Life</u>. And if we set out to be honest, intelligent, & unselfish, we'll accomplish much more than the feeble people who look to their own safety first rather than sallying forth & saving others, going & <u>doing</u> something. That's Christianity, going and doing Things.

... Beethoven's 9th last night was glorious – the best part was that the soloists were so good; Germans generally aren't too hot at that sort of thing, too. Oh but what a beautiful thing it is. Ron had never heard it before, & he was wildly enthusiastic about it! Had a box, we did, or shared one – very nice, though too near the orchestra...

Then yesterday afternoon I sunbathed & read my book, & to-day worked quite hard & talked Party Politics with the Christian Democratic Party leader. This evening had a long discussion with the German Teacher & Ron about war & the evils thereof.

[*4.7.46*]

... Mmm, what did I do Tuesday... Oh, wrote the report (Political Intelligence Report), & finished it at 3.0am!

You know, I <u>do</u> love that side of my job – Political reporting. I sometimes think How Nice It Would Be to do that all throughout my life, & write articles, but it's rather a secret thought, & not awfully hopeful. Do you think I can write? Anyway, dashing about all over the place doesn't make for a peaceful family life, really – almost as bad as a Travelling Salesman. But I wrote a Whopping Pol. Int. report – 6 pages of closely-typewritten foolscap. it's rather amusing we get copies of the Area Intelligence Pol. Int. report, & it's <u>always</u> composed largely of chunks of ours, word for word! In fact to-day they rang up to apologize for not being able to put one of the bits in..!

... News! I'm now getting 10/6 a day pay!!

[*7.7.46*]

... I went to Bremervörde yesterday, as I said, & had quite a good time in the evening with Dorothy – first we went rowing on the river at Plonjeshausen, & climbed onto the bank & went for a walk & sat on piles of hay & talked, & then back to B'vde & had summat to eat in her room, & tea. Then later on we went for a ride in the Volkswagen & went into the Höhne forest with it!! <u>Great</u> fun, whooshing along tiny paths & up inclines & on pine needles! How the car stood it, I don't know(!!!), er – I mean, why it never complained! But then I was going quite slowly... and the moon was up too & everything looked lovely. We looked at the river, & the pond in the park, & then back to her room & had cocoa out of a self-heating can! (Have you ever met those things – just light a wick in the lid of the tin, and in three minutes it's more or less boiling!). Then I went back to Frau Schlichting's to sleep. This morning I went & saw some Bremervörde people & had a glass put in my watch at our jeweller-friend's (& admired some of the semi-precious stones he had – a lovely Tourmaline for 2000 marks (£50), & Topazes, & aquamarine-stones – some set in silver, & all terrific prices. Still, they must be impossible to get, I suppose.)

Came back here this afternoon, & went to the opening meeting of a Trade Union there is to be here in the Kreis, & after that played the piano. I've begun to sniff at a horribly difficult piece by Chopin – goodness knows how far I shall stagger along in it – I know about one bar up to now! I will conquer it one day, though. And my Beethoven needs repairing and my Mozart needs patching up – gosh what a lot to do – it's like cleaning a huge pile of silver plate.

... As far as I know this is more or less what happens when one goes on leave: Münster train leaves M. at 3.30 a.m. on, say, Monday morning, arrives at the Hook of Holland at 5.30 in the afternoon – the boat leaves at 9.0 that night (still Monday), and gets to Harwich at 6.0 in the morning. After a lot of pottering about the train leaves H. about 8.0 and arrives in London 10.0-ish at Liverpool St. There are three or so trains, so I'd be on one of 'em. Oh sweetheart, I'd love to be met, I just can't say how much I'd like it, really I would! Ho, indeed!! So I'd be at L. St. from 10.0 – 11.0 (or whenever the train does come in), on the 16th (or 17th?) – no 16th, probably. Eee, I am getting excited!

[10.7.46]

... Lookee, I shall probably be arriving on the 17th, as I'm leaving on the 15th, & it takes two days, Hoke? That's next Wednesday – phew! I'm just about snowed under with work & trying to get it done in time, & feel hopelessly browned off, for some reason or other – probably feeling impatient, or something.

[*Douglas came home on leave from 17th July to 6th August.*]

[*6.8.46*]

Eee, it don't 'arf feel odd to be writing to you again...

And the sandwiches were <u>lovely</u> too. I thought I'd keep them for the boat, but was overcome by a Norful Temptation, and said that why should I let them get stale like museum pieces, and now am jolly glad I did! <u>Bless</u> you, sweet, very much indeed, and such a wonderful three weeks it's been, and all... These leaves always seem to get better & better each time, don't they.

[*6.8.46*]

Its a lovely night, & the sea calm & the moon bright (when it comes out from behind the clouds). Otherwise, quite dark, with the lights of Harwich receding into the distance. Being on board ship is very pleasant on a summer's night, but I'd <u>much</u> rather be in Coulsdon with you, bless you – gosh, & how...

... I got to Parkeston Quay at 3.30 or so, & got taken to the transit camp in a truck (began to get into an awful flap because a CMP seemed to be following on a motor bike but he disappeared), lounged, slept, ate, read, & went for a short walk at the camp till 6.20, when we all embarked. Nothing has been noticed yet about my lateness off leave – on the pass it now has "Your return train departs at 1400 hrs on the 4 Aug 46" <u>and</u> "Embarked Harwich 6 Aug 46", which looks a trifle odd! Still, what does it matter. I was put in charge of a Troop deck when I got aboard, which rather peeved me till I found that there wasn't much to it – simply detailing four blokes to get two urns of tea... & now the lights of England have almost disappeared, & are just faintly glimmering on the horizon.

... I wonder what I'd have to do if the ship began to sink – I mean, as "Troop Deck Commander"... ? Probably get my 100 men to stand to attention & sing "God Save the King"... I was about to write that the ship was in two minds about going, as it was revolving in circles, but it seems to have decided on some plan or other now, and is ploughing forward in a wavy line. We get to the Hook of H. at 6.0 to-morrow morning, & I hope to be in Cloppenburg by nightfall.

Oh dear, I do feel hungry – why was I such a fat hog to eat all the sandwiches you gave me. But I was just as hungry then, really.

[7.8.46]

Well, I've got so far – left Hook of Holland (where I posted my last letter) at 9.30, and arrived here at 4.0 or so. Telephoned Ron, who very kindly offered to come & pick me up in the car, for which I am very grateful, not feeling very bright or energetic. Then for a walk round Osnabruck – oh it's such a different place. You know, Germany is quite another world – the Germans themselves like ants creeping round heaps of crumbly bricks.

... I enclose an example of the new British money to be used out here. Isn't it Ever So Pretty? There are 3d, 6d, 1/-, 2/6, 5/-, 10/- (I think) & £1, all notes. You may keep it, in a sock, dear.

Oh, I finished reading "St. Joan", & liked it very much. Shaw is terrifically full of Common Sense, isn't he.

[*10.8.46*]

Yes, it does seem a long time, oh wooze, isn't it a B——business, all this getting used to being apart all over again. <u>And</u>, to make it even more difficult, I have just been to see "Brief Encounter" – oh it <u>is</u> good, isn't it. I kept on seeing & feeling things in the story that were <u>so</u> akin to ours – did you find that. I saw myself as Fred <u>and</u> Alec Harvey, & you, of course as the wife! Probably you did the same... but oh gosh, that feeling that she had when she'd been out for the first time with the Doctor, and when she got back, her small son had had an accident – isn't it <u>exactly</u> what one <u>does</u> feel sometimes after a high-running kind of day? Not necessarily with a person, but just any kind of enjoying-day. Oh it was a <u>terrific</u> film. And saying goodbye as they did – how well we know that... I think the music was well-suited to the film, & I loved little touches such as newspapers being blown along the alley-ways by the wind. Oh, & wasn't the "fore-runner" of the "film" in the cinema that they went to <u>wonderful</u> – "Flame of Passion" – gosh, I thought that was <u>so</u> funny, almost because it was so typical, and then to have an advertisement for prams directly afterwards – gosh, even the Army audience could see the humour in that!

... The Regimental Paymaster sent through a curt note to enquire why I was £29 in debt at the end of June! Probably because I drew that £50 earlier on.

Ah well, life here is more or less heaving itself onto its feet again, though I must confess I can feel no desire whatsoever to do any work yet! We went round the Kreis on Friday & had quite an interesting day. A lot of people think that were it not for the Black Market, there would be no food problem at all in Germany...

Gosh what a happy day we had last Saturday, didn't we... at Pevensey beach, & batheing – oh <u>sweet</u>...

Goodnight, my love,

God Bless us, & again thank you for a glorious leave.

All my love to you.

[*12.8.46*]

... This time last week we had just come back from seeing your relatives at Caterham & going for that lovely ride over White Hill; & then after supper & packing we listened to the Byrd Mass on the gramophone, and all that. Oh sweetheart, I just can't – oh well, it <u>was</u> a perfect time...

... I get <u>so</u> fed up with my bed clothes – the bottom of the feet is always coming undone – it's so demoralizing, really it is. I don't <u>like</u> the sides getting undone, but it doesn't make me a quarter as

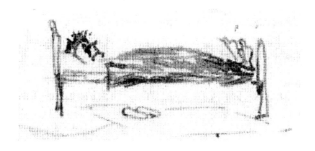

peeved as if I find my feet out in the cold every morning. Oh dear, what <u>can</u> I do about it? Tucking the blanket in doesn't seem to help much – it <u>is</u> a nuisance – I'm beginning to get a Thing about sleeping in the bed now – perhaps it's because the sheets are too short...? Anyway, it's all very browning off, especially directly after a leave.

... The Volkswagen is going through a Phase of General Obstinacy – I was very much disturbed to read a message on my desk which ran "No. 4660133 (my V'wgn) – driver to report Oldenburg at 0815 hours in overalls and with Haversack rations on 15 August." Sounds rather grim, doesn't it? Ah well, dear, think of me on the day! I don't quite know what they want me to do, at all.

Oh, & did I tell you that I probably shan't be able to draw any more pay for some time? (As a note came through stating that I was £29 in debt in my paybook at the end of June.) So I shan't be buyin' no more chocklit' nor cigs for a lawng time... snf snf.

... Do you know which music I have been thinking of lately? Petroushka! If there was a good recording of it, I wouldn't mind getting it, would you? It grows on one, doesn't it, & I'd like to see it again, too.

[16.8.46]

... Inspection on V'wagen went off very well yesterday. I went along there sans car identity books, & sans tools, & they were very decent, & tested it & inspected & painted little numbers on it – "40" on the back, & little "30's" & "26's" on the mudguards over the wheels (tyre pressures, dear) & there I was! And I'd brought sandwiches along, and my oldest battledress, & I was finished by 10 or so... so went back rather sheepishly to the billet in Cloppenburg & said I'd be in for lunch after all, & then went off on some job.

... Then to-day I had a lot of fun – went (by myself) down to the very southernmost tip of my area (quite near Osnabrück) and did a job there. Oh & on the way down I went over a bump, & the car stopped! So I looked vaguely at the engine, & twiddled about with the points, & tested the distance between them. Pressed the starting thing, & it all went off with a colossal bang... So I tottered weakly down the road, to where some RAF blokes had a billet, & one of them, a Canadian, soon saw what the matter was. A jigger had fallen out of the thing above the points – called a brush, I think, only it doesn't look like one at all. I don't see why it should go & make such an awful bang, anyhow. Then I went, waveringly, down to Damme, the village, & did what I had to do. (Vet a lady who was applying to go to Denmark.)

Then went into the church there, which really is rather lovely: very wide, like many continental churches, & with very beautiful stained-glass windows – very grand an impression it gave, though friendly.

Then, I thought I'd have my sandwiches in Peace & Quiet by the lake which I knew to be nearby – found it after quite a while – very nice one, about 1½ to 2 miles across, with the hills of Osnabrück in the background. Sniffed around for a while, till I came to a notice which read "Commander-in-chief's Yachting Club – Keep out!" or something, so I drove in, and there was a châlet by the lake, with some sailing boats moored up. I didn't see any Commander-In-Chief to spoil the peace, so asked the caretaker of the châlet if I could have some soup, & he let me sit in the dining room, which overlooked the lake – very lovely view. It transpired that this was a Yachting Club for officers & members of a certain unit or other, & all sorts of important people came down. None there then, though. There were little caravans outside for sleeping quarters.

So I came back to the main road & up to a place called Lohne, where I visited a photographer who does my photos now. He is from Brazil (St. Paulo) & a very nice chap. We spoke for quite a long time about cameras, & how hard it was to find Leicas nowadays (same old topic!) etc.

... Oh, "Il Seraglio" last night was great fun – it was done in the great hall of the castle at Oldenburg, not quite the right place for an opera. Acting was <u>awful</u>, as usual, but otherwise everything very good & I loved Osmin, the keeper, & his bumptious wickedness.

[10.8.46]

... I'm writing this in the car waiting for the doors to open for the Beethoven 9th, and am surrounded by letters, photos, money etc. Oh, & thank you <u>very</u> muchly for the parcel, which arrived to-day, bless you, what a time you must have had tying it up – I undid it after lunch, & everyone kept saying "Here, cut the string", & got quite peeved when I wouldn't! Everything is all right – the tins of coffee rather dented, but otherwise nothing at all. Eee, you are a dear to do such a lot of things for me!

... Oh, it <u>was</u> wonderful... not such a big orchestra, but beautifully played. I enjoy it more & more every time I hear it – also a very large choir, & a very good one too... oh, it's terrific.

Dorothy came yesterday and stayed the night at the house of the lady who does our washing – & went off again to-day at 5.0 p.m. She is in the depths, as All is Ended (with Terry Clare), & says she is incapable of feeling any emotion whatsoever, at present, & is all numb. Apparently on the last evening he was with her she said "Let's get it all clear", & after some humming & hawing he said No, because his family (Mother, & sister aged 17 – he's nearly 40) wouldn't like his marrying a German girl! Which upset D. very much because quite independently of the Terry question she has been trying to get naturalized British for some time now! And so she feels it rather unjust. Isn't it sad. I personally feel that he isn't anywhere good enough for her if he goes saying that – for Dorothy isn't an ordinary all-for-a-bar-of-chocolate girl! & can't be classified as a German female-trying-to-make good. I don't think so, anyway.

[20.8.46]

... & what a nice evening it is. I'm sitting out on the terrace in my deck chair, feeling quite at peace & <u>quite</u> content fat fellow that

I am. We've just bartered & bought two tins (<u>64</u> packets a tin) of milk-chocolate biscuits & one of Weston's Assorted biscuits, <u>&</u> a 7lb. fruit cake!

Yesterday was rather a full sort of day. We were sitting rather drowsily in the office when the phone rang... and I think I told you – (hem) – but I've been sniffing around for a Leica – er – for some time, yes? er – yes. Well, the phone rang, & our German teacher, one of the twenty odd people who have been co-sniffing with me in search of a Leica (for me) rang up & said that there was a <u>Contax</u> to be had in exchange for what I wanted to give! So Jupp, the Dutch Sergeant, Ron, & the German teacher & I all hared round to the address, & a scruffy-looking bloke produced a brand-new Contax! We took him to our billet, & he agreed to take cigarettes 'instead' of the Binoculars, for which I was very pleased. So he took my little wireless, the Robot, & 400 cigarettes, & that was that! I was a bit afraid that the camera mightn't have been his to give (to put it politely) but I was reassured when he explained it very thoroughly – so it was obvious that he knew a lot about it. Wheee! So there it is, & fair makes me gasp still when I look at it – Contax II, lens = "Sonar" f 1:2! Wheee, indeed! The only thing I rather need for it is a leather case to carry it in (Ever-Ready case like Gil has with his), as it hasn't anything. Then I'll have the filters, lens cap & hood etc to get. But they won't cost much, I hope. The camera in England was priced at £125 last December, too. I'm longing to get to work with it! Eee, isn't it exciting! Pleased too? I <u>do</u> hope you are!

And, if it doesn't sound awfully feeble, I don't understand <u>quite</u> everything on it yet, so could you get me a "Contax Guide!" next time you're near Wallace & Heaton's, or some such place? Please, darling? And get a rough idea of how much accessories will be for it? – though I shall try & get them in Germany first. We're going to Hamburg next Saturday. But if you could let me have an estimate of what price each thing for it is... ? So if I can get it through the customs without having to pay about £100 duty on it, you'll see it soon.

Oh dear, I can't stop talking about it. Never mind, Dear, I <u>do</u> love you more than I do it – Never Fear!

To-day we went round the Kreis, seeing people & having quite a pleasant & sleepy time, really – awful, we don't seem to be working at all hard!

[*22.8.46*]

... I see in the newspaper to-day that they <u>are</u> continuing Class "B" after all – I wonder if there is any hope – perhaps in January?

... Oh aren't things in a mess, in Egypt, Palestine, India (?) etc. I just don't know what to think about Palestine – not that I know much either, but a <u>solution</u> is so hard to get at. It is all very well saying that the Jews make much more efficient settlements etc. but even then would you like it if the Coulsdon Council (or whatever it is) came & said that as the house could be much more modernly run by the Higgins family, they would be moving in to live with you – <u>and</u> you could see perfectly well that the Higginses had every intention of running you as well, ultimately. Oh dear, it's a mess.

[*25.8.46*]

... Well, what have I been doing lately? Friday went around the Kreis, main visit being to a Dr. of Theology who is very interested in starting up the "Zentrum" (Centre Party) – of Socialist Catholics – very good idea, I think. He is very interested in photography, too, & lent me a ball & socket (tripod-head) for my Contax – which will be very useful. it's <u>such</u> great fun taking photos of oneself! The first film will be developed soon. I do hope it turns out well.

We went to Hamburg yesterday. I wanted to deliver that parcel to Dawson Jackson's friends. I found them after a longish search. They have a lovely little flat in the best part of Hamburg, seem very prosperous too. Herr Brinkmann has a car, which means a lot in Germany these days. I mean, a person is quite important if he has one. They were very kind & nice, & delighted to see me, said they'd be glad to put me up any time I was in Hamburg. I took them Dawson Jackson's parcel & some odd extras of NAAFI & rations I thought they might need.

[*27.8.46*]

... Here a change has taken place; just yesterday we were told that a C.C.G. Officer would be coming, to be in charge of the detachment! Which fed us up, rather, especially, as I didn't like the idea of not being in charge any more. Anyway, he came in the afternoon, & is a <u>very</u> nice bloke, we think, but as for knowing anything about the job it's rather dreadful – he doesn't speak one word of German, has never done <u>any</u> Field Security work ever before – was a Naval Officer on a motor launch in the Far East, & was an Engineer before the war! Earns £650 a year plus keep! So that he's rather an Encumbrance, & will have to be taught everything. Oh cor... but it does peeve me that he should be (nominally) in charge of the Detachment – silly of me, but there it is – or it's not silly, but petty of me.

[*31.8.46*]

Rather an appalling thing has happened – in fact, very appalling: the parcel you sent containing the negatives & filters was stolen, I'm afraid. Unfortunately it went to "13 F.S.S.", & the bloke who collected it from the Post Office in Oldenburg went in to have a cup of tea at the NAAFI, leaving it in the car (locked up), & when he came back it was gone. I was only told about it the next day, which wasn't very bright of them, & spent all the morning going from the German Police to the British C.M.P., putting an advertisement about it in the newspaper, getting a notice put into all the Military Units' Daily orders, & so on. Oh Bear, it is maddening, isn't it. I felt <u>so</u> enraged about it, & so helpless too, & despaired of everything. It <u>may</u> turn up, but I should think that the person who stole it would have thrown it away as soon as he saw that there was no value in it. The Post orderly was quite helpful, & said he'd supply £5 for a reward if anyone did find it.

... On the evening that I was more or less upside down with anger, & lots of discord, I began reading a book by Peter Howard called "That Man Frank Buchmann" – which I didn't stop reading till I'd finished it. The A.I.O. (Area Intelligence Officer) is a keen Oxford Group man (called Mr. Coleman) & knows a lot of quite important people in it. Pooh, tell me something about it all, eeee? And what they think, & feel, & do. The book was mainly on Moral Re-armament. And tell me what you think of it, too...

Bless you my Love, you're very wise and I'd trust your judgement to be honest on any subject or about anything.

These last two days have been mainly occupied in showing Mr. Parker round & introducing him to various political heads. It's all rather awkward, as I'm not much use as an Interpreter, quite forgetting there's one poor chap with me who doesn't understand what's going on at all, & is patiently waiting for someone to explain. Still perhaps I'll get used to it & remember to do so. But it's difficult to switch one's mind from thinking in German to start thinking in English, right in the middle of a conversation.

Last night I went down to Lohne (near Vechta) to see the photographer, & he showed us, through a magic-lantern, most of his colour negatives – really terrific things, of Autumn, & rivers & reflections, & flowers... he's a very good bloke, indeed he is, & kind. I told you he & his came from Brazil, didn't I?

[2.9.46]

... I got to Nijmegen on Sunday all right, took Jupp home, & then went to Cuyk, & saw everybody again: the Telkamp family (Truus), Manders family, Walters, etc. I stayed with the Telkamps, & went to visit the Manders in the late afternoon – they are a lovely family, all 10 children round the table having their tea – it's so nice. Mr. Manders is obviously very well off, and so they can spend a great deal on their children. The Walters family had increased from 5 to 7, too! Mr. Manders showed Truus & myself over his leather factory – masses & masses of cow hides in various degrees of "tanned-ness" – very interesting, really. And gave me a leather camera case which I hope to be able to convert to house my Contax!

[*3.9.46*]

... To-day we went round a bit of the Kreis, had bread & ham & hot milk at a farmer whom we know very well. Mr. Parker is slowly thawing into shape – he's very keen on the job, I think – & that's a great blessing. Hilda is back from her honeymoon, very bright & happy.

[*9.9.46*]

... I went Saturday to Bremervörde – spent quite a nice weekend there – saw Dorothy, & dashed round visiting people, & taking reels of cotton & silk, & forgetting who was supposed to have which from the things I bought in England, & getting into a muddle, but emerged nevertheless cheerful. Went riding on Sunday with Karl & Dorothy and took some quite good photos – I hope – all quite fun. But I was awfully browned off most of the time, 'cos I'd seen Martin, & he told me that someone's given an order that we have to become ordinary Sgts again! Isn't it cheesing off – one damned thing after another, really... apparently some silly sod up in Hamburg or Berlin doesn't like Acting or Local rank, so down we all go – it's so idiotic & uncomfortable for us – just imagine walking about a small town like Cloppenburg with everyone noticing you & seeing that you've not got a crown up (Germans are very Military minded & notice those sort of things) and whispering away, & everyone firmly believes you've been demoted for being drunk or inefficient, or something! Really, it is annoying.

[*10.9.46*]

... Oh <u>yes</u>, how I do agree about "Saying the same thing" – I'm sure it's like an enormous weed, with roots spreading everywhere, though.

... It's such an easy thing to talk <u>unconsciously</u> – just as if you are playing the piano & talking at the same time. The words come easily, but your thoughts are somewhere else.

It would appear that the older one gets, the more automatic speech becomes – and when your Mother has spent a great amount of time running a house, the channels of her thought on various things will not change easily, & won't widen either.

... It doesn't do to get sensitive over that kind of thing – it certainly doesn't lead to happiness or peace of mind. It is a human failing, & we'll do it a little anyway, however hard we try, don't you think?

[*14.9.46*]

... I saw a film last night I liked <u>very</u> much called "The Years Between". I can't quite remember whether you have seen it or no; it had a fine moral to it. I thought; jolly good, for it might help a lot of people: Michael Redgrave, Valerie Hobson & Flora Robson were in it. Oh dear, now I wonder if you <u>have</u> seen it? All about a Colonel going 'underground' from England to Germany (I think) and to cover his disappearance he had to be reported killed, & couldn't tell even his wife... & so she thinks he is dead, & takes his place in Public Life & finally gets over it – is about to marry again when he comes back. And the actual plot is their getting used to each other again, & allowing for the changes in each other. (The only thing is that the film ends up with them both in Parliament!) Still, it <u>was</u> good, & <u>so</u> English, I loved it.

I get very impressed with good films somehow – & go around the next day thinking about them & what use their story can be to us – I felt this one had more moral than most, for I've a feeling that separations are the greatest dislocating things in marriage – much worse than rows on the spot, however great they may be. Mother & Unk are examples of that – bless them – for separation has led to practically everything, with them. And a film which tries to help with a problem like that is doing a good bit of work, I feel.

... The Elections (community-village-ones) take place to-morrow, so I shall be buzzing around a great deal – visiting polling booths & whatnots, seeing how things are getting on. I hope to be the first in with the results on Monday – together with a report on them (rather reporter-ish! "Waal, I work for 'The Mirror'... !"). Mmm, well... & I shall take photos, no doubt. This is the first of the elections – the next date for them will be October 14th, when the Kreis-parliament elections will take place. There is not much doubt as to the Party which will win the majority here – it'll be the Christian Democratic Union Party, of course.

The party, as far as I'm concerned is the Social Democratic, but they started too late here, I fear, & have only put up candidates in two places. I enclose two small posters which their chairman gave me. One reads:

"If you want to play at being a Blind Cow (i.e. to play Blind Man's Bluff), Vote for *F.D.P. & *C.D.U. But if you lay stress on clearsightedness, you'd better not vote for either – neither C.D.U. nor F.D.P. Who loves Germany votes SPD"

& the other:

"Black Market – The overcoming of it is in your interests – the SPD fight for that." (The *F.D.P. = Free Democratic Party – horrid lot, *C.D.U, I've mentioned).

Keep them, will you, Pooh, they're quite interesting. I think I'll make a collection of them!

A bloke in Wilhelmshaven made the poem up – it reads very well in German. The CDU is in its heyday just at present, but will probably decline in the future, as it will be split in two. The Berlin CDU, led by one Joseph Kaiser, is more socialist, whilst the Cologne CDU, led by a man named Adenauer, is very right wing. Again, the "Centre" Party is growing again, & is likely to gather to it all the Catholics that are at present in the CDU. They (the

Centre) are neither left nor right, but are more socialistically inclined than the CDU, which is composed to a great extent of rich farmers. In the past (pre-1933) their support used to be much sought after, as they swung from side to side. The main parties in Germany are now:

1) SPD – Sozialdemokratische Partei
[LEFT] Deutschlands.

2) KPD – Kommunistische Partei
[LEFT] Deutschlands

3) CDU – Christliche Demokratische Union
(Formerly Zentrum – centre
[RIGHT] Protestants + Catholics Party)

4) Zentrum – just starting – all Catholics
[centre]

5) FDP – Freie Demokratische Partei
[RIGHT – + how!] Formerly Liberal Party

6) NLP – Niedersächsische Landespartei
(Lower Saxony Party – formerly
Hannover-Party, wanting
Hannover as a federal & independent
State § - or kingdom – very strong
in Kreis Bremervörde – amongst
[RIGHT] farmers.)

7) DKP – Deutsche Konservative Partei
[RIGHT.] Conservative Party

Then, in the Russian zone the two leftist parties are united, making the

It will be noticed that whereas the leftist tendency is to unite (even here they work quite closely together), the right-wing parties don't, & have several smaller factions. In Bremervörde, the farmers' party was the N.L.P., & here it is the C.D.U. In the north I believe it is the F.D.P. In Austria the CDU, I think. They (CDU) being very Right-wing, still have many old Nazis amongst their members – & that is held up against them. For instance, the former leader of the CDU here had to be "denazified" – i.e., removed from his position in the party as he had been a Nazi Party member since 1933, & a "Blockleiter" of it too! Funnily enough the CDU leader at Kreis Vechta had the same happen to him!

These Catholics – they're a bit odd, politically, you know – they <u>must</u> bring their religion into party politics (<u>&</u> aren't particularly addicted to telling the truth!), & have always done so, around here & Münsterland. There haven't been many <u>bad</u> Nazis here, but there also haven't been many very great <u>anti</u>-Nazis, either – with one or two exceptions. The best anti-Nazi I know – well, there are two actually, but the most striking is "Pater Steiner", the head Dominican Friar of Germany, who lives in Vechta. He was much in the habit of having to climb out of windows (in his robes, I suppose!) when the Gentlemen came from the "Stapo" – but did serve two years behind wire nevertheless. He is one of the most interesting people I've known, to talk to – he's now gone off to Rome to a conference of Dominicans.

The other one is also a priest, a Dr. Göken, who has amassed a terrific collection of pamphlets, records, & stuff, but I think I told you about him, too. Mmm, it's all very interesting. I could go on doing this for ages – if <u>only</u> I didn't have the other part of the job – counter-intelligence. Mmm, well, I've gone on for ages.

[*16.9.46*]

... Well, elections took place yesterday, & I spent the whole day buzzing round & Observing. Some people were very interested in the affair – though only 67.5% of the people allowed to vote did so. The CDU got 185 seats, the SPD 3 (!), the KPD 2, and the Independents 5. So there we are. Those are the Community or village elections, of course. Then after that I had to go to a party, at which I got so bored I nearly burst into tears. I managed to persuade Ron to come too. It was Blackie's (the other Sgt. – Sgt. Black's) birthday party, taking place in Vechta. And the thing about it was that it was his engagement party as well! That is, he'd got engaged to a German girl there. It's not for me to judge, but Ron & I are rather doubtful as to its desirability. The girl, or woman, is 27, Blackie is just 22, for one thing. Still, that is the least important thing about it, really.

... Well, & then to-day I was engaged in writing out the election report & getting the results, then this afternoon went to hear Pastor Niemöller speak in Oldenburg! And took in the car the Protestant minister, the Protestant Youth Leader, and a Sister who looks after 30 children, part of an orphanage which came here from the East of Germany. But Niemöller spoke wonderfully – he is a great man & a great Christian. He spoke on the Rebirth of the Church, for 1¼ hrs., telling of the Church Conference in Ghent, & the new Spirit he found there. He's very gaunt & thin, but dark-skinned, with a very fine mouth and intelligent face. He was in Conc. Camps for 8 years (ever since 1937), the last four of which he was in Dachau.

[*25.9.46*]

... To-day I wrote the Counter-Intelligence Sitrep – a more lousy report I have never seen – however, such are results when one has to write a report on nothing. Some parts are faintly interesting – 36 burglaries & thefts in the Kreis in a week, 120 cwt of Black Market potatoes & fruit going out through just one of the railway stations, everyday...

Yesterday Ron & I went for miles & miles, & came to the most queer town, supposed to be quite a big one, but very queer. It was just set along the opposite sides of a canal, for miles – about 5 from one end to the other! And the canal kept on turning at right angles, it really was amazing. The land around was terribly poor, too. Peat-diggers, & barge-owners who take the peat away. Ron & I went to a "factory" where it is pressed – very poor people, with a wee office and an undernourished girl working away at ledgers. The whole soil there is peat, and it shakes under your feet whenever a truckload of bits of it comes rumbling past. Well, we didn't get our man, but it was certainly an interesting experience.

[27.9.46]

... Hrmph... Well, what did I do yesterday – mmm, went to quite an important meeting of the CDU, at which one of its leaders, a Dr. Adenauer, from Cologne spoke to an audience of about 1000. Very interesting, in that it showed them up awfully – he just plugged away against the SPD for ¾ hour, then against Mil Govt. for ½ hour after that! Honestly, the things he said! Talk about mud-slinging: "The SPD say that unmarried women have a right to motherhood", "1,500 calories a day, 500 calories increase? – well, we just starved a bit quicker on 1,000!", etc. etc. I've never heard such a lot of applause, either, when he made all his points! But that is the way of the CDU – they get hold of problems that lie close to people's hearts: problems which are hopelessly difficult & well-nigh impossible to solve, even by the most willing Mil Govt. – because of the circumstances in the world. Then they work on the problems, tear Mil Govt. to pieces over them, & of course get a lot of cheap & ready-made popularity. If they only tried to be even a little constructive... but no, they haven't the people's interests at heart, they just want to get masses of votes & become the strongest party.

... It's been lovely weather these last few days... This afternoon we ran down to Lingen, to arrange about getting a month's supply of coal – the air was scented with very sweet smells... it would be so wonderful if you were here, Hazel. I think of you terrifically often when I drive along by myself, & half-talk to you, & tell you about everything, & think about us, & wonder what it'll be like back at Oxford, with you – it sounds just perfect, bless you.

Eee well, pour le present il faut cultiver notre jardin.

[*4.10.46*]

... And Love *is* hard to define – one knows the bumpings of heart & feeling sick & excitement that comes from one as a result of it, but those are very small things in comparison, though I feel the best way to set about defining it is to start with them & climb upwards even though the summit be covered in cloud. After saying which, I'm still no nearer – but can one define early morning air & its electricity, or the feeling you get when you look at a star? Or when you gaze into the depths of a fire? Or sleep? True, they're easier perhaps than Love, which is more or less like a searchlight, bright & intense, shining from one person to another.

Or a blinding ray? – no, defining it *is* a bit hard! All I know is that I feel definitely queer & unusual when I think of, see, hear or feel you! & would that be being in love?!! Well, *I* think we are! It's obvious, too, that no two couples of people are in love the same way. Just as Man & Life, Love has its own individuality. Therefore it becomes doubly difficult to define, just as man is, & one can only state the principles and characteristics of it. Also, it varies in intensity, & there is such a thing as infatuation (Horrid word, somehow).

... Oh dear, Ron W. *does* go on talking, & never takes any notice whether I'm writing or not, it seems – it's so difficult to concentrate sometimes. He's been here most of this page, on & off. There, now he's gone off to Bed.

Yesterday we had a day which I hope I won't forget. We went up to the North of the Kreis, where there are small moor-villages – not rich people by any means. And visited a baker there who is member of the Provincial Parliament. He criticized Mil Govt. very sharply, & when I endeavoured to defend it he said "Come with me & I'll show you why I criticize!" – and we went around the damaged part of the village – pitiful little houses in various stages of repair – a lot quite repaired except for the roof, & of course the rain poured in & was rotting the wood. One family of three had lived in a small hut with 5ft × 4½ft living space, for a year. The worst part is that the tiles, wood etc *are* there in the factories, but

Mil Govt. just won't release them or let the Germans use it. That seems so unreasonable.

You see, being poor people they haven't the goods to buy material on the Black Market. One house without a roof there was, & five people living in a tiny room. The furniture they had saved had to stand outside the room (which was covered) & get rained upon. All the wood was going green, the furniture mouldy. The old lady there was blind in one eye, & hobbled about. It did seem sad. And as a last straw, she stood in the door of the shack as we went & had two apples in her hands for us, not saying anything or even daring to ask us to take them...

Ron just fled, & I <u>couldn't</u> go, and talked to her, & asked her if she needed anything that we possibly could bring, apart from tiles, & she said that they hadn't any clothes, & that Polish civilians came & stole things every night – a hen last night, & so on. And wept at the same time. Oh dear, it sounds awfully sentimental & trashy to read, probably, but as it happened it was pretty grim & saddening. I decided that Right thinking about it wouldn't be so much good, unless I could do something. I went to the Housing Officers in Oldenburg to-day & got them to release 10,000 roof-tiles for the civilians & asked that as many should go to Idafeln (the village in question). Of course, 10,000 tiles aren't much (enough for 4 houses perhaps) but they'd help a bit. Oh it's all very sad.

Still, clothes – have you any old ones perhaps? And I'll ask your Mother to send on the ones that came in the C.S. parcel, too, I think – they are so needed here. Food isn't such a problem for them in a country district, but things like shoes – do you know that 200 out of 500 refugees from Silesia hadn't <u>any</u>?

[6.10.46]

... We <u>are</u> a pair, though. I quite sympathized when you wrote that you'd talked to Ron T. about your ideals on marriage & consequent despair of ever attaining them. I often despair of ever attaining them. I often imagine the most awful things, & wonder how we'll ever get to be what I want us to be, & think about my own impatience & snappiness-without-meaning-to-be, & often feel desperate too. But there is surely some Mathematics in pairing off two people, & if you put two positives together, the result is very likely to be positive? Haven't we got a particularly good chance of attaining these ideals of ours? We have the same interests, think pretty well the same in regard to relationship with God, same standard of living, quite alike in character, quite alike in sense of colour & beauty, both love the same music, both like collecting junk (!?! Well, I know a certain Person who hoards books!! Not junk? Well, sporrans & red socks & small porcelain animals aren't either!!)

[*9.10.46*]

... Mmm, what have I been doing – rushing about a lot of the time. To Oldenburg to help make a confidential report on Blackie (for his application for C.C.G.) on Monday – wrote the Political Intelligence Report yesterday evening, and took till 3.15 to finish it! It was the longest one yet – seven pages of foolscap for Cloppenburg and for Vechta, making eleven in all! And a good one too, it was – if I may say so (which I do... !) full of rumours and opinions about the Nüremberg trials, the lifting of the Curfew (at which most Germans are pretty sick, or did I already tell you), grouses about the German Denazification Panel, the German Administration, etc.

To-day I wrote the other report to be done, & in the evening went to hear a very famous CDU speaker, one Maria Sevenich, speak in Cloppenburg. She spoke wonderfully clearly & well, & put over the CDU argument in a most reasonable way. She is about 39, and a Lawyer from the American Zone. She was prohibited from speaking there because she was too strong in her criticism of American Denazification policy. I went up & spoke to her afterwards, & she seemed very pleasant & hearty. Then Ron & I brought the Mil Govt. interpreter who had taken down the speech for us by shorthand, back to the billet & had some tea & biscuits, & talked for hours & hours & listened to the gramophone. The interpreter is a little round fairheaded German girl, quite sound in every way! But she can write shorthand very quickly. Name is Gisela, not a very usual one, is it.

[13.10.46]

... Mmm, well, to return to this band of children, we had the "Kreis" elections to-day, & Ron & I spent the whole time rushing from one place to another, looking at booths. I had my Mil Govt. pass stamped in each Gemeinde (community) so that you can see what the Gemeinde stamp marks are like. They go on every document from the administrative offices, & more or less symbolize each community.

... There are two different sort of stamps for Barssel, so I had them both put down. Will you keep it safely for me sweet? Eee? Put it with my diary or something?

In "Saterland" they speak a special form of German, did I tell you? Quite unlike any Low German dialect, and much nearer Dutch than anything else. It is interesting though, the German

Community stamp: in rabidly Nazi areas they were all like this. Cloppenburg wasn't so bad, though, so it didn't have any difficulties like that. Friesoythe has a luverly stamp, hasn't it, & Altenoythe is rather fascinating. The word Friesoythe comes from "Friesland" (which is the area to the north of the Kreis, and whose influence has reached down to, & formerly ruled as far as, Friesoythe), and "ort", which is the German for "place". Altenoythe is "old place" therefore. Did I tell you, too, of the spreading influence of Friesland in the realm of architecture – that the "Friesisch" type of farmhouse is growing more and more popular? The difference is easy to see:

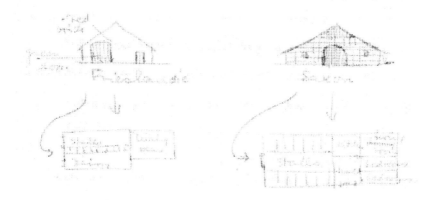

Actually I've gone & done two small Friesland types of farms – they're just as big as the Saxon, really, but not nearly as picturesque, though rather cleaner and healthier.

... The elections were a bit of a scream to-day – some polling booths were The End.

In one village the inhabitants had no idea at all where the booth was (!) and when we got there, all the election staff were sitting round having a meal (in the booth!), beer bottles on the register-table, & had lost the ballot box! – found it in a corner, unsealed (and very easy to open), & looking rather forlorn.

[*15.10.46*]

... To-day I went to see Maria Sevenich. She is staying near here, so I thought I'd grab the opportunity and visit her. She is most interesting – has been a Communist & lots of other things. It was said that she had been exiled from the American Zone, but she denied it very firmly. I heard her speak a week ago, and she is pretty terrific, quite the best speaker I have heard yet. She is living in the American Zone (Darmstadt) and is said to have been exiled because of her very sharp criticism of Mil Govt.'s denazification policy. She often gets an audience of 10,000, which is a lot for Germany. Mmm, it was an interesting morning. Of course I couldn't very well take notes as she was in conversation with us, so as soon as I got to the main road I stopped & spent half an hour writing down what she had said!

Then yesterday we spent the whole day writing a report on the elections – the results are even more unsatisfactory than last time: 41 seats in the Kreistag for the CDU and 1 for the SPD! That was in Cloppenburg. In Vechta there were 39 seats for the CDU & 3 for the SPD – rather better.

Then this evening one of the Mil Govt. interpreters was around, a Frau Schenetzky, & we talked to her for quite a while. Poor soul, she has had quite a hard time of it. She is 26, married when she was 18, has two children. Her husband was a major in the army, degraded to Lieutenant & forced into the SS, ended up in Oranienburg concentration camp (for being implicated in the attempt on Hitler's life), and was shot there. So now she has 2 children & parents to provide for, and rather dim prospects, as is most probably leaving the Mil Govt., & she will be without a job...

[*18.10.46*]

... And we'll sort each other's junk out, all right! We'll make it like the denazification here – first we'll de-junk the junk, & then it can make appeals to be reinstated again, & present its reasons for being useful – O.K.? It'll end up in a most appalling fight, I expect!

Ah, I'll be laying my plans, anyway! And don't be a Snerge & go & look at all my things while I'm still here & decide what to de-junkify!! <u>Horrid</u> girl, I bet you do...!

... And yes, I feel quite the same as you do about the early days – it surprises me sometimes, for I get the feeling that we should have been Ever So Polite & Refined to each other, not having known one another at all well! But we weren't polite.

... Of course, we'll feel just as much 'past' our stage now in ten year time as we do 1943. The Oxford days did teach us something, though, & that was, in a way, conversing and talking honestly. I somehow feel that they were something to be gone through, either then or later.

... I spent to-day with Ron going round the Kreis. I have a colour film in my camera but the sun just <u>won't</u> come out! But we had some fun, especially with a friend of ours who is a butcher and a communist friend of his – a terrific discussion – very good too, considering we were in agreement all the time! But the CDU are stinkers, they really are. I've not really met <u>one</u> yet who is quite all right. Either they're former Nazis, or they're Black Marketeers, or something. One can tell almost at once by the impression they give of insincerity & falsity, of just acting. The greatest enemy we have here in this Kreis is the power wielded by the church through the CDU. The power they have over the Kreis administration – it's just as complete as the Nazis' ever was. <u>They</u> appealed to their party members through Nationalism, and that was the life blood of their power. But these appeal through the Catholic religion, which is far more engrained than nationalism ever was. It is a stronger power altogether, and I venture to suggest that as many atrocities are liable to be committed in its name as in the Nazis'! Quite honestly & truly, politics wielded by the church are not honest or right because the church doesn't stop at anything, is not democratic, is unscrupulous. They are narrow-minded and intolerant, what is more. It's an appalling prospect, this surely growing strangle-hold by the CDU and the Catholic Church. Ugh. They <u>must</u> be split up into two; in other words, the Zentrums-Partei must grow, and the SPD will outbalance two smaller parties, just the job. (Er – am I disinterested? Oh yes, <u>of course</u>!!) I may be a bit impressionable, but with these political parties I've generally gone by the type of people I meet <u>in</u> the different parties for my first opinions. And really, the SPD & the Communists have been by <u>far</u> the most decent and honest people.

... And now this morning they've all heard that Mil Govt. is finishing on November the 15th, so that they'll all lose their jobs! Which doesn't worry people like Gisela (the little round girl) or the others, but it does rather do Frau Schenetzky in the eye, as she has two children & parents to work for. No doubt they'll all find something to do, but the trouble is that the people of Cloppenburg don't like them at all (such are the good Catholics here!). A resident officer will be staying, but won't need many interpreters – in fact, he'll probably only be allowed to have one. Mil Govt. H.Q. will be in Oldenburg from Nov 15th onwards. Ah well, it sounds rather callous, but I'm <u>very</u> glad we're not allowed to have interpreters! The idea of Frau S. or Gisela or anyone in our office is a bit appalling. Still, that's rather unkind, I suppose.

... The American denazification policy is a bit sweeping: <u>all</u> Party members were kicked out of office, whether they were guilty or not. So that now the tendency is for all sorts of Concentration Camp internees (quite a lot of which were there for Crime, sexual perversion etc.) find their way into the administration. My opinion is that Nazi Party members should be pushed down a few pegs, yes, certainly, & put reliable non-Nazis in at the top. But to kick everyone out & to fill up the whole machine with new & somewhat

doubtful blood isn't all that good a thing. And of course, guilty
Nazis should be chucked out of the administration altogether. But
the innocuous Party members, I think they oughtn't to – when
their job in 1937 would have been taken away from them had they
not joined.

[*20.10.46*]
... Then to Oldenburg, picking up the Cloppenburg Protestant
Youth Leader on the way, & so to a choral concert – oh Pooh it
<u>was</u> lovely! Telemann, Schulz & Bach. Mostly Motets (Bach's
'Jesu, Meine Freude') & also two sonatas for flute, violin, viola de
gaba & harpsichord – music <u>very</u> akin to the likes of Rosenmüller –
I did so want you to be there, all the time, & was making plans for
you to come to Germany with me, half the time! <u>And</u> such a choir!
Really, they have to be heard before they are believed, these
German choirs – <u>so</u> exact & disciplined – yet so friendly & jolly
amongst themselves afterwards. I stuck around with the people I
was with, after the concert, & said hallo to the chief performers, all
of whom I know.
... I spent to-day mostly visiting people, & doing an appallingly
difficult translation, or helping do one, with the little interpreter
from Mil Govt. – Gisela. Then in the evening to the S.P.D. leader.
I've decided I don't like politics (though I don't mind observing
them!) Never never am I going to have anything to do with any
political party whatsoever, & neither are you, I hope.

[*22.10.46*]
... Gosh, <u>what</u> a busy two days since I last wrote – to-day about
120 miles over <u>the</u> most bleak moorland (near the Dutch border)
to get witnesses and victims of a very brutal Camp-leader in the
north of the Kreis. Although none had died, they were often taken
out & beaten (Polish people) by him & others, so that life for them
for five years was rather grim. Now we have arrested the camp

leader, we have to provide a case against him. But the moorland is just unending where I went; a <u>completely</u> flat horizon, & from time to time little camps comprised of wooden huts, now inhabited by Poles & formerly either Concentration or P.O.W. camps. The roads were <u>awful</u>, & bridges over the frequent canals weren't too good. But it gave me a sensation which was terribly queer, though bleak & wild at the same time. Miles and miles of orange and yellow grass. Mmm... one sees & learns, & it's the least glamorous & ordinary places which often impress the most. Oh I do want to travel Pooh, <u>so</u> much...

... The Nüremberg trials? The general attitude (& we have been reporting it solidly for almost a month now) is

a) That the Germans should have tried their own countrymen.

b) That, now having tried the German War Criminals, this international tribunal should go on to try Russian, Polish, English, & American War Criminals too – for there are many (they say). Otherwise, the whole thing is obviously a matter of Might over Right (if they <u>don't</u> try them). They all seem quite unanimous in that they agree with the punishment meted out. A good % agree with the Russian point of view.

c) A small number of exceptions are always to be found. Last week a notice was pinned up on a tree in a place called Barsselermoor (W. of Kreis) which ran like this: "You hung our brave ones on the trees – wait! The hour of retribution is not far off!"

d) There are lots more isolated opinions – that Doenetz should have been more heavily punished than Raeder, that Goering's guards were bribed by Nazis, etc. That von Schirach, a poisoner of German Youth, should have received the death sentence.

As I said before, I don't agree with the principle of the thing, so it's all wrong to me anyway. But it did seem that they took great pains to be as just as they could.

[31.10.46]

... Sorry I haven't written yesterday – really, life is <u>so</u> full just now. Political meetings, Youth Group meetings, & this & that – one endless dashing about... but it really <u>is</u> wonderful work, I think, especially the Youth work (said he, hardly having done any – still) on Tuesday I went about the place with Mr. Parker, & took Ron to Osnabrück for his Brussels leave in the evening. Then on Wednesday to a big CDU meeting of all the village councils in Cloppenburg & Vechta. Maria Sevenich spoke again – she really speaks wonderfully, & gave an excellent talk on Christian duty. If only all the CDU leaders had her words at heart, but they really <u>haven't</u>. But do you know, the reason why areas like the Ruhr voted right-wing & CDU is, I am convinced, because of her speeches there, which won them over.

... Then yesterday evening we went to Vechta to an Open Youth Discussion there taking Herr Bergner the Protestant Youth Leader, & little Gisela the interpreter, who also has a small group of girls herself. It was rather a rowdy discussion, with a rather smooth but terrifically witty Canadian officer (C.C.G.) in the chair who just would <u>not</u> take any question seriously. I got annoyed afterwards when I thought of it, for he only provoked the youth there, I'm sure it <u>didn't</u> do them any good – one got <u>so</u> angry, & the Canadian made such witty remarks at his expense – things like:

Cdn Offr. "So you don't believe my figures for German coal production?"

Youth (emphatically & almost in tears) " No, I jolly well do not!"

Cdn Offr. "Good, that's a good thing, it's time you stopped believing everything you hear" (meaning Nazi propaganda) (Roars of laughter)... but somehow it wasn't very fair, & so off the point.

... Oh well, it was a messy uproarious discussion, but it was useful. The main thing was that there were too many old fellows there – one ancient sage, leader of the CDU, who by an impassioned speech got the audience terribly excited! & so on. After that, Bergner & Gisela came to the billet & I made some cocoa which we had without milk & with saccharine (such is our desperate food situation from Tuesdays till Thursdays!). We had a very pleasant & comfortable discussion – <u>so</u> agreeable & quiet after the uproar of earlier on. One of the main themes was of 'Mens Sana in Corpore Sano' with regard to refugees and the suffering German population, & how, if ever, they could get over it, or come through it. That doesn't sound very deep as it stands written down, but it was really much more than that, & as I say, so very warm & comfortable & friendly. Bergner is really an <u>excellent</u> fellow, so open & honest & full of ideas (he's 22 or 23) & Gisela (also 22) is too, & very serious about life & German problems. Actually <u>the</u> main characteristic of a lot of German Youth to-day is their great seriousness. Believe me, they'll produce something some day with it, & there will come a day when Germany really <u>is</u> a great nation, not through military force, but – as before – through her thinkers & works of literature, science, religion, & philosophy.

... Then at 4.30pm to a Protestant Youth discussion, in Cloppenburg. I went rather quaking to tell the truth, as the questions in last night's discussion were such appallingly difficult ones (about how much coal & wood were being exported – for example). And as I <u>hadn't</u> much of an idea about the figures for such things, I felt that I would be wiped off the face of the earth in a few minutes. But it was <u>so</u> different, & they welcomed me so very warmly & kindly. It was about the reverse of the Vechta discussions, went much deeper though quieter & more calmly. I did enjoy it, & talked a lot about the Church in England, Boy Scouts & so forth. They were so eager to find out things, & how they were applied in England.

[3.11.46]

... And good news about the Christmas cards. I finished a design on Friday night – I do hope you like it. The whole tone is green – green sky, dark green earth, etc – being at twilight. The painting was about 10 ins × 5. I took it into Oldenburg on

Saturday morning, to a good printers. Did my usual act of saying that I was the Security Police & wanted to see the manager at once, saw him & explained. Whereupon he said that I must get permission from the Mil Govt. first – whereupon I pooh-poohed the idea & said that I had no time for such frivolities, & that it would take till long past Christmas to do it, & couldn't we do the thing privately? And after that I didn't hear anything more about Mil Govt. permission! He called various people in, they all went to the window & admired (!) the painting, got quite enthusiastic about

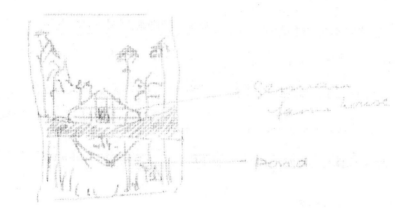

it, & said I could have 300 postcards of it by the end of November! So there we are!

... Then this evening I am going into Oldenburg to a concert with the Protestant Youth Leader. Next Thursday there is one too – J.C. Bach, Beethoven & Brahms. Mmm. I've got two tickets, & asked Gisela to come, as she's missing to-night's. I think <u>my</u> reputation here is far more 'kaput' than yours – I'm always seeming to be out in the V'wagen with Frau Schenetzkey, getting vegetables or eggs, as she knows where they are to be bought, or with Gisela, with whom I've become quite friends, or taking the maids to Oldenburg for their shopping, or other interpreters to Oldenburg. I think my reputation always goes very low, wherever I am, & the raises itself later as people realize there's nothing at all Interesting (to them!) in that which I do! Mmm, the Rake's progress, it always looks like, no doubt.

[4.11.46]
... Then the Protestant Pastor & Youth Leader came to our house, & we drank Bovril & talked about Martin Luther, & whether he was responsible for Nazism or not! Many people seem to think so. Their argument is that by divorcing the Church from the aristocracy he made the latter independent & eventually unchristian, then > militarists > Nazis! But if that's the only argument (it may not be – do you know?) then you can say that anyone, even Jesus, was responsible for Nazism! Still, there may be more things against him.

[6.11.46]
... Oh, I suppose I'm in a muddle what with all this work on top of me, & can't think very reasonably, but it just seems that the Reality in my Life just isn't here – it's with you in England. And I get so full of Pol. Int. & Security sometimes that I feel I have no balanced & experienced outlook on life at all & am just full of petty complaints! Goodness knows how I shall ever get back to writing essays on Spanish authors.

Oh Bear – how can I say it: I'm essentially a creative sort of person – that is, I create with ease, whereas I receive only with an effort, & need plenty of imagination to help things down. When I'm reading a book, for instance, it's my imagination that makes the reading run smoothly, & if the book is one that is rather boring, I can only plod along rather like a blind horse.

[8.11.46]

I don't know why, but I always seem to have a different job to do in all my various friendships – to Dorothy I am a General Comforter & Consoler, to Peggy I was a Companion & Canteen-manager (!), to Ron I am a sort of Mother, Father & Aunt rolled into one; to Stanley I was General Help & discussor, & to Gloria I seem to be a Teacher & Lecturer! I tell her what I think is the right attitude to take & what not to believe, & how to be Prepared. I often seem to preface my remarks with "Hazel says, that... " etc. Last night I was laying down a strict rule that she shouldn't ever say that she was unintelligent or feeble (as she does) & had the honesty to add that I was often under that law too, as it came from you!

[*14.11.46*]

Yours of the 12th arrived to-day – oh darling...

Yes, I found out about demob. just to-day, & can assure you I am very depressed over it! Everything seems to have shifted from a point visible away right over the horizon to where I can't see it, & I'm in a muddle again. Whether to take a commission or not (! it seems to come up regularly every year, that question!) or to apply to have you out here (providing you said yes) & whether it would be allowed, etc. Oh I'm so cheesed off, I really am. There's Fred Kingham coming out at any time now, who has a higher group number than I – oh I don't know, Bear, I long to shake myself free from it all, free from this eternal separation from you, & this clamping down on my movements & where I am allowed to go or not. I am lucky in having the best job in the Army, good friends, being successful &-all-that, but oh dear, it's just nothing compared to the weary & blindly-plodding hope which keeps on getting squished time & time again. It just takes such a great chunk out of life. Then times I wonder how awful it would be if you did get tired of waiting, as you have quite a justification to do, & then I get desperate because I just can't do anything at all about it, & just have to keep on disappointing you time & time over, never really

LETTERS TO HAZEL — 1946

being much of a help in the matter, as I don't have any definite information.

Oh well, & so on – it's just bloody, that's all.

And I <u>do</u> appreciate how you feel, sweet, having told people that we'd get married next summer – I've told a lot, too, but I'm afraid I'm so busy being sorry for myself that I've not thought of how I must appear to others! Oh dear, I suppose it all makes one selfish.

The Army, of course has now its own reward to reap. It can't get volunteers enough because it formerly treated soldiers like dirt, & naturally has a notorious name. <u>I</u> certainly wouldn't volunteer for it. The miserable life of degradedness & unchristianity that the ordinary infantryman is forced into is nothing to volunteer for. If a soldier emerges from his days in the army as a Christian it's in spite of it... When <u>will</u> it cease to evade us & come to a standstill?

I've never quite been so definite in my mind as to my need of you, & sureness of <u>Us</u>, <u>&</u> love of you. If we were married, it would be a bit more comforting, I suppose, but the price would be higher too. Talking of prices (such a muddle I'm in, in a way!). We'd get Quite a Fat Army Allowance, or you would. Something like £70 extra. Sorry, I'm wandering off the point, & no, that wasn't trying to push you into it – though sometimes I rather wish I could. Oh Pooh, I <u>am</u> so fed up, really I am, I could sit down & eat the electric heater, or something...

Mmm. Well, what did I do yesterday. In the afternoon a Youth Discussion Group on "Faust" which was in such learnéd German I couldn't follow half of it – also, a rather ancient fellow made terrifically complicated references to bits of the play which were almost as obscure. One idea I got out of it is this – that Imagination binds the Supernatural & Power to-gether, makes it possible, desirable & attainable. Understanding pulls it to bits, makes it look rather incomprehensible, muddled & undesirable. Perhaps "understanding" is a bad word – I really mean a realistic attitude rather than the achievement of understanding. I suppose those two opposite ways come into – or try to influence – marriage, with curiosity (horrid word) & everything-will-be-fine attitude before & during the first year, & Oh-Lor-is-this-what-it-is after that, for a while till something substantial is built up. That's with Ordinary People, dear, no doubt with us, being Rather Different & Queer we'll get the two viewpoints in reverse order, starting off with Doubt & Apprehension, & finding out afterwards that it isn't so bad at all!

After that discussion (Protestant Youth) I dashed back, scoffed down my supper, picked up Gisela, & then another youth (a son of the head of the German Red Cross in Oldenburg), & so to another discussion – a larger one with 350 chaps there – the egregious Mr. Berenson taking it again. He wasn't much better, & never answered anything directly. I generally completely forget I'm English at things like that & enter into the spirit of it very wholeheartedly – which isn't really as it should be, I suppose – British Mil Govt. prestige & all that – though I'd rather be a D. Gifford than a True Briton – or would I. That's something on which I'm not quite sure, now I come to think of it!

Then had coffee, & helped Gisela with two translations, took her home & talked for a while in the car (what is the temptation always to go on talking in a car after it's stopped?! It's so cold & windy & draughty, not comfortable like the drawing room) & then on to join Ron & Mr. Parker at Frau Schenetzky's (written Czarnetzky, I found out!) who were talking with the former German Consul General of Barcelona! He must have been there at the same time as mother & Unk. We didn't stay long, & went home after eating masses of cake & sausage sandwiches.

Then to-day we've been in Oldenburg – hearing that news about demobilization, also that 13 F.S.S. was to be on its own once more, apart from 4 Area Intelligence Office – oh, perhaps I should explain, this is the set up of Intelligence organization in Germany to-day. I've just fitted in one area with examples!

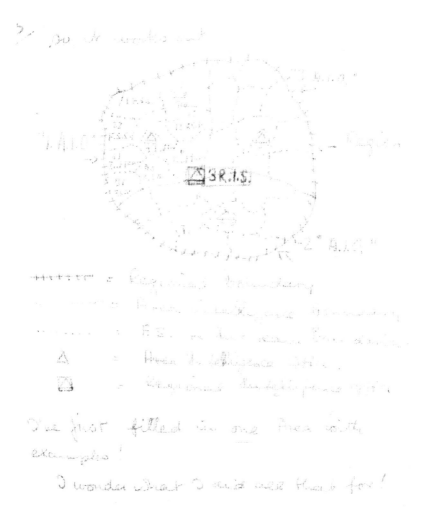

To get back to this business of getting out of the Army, I should think it <u>quite</u> possible that in next October in Class "B" limit will be raised from Group 55 to 60 or 70, & <u>that</u> would get me out – next October. I'll write to Mr. Russell. I really <u>do</u> feel for you about your job, darling – but you <u>haven't</u> made a fool of yourself – is it making a fool of oneself saying "We'll go for a picnic to-morrow" just because it pours with rain the next day? It's <u>not</u> your fault, sweet – oh bless you, I <u>know</u> how you feel, but it's not you who are the fool, it's you-thinking-other-people-thinking-you-are! It is, when in most cases they're not thinking that at all. Don't take people's tones to heart so, Bear – those sort of people's tones are about as worth listening to as those of the catty little schoolgirl of nine – they're ignorant, narrow minded & malicious & not worth the while.

... Gosh I wish you could come to Germany. Do you remember what you said about my being in your world in Kettering? I'd so love to introduce you to mine - 'cos I feel you'd be very interested in it, it's so broad & all-embracing.

[17.11.46]

... Mmm, yes, I think some of my Oxford friends I didn't admire all that much – but then I never regarded them as friends, really. I very much like my ones over here, they're all just terrific, & so different from one another, really. I'd give anything for you to meet them, I really would. The main thing in having friends is always striving to give to them all you can, & of your very best. I sometimes feel I belong to half the world, I have so many – or so it seems to me. Practically all my spare time is taken up with & ministering (?!) to someone or other! No, "ministering" sounds much too patronizing – quite the wrong word! I think your friends are nice, too – bless you, & think you choose (or are chosen) every whit as well as I.

... Oh & I am now the proud owner of a Jeep! Really! Had to give in my Volkswagen. The jeep is a much better thing, but not comfy or warm like the V'wagen. We're getting two new men, one of whom is only 18 or 19.

[20.11.46]

... Then this evening I spent round at Frau Czarnetzky's, talking about everything in this Kreis, & how it needs improving. She's an interesting sort of character, I think – a terrific energy with a desire for a lot of society, has many friends, is sincere, <u>very</u> German & nationalist, sensible, & excitable, demonstrative & impetuous. Terrific mixture, isn't it! But she always reminds me of the parable of the Good Samaritan, for whilst many so-called good Catholics pass a sufferer by, she, for all her rumoured free thinking and living (which may or may not be true – I don't know) helps everyone she sees. Mmm, German people are interesting, yes – but they are <u>all</u> the same (it would seem) in that they pour out their life troubles & speak always with relation to themselves. In other words, they're so subjective, or ego-centric rather. Still, I like them, mostly. Oh I <u>would</u> like you to meet masses of Germans, they're a people & a half.

... Hoggle-wuggle! Well, please accept a Present or Do at the weekend, if you would be so kind – ho? And I do hope you like it (<u>or</u> them) & press the right knob...

[*24.11.46*]

... A lot has happened. There is a lot of disquiet, because of Polish troops & D.P.'s [displaced persons]. On the 15th, a D.P. went into the little prison, told the gaoler he wanted to see a prisoner there, & when he came out into the ante-room, the D.P. shot the gaoler six times in the chest, & made off with the prisoner. The gaoler died on the spot, & the D.P. hasn't been caught yet – is rumoured to be wandering around Cloppenburg. Though I don't believe that.

Then, at a small party after a football match between British troops & the German team here, Polish troops & D.P.s forced an entrance, shot two youths – one in the head, the other in the leg – both were only wounded, however, though one of them lost his leg through it.

And lastly at a little village near here, two youths were shot by the Polish Military, one through the neck (just under the ear) & another in the thigh. Both are now in hospital.

Hope you don't mind all this, but it was to show you what things are like now. Really, all yesterday evening – no, Friday evening, there was shooting going on next door (Polish troops billet) – once a grenade exploded, some time ago.

[29.11.46, Brussels]

... I do wish you could be with me here – it just doesn't seem complete without you, at all – oh Pooh.

I arrived this morning at about ten, washed, & have been roaming around the town ever since. The bookshops are just terrific, & have English books too (I looked at "No Orchids for Miss Blandish" – Gosh, what a book). Oh, & saw "Physiology of Sex" in Smiths, so got it! (the Pelican edition), I'll send it to you when I've read it, if I ever get through it. But oh, I've spent so much money, & can't think what on! Well, lunch cost 104 francs (about 10/6d)... Then this evening to the opera, "Carmen" – I love going to that opera house – it's so grand, & I enjoyed "Carmen" very much – the last time I saw it was in September '44. And I kept on longing for you & wanting you to be there with me. We really must come to Brussels, too, on our honeymoon.

... The shops are so full of wonderful things, gosh & bananas being sold in the streets! Sorry I didn't write yesterday, darling. I was in an awful hurry. The train journey here was absolutely awful, 14 hrs on wooden seats.

[1.12.46, Tilff]

And here I am at the Collas', very happy & (for a great change!) wishing you were here – oh gosh, sweet. I came here yesterday afternoon, & M. Collas & Arlette were at the station at Liège to meet me, bless them. They are all three exactly the same, Mme Collas looking a bit younger if anything. I arrived there, had big pieces of egg-custard tart & coffee, then we went into Liège to see "La Grande Illusion" which I enjoyed very much – though it was a bit badly cut in places, being so old I suppose. Then after that we had a wonderful dinner in Liège – Oysters, chicken & ice-cream!

... Pooh, don't send me any parcels to Germany for Christmas, please? I mean, latest date of posting & all that, keep them for when I come on leave. I just don't know what they do to parcels in the Army post office – I've hardly had one which hasn't been looking as if someone has been at it with a sledge-hammer!

... This afternoon we're going to the conservatoire de Liège for a concert, & then dinner there. Eee, they're talking about you all the time here – you know, you'll like them awfully much, they've such good sense & are practical & thoughtful & happy together. I think Mme Collas is from farmer's stock, & is so full of character & strong-minded. They've built up everything themselves – got married very young, & rented a small liqueur shop in Liège, now have a very big distillery.

It's so lovely, too, to hear the river rushing past at night as one lies in bed.

[3.12.46]

... Before I go any further, I'd like to tell you my little bit of minor news – or rather, our news – would you mind so very much plodding through the rain to Liverpool St. Station (know what's coming? eee?!) to meet a (no doubt) bedraggled & scruffy fellow – with whom you will one day share bed & board – at 9.30 a.m. on the morning of 22 December? That is, in just over a fortnight's time? Eee? Or perhaps not? Well, I just thought I'd ask in case you did feel like it... !

[*5.12.46*]

Did I tell you I've got hold of an Alto recorder?! I'll bring it on leave – it has a lovely tone.

... The last two days have been quite busy doing nothing very much in particular getting the Jeep out of workshops. I don't quite understand, every time I switch the headlights on, clouds of smoke & a burning smell comes out from under the dashboard. I'm sure it's not supposed to do that at all – it never did it before. Queer, isn't it!

... I wrote & told your Mother I was definitely coming for Christmas (she knew before that I was hoping to, but no one else did, I think! & there were very strict orders that you shouldn't know in case it didn't come off!). I am sending most of my things by parcel-post too this time, as I don't want to have to carry too much.

[*16.12.46*]

... Mmm, something else happened on my jeep – don't laugh, you horrid wench. Well, I was going along when I smelt a strong smell of laundry & washing, and since it came from inside & not outside, I stopped & looked. The water thermometer jigger pointed to 220°, so I thought "Ha! Water a trifle too hot." So went into a shop nearby & topped it up with warm water. (Actually, it had all boiled away.) Well, in it poured, & off I went about 50 yards further, the same smell of washing & steam pouring out from under the bonnet. Again, water all gone. So I telephoned Cloppenburg, & they couldn't tow me in, so I poured more water in, & proceeded very slowly... It was very odd, as the water just disappeared to nowhere. No water dripped out or anything! Odd, wasn't it. Anyway, the workshops in Cloppenburg said that a gasket was gone. But it's ready again to-day, so that's all right.

Then yesterday I went round the country giving out questionnaires to returned PW from England – in an open wagon belonging to the Police! Gosh, was it cold! And to-day we have been shivering & dreading the thought of even looking out at the snow. It's <u>so</u> cold!! Whew... !

Every "leave" was precious and Hazel's wedding veil came from Brussels

13th Field Security Section, Intelligence Corps, "at ease"; crossing the Rhine

Bremerhaven: the Victory March Past, May 1945

Post war Germany; Winnie, Hazel's Morris 8, 1934; Douglas in a cherished Volkswagen

1947

[*13.1.47*]
Oh sweet,

& here we are, <u>again</u>! I wanted to write a little earlier, but the N.A.A.F.I. was opened, so I rushed off with me mug, as I was well-nigh starving – but it was about 8.30, & I could <u>just</u> imagine Mrs. Potter saying "But I think 'Sons & Lovers' is so very <u>depressing</u>, I remember when <u>I</u> read it" etc. etc. – now, didn't she?!

Oh Pooh, & there's so much to say & all, & no-one knows where to begin except to say thank you for a very wonderful leave – each one as it comes along seems to dwarf all previous ones – I feel the same about this, that it had qualities about it that no preceding leave had ever had – so much more real & true, somehow.

Gosh, I'm longing to hear from you! You know, I didn't mind leaving <u>England</u> so much this time – but I did mind leaving you. Awfully much.

... The train arrived in Harwich about 7.0, & we were taken to the Transit Camp to get a blanket, brought back again, & Oh! the customs! & oh! Arthur Morris! The officer singled me out & asked me whether I had any foodstuffs with me – to which I said no – just some coffee. So he said, "What's in that Parcel", so I said, "I don't know" – which sounded distinctly fishy, of course. And of course he had it open & there were masses & masses of food, to my horror & shame. I rather thought he was sending clothes to the people. Anyway, this appalling customs official then began to ransack my big pack. "Ah, a camera tripod" – to which I said "Yes, a camera tripod", & didn't volunteer any more information. Luckily he didn't find the camera. Phew, & it <u>was</u> a do packing everything again! He allowed the parcel to go through, but told me never to do it again, as it was strictly forbidden! Mm!!! I must say it's something I didn't definitely know, though.

[*14.1.47*]
Oh Darling,

My very dearest one – how awfully I miss you – it's descended on me with a vengeance to-night. I arrived about 4.30 at Osnabrück, got a truck to take me to the Cross-roads near Cloppenburg, & there was Ron waiting in a Volkswagen for me... full of all the appalling things that seem to have happened... "Jeep crashed into ditch & overturned", "maids stole all our tea", "20° below zero", "police have taken our garage", "coal running out" & "house freezing" etc. The truck's big end has gone west, no jeep left... oh dear. Now all we have is a Volkswagen... and so back to the house, to supper, & to unpacking and to bed after it. And here I am, feeling ever so lost & strange & very much wanting to be home again. The journey was very army-like, men brawling & swearing all over the place, others fondling German girls they had probably promised to marry, children looking pale & thin & crowding round for chocolate & cigarettes, lorries speeding along, kit-bags, thick air & smoke...

Well, it was good to see Ron again, at any rate – he didn't have much of a Christmas, poor lad – for one thing (I think I mentioned it before) someone had stolen all our tea-ration, & Christmas dinner consisted of sausages cooked by themselves... all rather a shame.

... I <u>loved</u> "Howards End" – it really is a perfect book (if there is such a thing!). I was so sad when I'd finished it.

[*15.1.47*]

Darling,

'S no good. I feel Utterly Fed up. Yes, self-pitying, as much as they make 'em. It's just the world of "Telegrams & Anger" which is forcing itself on me so just to-day – brutally telling me I must forget my leave, home; memories of you must remain strictly memories. I must sink into oblivion & do my job. New Pol. Int. officers, swelling with incompetent conceit, telling the world that they are really fine fellows, things going wrong with the house, the garden gate disappeared, telegrams & anger, anger & emptiness. And you, my darling, you're fading away behind the rush of it all, & only the written-you will remain, the Pooh-letter & the Bear-memory. That's what's so upsetting. If it all wasn't so <u>different</u> here.

... I am not going to Vechta after all, a C.C.G. Pol. Int. Officer has been sent there (the conceited one), & I am required to stay here. Ron will be going in a few weeks time, probably. Gosh. Blackie, the fellow with the German girl in Vechta, has been sent away & will soon be posted out of the Intelligence Corps, poor fellow. Wilson is said to be going away soon too. That leaves me with 4 Lance-Corporals of 19, all hearty eaters!

Dearest, here is the £10 – all right? The cheque for £10 too. £7.0.0 I owe you, £1.0.0 for Mrs. Coley, & £1.0.0 for all the bits & pieces, & also some things I'd like you to send out to me – please?

1) Two packets of shampoo (Dorothy)
2) a packet of pepper
3) some cinnamon
4) Saccharines

(2 & 3 for Bertelt, the German teacher who gave us that box)
Oh, & some lighter flints (two packets)...?

Later / Bless you for your first letter, which was terrifically welcome & made me feel a new man – it really did, Darling. I felt so miserable before.

... I'm wearing my orange socks now, & have to show them to everyone I go to visit in case they take him unawares... sort of Gorgon's Head, really.

Yes, <u>bless</u> you – our leave certainly ended well & reassuringly, in all it was what one might term a Great Leave, much deeper & realistic than previous ones, somehow. Do you know, the things that stick most vividly in my mind are the wonderful meals you prepared! – aren't I a P.I.G.! I've been giving glowing accounts of Vegetarianism & Cheese Puddings to my detachment till they began positively to abuse all the meat that there was!

[17.1.47]

... I have (Lord, what a lot of "I"s! Isn't it terrible!) got a very interesting report from our chief informant containing a general picture of things in Germany – most interesting it is. I'm having it translated, & will send you a copy. I'm also conducting a sort of survey to find out how far below the food ration standard the people are dropping – questions like "Have you received less than your due ration? Have you been given potatoes in lieu of meat &

bread at any time?" etc. Then I am getting 10 Refugees, 2 railway workers, 2 electric light station workers, 2 small officials & 2 teachers to fill in a questionnaire each. I asked those sort of people, as asking farmers is obviously no use as they have a surfeit of practically everything.

Sunday / Excuse my not sending this off this morning or yesterday, but a Party took place last night, or anyway Joop & his girlfriend Maria came to see us, & we sat round & talked; had supper, then Ron & Joop polished off a bottle of cognac between them (!) whilst we others talked, & watched Ron dancing with Maria. He really is a good dancer. I danced once – this was in our drawing room, which is quite large, & suitable, & the evening broke up at 1.0 or so, when Joop got unsteadily into his Volkswagen & drove off – oh dear. Well, I won't say it, but blow me if I'm ever going to very "sociable" unless I can help it. The Army has certainly shown me the emptiness of drinking, that's one good thing about it. It all seems so card-castle-ish, somehow. Zzz. (He said, inevitably!)

Bless you for a very sweet letter of Thursday, Darling. I still feel rather empty & cold, I suppose that's the way feelings work every time after a departure – person left behind feeling there's something missing, & the person who's gone off feeling isolated & fish-out-of-water. That's exactly what I feel like, yes I do – a fish on dry land. A jolly fine analogy, or simile, & don't you deny it, 'cos you're still swimming about in water, lucky old swig.

Huh! Well you are lucky – mainly to be in <u>surroundings</u> which are quite like Us in sympathies, books & so on. <u>Yes</u>, that's where the water, in which you are a fish, comes in – how very clever of me to have thought all this – definitely a very fine simile. (!)

... I've been quite happy this weekend. Yesterday afternoon I typed out our Gramophone Record Card index, to be completed when we get back to our records. You see, in my diary there is a list of nearly all! records bought or given since 1941, so that's how I was able to do it.

... We have 46 records of J.S. Bach – no, more – 49! Putting all the "B"s under one index marker was no good, so I made out three "Bach", "Beethoven" & "Brahms" – otherwise they are all in alphabetical order.

Then this afternoon I cleared out my cupboard & put everything back Very Tidily & according to a new system – also listened to various concerts amongst which was Vaughan Williams' 5th symphony, which I enjoyed very much indeed. Also Brahms' 2nd piano concerto – part of it. The Mozart's symphony No. 39 & finally part of "Rigoletto".

[*20.1.47*]

If you saw me now, I've no doubt that you would give a sympathetic though heartfelt giggle! I'm in bed, as it's the only place where I can be warm (we have no coal) – the electric light keeps on going off (hence the candle), the electric heater cannot be used, I'm wrapped around with a dressing gown, the bed is half-collapsing (sort of) & one or two other things...! Gosh, what a good idea to get married before next winter!

Lots of reports are coming in just now – on one I see that the amount most Germans get from their ration cards is 1260 calories a day – oatmeal, flour or fish they don't get though they should. That would make up the calories to 1500, I suppose.

[*24.1.47*]

... The Germans now have their local government completely back in their hands & Mil Govt. at Kreis or District level can only advise (& not order) them to do anything. All I can say is that it's a tragic mistake. Perhaps I should do like Fred & write a report to my M.P. about it! Oh, he's not much is he, though, I remember you telling me. And I'm not allowed to write to the papers or make communications to the press, hmm.

[*26.1.47*]

And yet another Sunday passes & yet another lot of telegrams & anger – this time about the billeting of English families in Cloppenburg. 20 Officers & families are coming in, & where are twenty houses to accommodate them, etc. Actually it is a bit grim, the whole Kreis has a "saturation point" of 83,000 – that is the maximum which it can be expected to cram into its living space. Well, through more & more refugees coming in, the present population is 92,000, & there are 7,000 more on the way here! So where is the room to put them? As well as the 20 officers & wives... ? The inhabitants are threatening demonstrations & goodness knows what else! Mmm, & the K.R.O. (Kreis Resident Officer) has just come back – is privately rather pleased that he was away when all the other happened. Did I tell you the whole story? Perhaps I did, but here it is, summarized.

   a) June 1946 – Dobelmann, Catholic Party leader, tries to form
      a Trade Union, fails because he's not liked.
   b) Same time Frese, a social democrat, forms a TU with
      success. He is not Catholic, & a stranger in the Kreis.
   c) August – Dobelmann starts trying to get Frese out of his
      position as TU leader. To do this he thinks that it will be
      best to get F. sacked from his position in the County Office
      (Kreis-amt), thus rendering him penniless & forced to go to
      another area for work. F. is very poor anyway.

d) October, November, December – officials in Kreisamt, having been told what to do (they're all as thick as lice) tell Frese to get proof that he has been Anti-Nazi, & that he really had to flee from Germany. F. finds this hard to do, but goto documents which should be satisfactory.

e) January. Officials say these are insufficient, Kreis Parliament is held & resolution passed to sack F. K.R.O. gets up and says F. will not be sacked – there is no reason for it. (That is to say, official reason.)

f) Landrat (Political head of Kreis) goes up to Oldenburg to a minister-friend of his who goes to the chief Mil. Governor of Oldenburg – complains & is told that the K.R.O.'s decision will be reversed, also that the Kreis Group Commander will come down & clear the business up. The muddle being that our K.R.O. had been told by the Oldenburg Mil Govt. to order the Kreistag not to sack F.!

g) Kreis Group Commander comes up (by the way K.R.O. has by now gone on leave & knows nothing about all this row!) & Landrat is told officially that though the reason for F.'s dismissal is very doubtful, the K.R.O.'s decision will be reversed, & they may dismiss F. if they want. Result: enormous loss of British prestige. Germans have put it to the test & found that they can get away with things like the above.

h) That's the Frese incident, & now our idea is to send the matter up to Hanover with the idea of getting the K.R.O.'s decision re-reversed there! Because it's a definitely bad thing if the Catholic Party (C.D.U.) get control of the T.U.s anyway. The Landrat is a nasty piece of work & an awful liar, too.

Phew! And now the billeting business is coming up, but it looks like being a far simpler thing altogether.

... It's extremely cold weather – is there a lot of snow in Kettering? Col. Dent (our K.R.O.) returned to-day & said there was quite a lot of snow about in U.K. Sweet, could you send me some candles, do you think – the lights here are cut every day, and there is now ½ candle left! If you could send a dozen it would help terrifically, as it's rather maddening having to sit in pitch darkness for anything up to an hour.

[*28.1.47*]

... I wanted the flannels & tie to make myself into a civilian-looking fellow here & be able to lounge about on Sundays, and also attend political meetings without attracting much attention! Any ones will do, sweet. But the reason for them is not so very exciting, as you see – though they <u>are</u> a good thing to have out here, & prove a good disguise.

[*9.2.47*]

I love you an awful lot to-day – or have been thinking of you, which is the same thing. I've read the whole weekend, too! First finishing "Passage to India" (which was wonderful! The satire on Englishmen at a time of crisis – isn't it good!), then looking through the novel called "Kathrina" by Hans Habe – and am now in the middle of "For Whom The Bells Tolls" – which is <u>very</u> absorbing. Oh sweet I got so homesick for Spain – what with descriptions of Life, & Food, & people – they're all just all I knew them & loved them – but feel happy just the same – probably because I'm so full of colourful memories – the book, the music I've had on the gramophone – mainly C. Franck's symphonic variations with particular regard to side no. 2

... Dearest, just in case – well – hoping it won't Be A Mistake – would you send me two pairs of brass C.S.M.s crowns. I mean C.S.M.'s brass crowns? They're still not sure yet, but one might as well be prepared. Thanks, sweet.

... Yesterday I had a talk with Mr. Vernham, who is the Area Intelligence Officer (formerly one of the five Brigadiers in Military Intelligence) & discussed my future! He said that I should finish my degree at all costs, but would be very glad to help me get back into C.C.G. after that, & that it would be a very useful stepping stone to the foreign service. The contracts were (provisionally) ending in 1952, however, so I would have to get in soon as possible. He himself only got a Pass Degree at Cambridge after the last war, by the way. Yes, Mr. Parker is in Oldenburg now, with a very interesting job. That man will be A1O one day – he has the knack of getting on splendidly (awful word!) with everyone. Didn't he strike you as being a Very Good Mixer?!

[*12.2.47*]

... Yes, the cold here <u>is</u> pretty awful. We have had electricity cuts all through the winter – once or twice 20 hours a day, but generally only about 6, spread over the whole 24 hours in pieces. The weather here now is the worst ever, for it's snowing all the time & a freezing wind blowing hard as well! We don't go out any more than is necessary, as one's head is feeling like a lump of ice after a short distance. Still, the snow doesn't lie as deep as in England (only 3 foot in <u>drifts</u>, & <u>much</u> less on the ground).

[*17.2.47*]

... Dearest, I've thought about Mother & have come to the conclusion that the most fair would be to say that I'd spend my leave in June with her. You see, I'm hoping to get out of the Army in <u>September</u>, & we could get married then. I somehow feel that she'd like me for a time, that's all – before we were married. Oh dear, I'm saying this because I feel it's the right thing, somehow – not because I don't want to get married in June at all. And to my shame be it said that I would never have thought of that had you not suggested it. Of course, in October term starts again, so that if I possibly could I would start again in Oxford then.

[*19.2.47*]

... I enclose Mother's next letter, which wasn't so depressed as the others, bless her. Don't you feel she wants you to come? You know, she must have got into such a groove of despondency after 3 years of it all that she'll be liable to say 'no' to everything – don't you think so? (I've said that before, haven't I – sorry!) It's more or less a matter of doing what we feel we ought to even if she doesn't say yes. Oh, it's all very slow going somehow. I do so wish June was here & September, & that I could get out of this & be free once more to travel & move about.

Yes, sorrow is lonely, – or is <u>individual</u> in its working out & goes the opposite way to joy, which gives <u>out</u>, seeking to share with others.

[*21.2.47*]

... This is going to be short & empty. Pooh – I feel in such a muddle, & am in bed with very cold feet – also am exceedingly fed up. I just don't know what to do. I realize that Life isn't at all the same as one thinks – almost like a cave which shows greater & greater depths as one goes forward with his faltering candle. Great holes suddenly appear, & the worst is that you suspected they were there before – so that though it isn't a surprise to find them, you feel a kind of feeling of fatality, something far greater yet terribler than man or human life. When one turns, for an instant even, from the light & warmth of God, then how awful are the gaps & dark caverns of evil! I always associate the grotesque & weird & fantastic with evil – like the painting by Goya – evil & the so-called supernatural – which <u>is</u> but a wandering of the mind – the shapes, the premonitions, the clenching of hands & the shutting tight of eyes, the thin music & the rhythm of nightmares, the feeling & the musty smells, the growing louder of noise, the coldness of heart yes, even the goats' heads & human hand – all & through all, pervading is the fog of evil, with naught to do with hate nor selfishness – just cold & absence of every thing & the utter

<u>loneliness</u> of it all, with nothing but your hollow self to look round in for comfort. No. Oh Pooh, there is such a lot to be achieved & done in this world, & they're so far from even seeing what they have to fight... a little evil can cause such unhappiness. God, give us light & warmth, & colours, & fleecy clouds & green leaves & long grass & summer's hay & the positive & helpful things – for all the creative & positive come from You & from no one else – all the solid, real things.

[*26.2.47*]

... Yesterday we all went right up to the north of the Kreis, through snow & the like. All to make a house search, & when we got there we found that the name we had expected to find there just wasn't! So went round to various contacts – there is a scandal up there because one village councillor wrote a letter denouncing another councillor to a Communist newspaper in Hanover! And the newspaper very cunningly printed it & circulated copies of the edition in the area concerned &... the man denounced had black-marketed a lot of peat in exchange for motor-car tyres...

[*27.2.47*]

... Well, we saw Figaro last night, & very enjoyable it was too. The singing as usual was better than the acting, but that seems to be a German (or Oldenburg) trait. I think the music is so <u>very</u> wonderful. I'd like to listen to it again & again.

Did Mother tell you she wanted to pay your return fare to Spain when you got there so that you would have a lot to spend on clothes & things. Also that you must apply to the Spanish Consulate in Cavendish Square for permission to go to Spain, letting her know at the same time of your application – reason is to be the visit of our future father & mother-in-law. Oh & a Miss Colas is a friend of Unk's in the Consulate – she would help you. Also that it would be better that you book your ticket all the way through Cook's as Dean & Dawson's don't seem to book after Hendaye.

... To-day, as I said, we've been wafting about – to the R.A.F. police, to the administrative officer in Varrelbusch (the big Vehicle Depot near here – R.A.O.C.) & talked about drawing coal from them, then this afternoon went to buy a goose, talked for an age to an old fellow who was full of prophesyings "When the apple blossom appears on the trees, there will be another war": Oh Pooh, there just mustn't be one – it would be so awful. Then got some potatoes, & got stuck in one or two snow drifts out in the country & so back here. Then when it was dark tramped through deep snow to get at an informant in a farm, & he wasn't there. So I wrapped my shoes in paper later & put them in the oven.

[*1.3.47*]

... Oh Bear, I love you. This demob. change has got me all unsettled, & I keep falling in & out of touch with you, mentally – next month seems such ages to wait, & so does next August. It will be funny to be together for evermore, won't it – we'll keep on feeling "How many more days have we?" & then realize we have a lifetime. It's no use speculating our reactions & the like, though there will no doubt be some. But there isn't any need for turbulence or peevedness. I know that you get on well with anyone & I do too – with nearly everyone, anyway – a person has to be awfully squiffy if I can't. So there's not the slightest reason why we shouldn't be quite all right – if only we take time to consider things & not blurt out silly & aggravating sayings. I have been experiencing that a lot just lately. Nigel & Jock are both rather younger than I, & I often am on the point of breaking out impatiently when I stop & think "Well, why are they slow? – wouldn't you be the same in their place – only been in Germany a few months & can't speak German" etc. & then I don't break out, because I realize that I'd probably be far worse than they, were I in their place.

[*7.3.47*]

... About "being possessive", it all goes quite deep, somehow. I don't do those things (like more or less patting you!) because I don't feel possessive. I hope it's not ever going to be a very great disadvantage or anything (in any case, we will get used to it!), but I don't feel in the slightest that way towards you. You're quite a being of your own & don't belong to me particularly – oh that isn't quite right, because underneath everything, I do, most strongly – but feeling we're one doesn't mean feeling you're a personal possession of mine. Physically, anyway I don't. I think I'm acquisitive rather than possessive, somehow! Or are they the same thing? They could be, but there is a difference. Mmm.

... To-day, I was with Dr. Ortmann in the morning for two hours (The Oberkreis – direcktor) talking of this & that & saying what we thought about Nazis. I think that I'd prefer an honest & formerly convinced one than these awful slimy people who "weren't ever very active & only joined for personal profit" managing at the same time, of course, to convince everyone they were violently anti-Nazi!

[*9.3.47*]

Eee, & what a weekend! Yesterday afternoon we went out with skis to a wood nearby and slid down gentle little inclines & gave Jock & Nigel lessons. Tella the maid came too, as they were her skis. Oh sweet, it's so wonderful going through pinewoods with the snow lying deep around – everything so silent, & a fresh smell of snow with a faint twinge of pinewood about it, & no noise but your skis shuffling on & on. We got back feeling happily tired & hungry!

[*12.3.47*]

... Now, one thing at a time. Firstly, I've found out that I can go to Spain for my leave after all. I don't want to in the very slightest. a) It'll muddle Mother all the more, to have an open battle or whatever it will be, going on & 2) I don't want to. Still, if Mother can't get out, I will have to.

And Sweet, I've thought about your idea & if you want me to be definite, then I will, & let's get married after demob. There! Firstly, I've realized that having it all in one week isn't doing it at all properly. I wanted to go to Tilff with you, & I've planned that quite as much as anything else. Then again, though your side has most of the preparations to do, surely I need a bit of time, to get measured for Moss Bros., or get the suit – which would cut it down to less than a week. And couldn't truly attend to Mother very conscientiously for two weeks before that, 'cos I'd be thinking only of the wedding & nothing else. And it's squashing it up so much. Bear I am really upset that I didn't tackle this problem months & months ago. I'm too selfish, & haven't looked ahead enough. But you did ask for something definite, & there's the clearest way I can see.

[*14.3.47*]

... About the money for our honeymoon. I'll provide it somehow. How much do bouquets & licence & organist generally come to, do you know? 'Cos my Army Savings will cover that (£25? with hire of suit) plus £22 Journey to Brussels plus £20 to spend there. And it doesn't matter if it's more, I'll manage. Only Nat. Savings has such a good rate of interest that I'd like to invest as much as possible & leave it there a long time. But we'll be all right for money for our honeymoon, eee yes, bless you. Gosh, but Bridesmaids' presents – mm, it'll be a bit of a rush – or can we buy them in Brussels – oh no, I must buy them by myself, perhaps?

... I wonder if we will change, or whether we'll just get more 'us'. I have patches of very ordinary ordinariness where I seem almost to lose consciousness altogether & go about in a trance (!) – then other times when I seem to get awfully impatient with other people... Still, on the whole I do get on well with everyone, & I'm quite pleased that I do, & happy that people like being in my detachment etc. etc. (both Nigel & Jock have put off their German Language Courses because they didn't want to leave) – and I think it's probably because they can lead their own lives & not have to be interdependent for everything. Mmm, but I <u>am</u> quite grateful that I can run something happily, & most of all that the <u>others</u> like <u>each</u> other a lot. But I think that if I <u>have</u> any fears it would be of going ordinary or you ultra-womanly. Somehow, though, I don't think we will!

... Sweet, will you send me two pairs of brass C.S.M.'s crowns, please? Mr. Taylor told me to put them on, it might be 3 months before we get any confirmation of it, & even if we don't, the A.I.O. will see (I hope) that it is brought in order, etc. etc. They shouldn't be too hard to get. I have a pair of cloth ones for my great-coat.

It thawed a lot to-day & now it's freezing again, Oh gosh – won't it <u>ever</u> give up. I'm so longing to see snowdrops & daffodils & spring birds & Interesting smells & Breezes & am <u>fed</u> up with puddles & slippery pavements & brown-purple trunks of trees glistening damply, blackening snow & wet feet & always looking at the barometer & wondering if the heating has gone out, & pushing the car out of places where it has got stuck & Germans with red noses & pale faces & glowering at the snow falling silently... yes, & a feeling of not being able to <u>do</u> anything till the weather does clear up.

[*17.3.47*]

... Really, the photos <u>aren't</u> costing a lot at all. I can't say they are 'cos it wouldn't be true. Up to now I've paid out about 100 marks on them – that is 200 cigarettes, which costs me under 10/-! And two cigarettes for a mark is a very generous rate of exchange for the photographer – there are places where <u>one cigarette</u> costs 10 marks (5/-!), and the usual price anywhere is 5 marks (2/6), a cigarette. So there's not much point in charging anyone, & I do it all very gladly as the family gave me such a wonderful time at Christmas anyway.

[*24.3.47*]

Darling One,

It's three days since I wrote – sorry, sweet, eee - & it's quite a while (well, one week!) since you wrote the last letter I received three days ago. Oh, I'm <u>so</u> full of Complicated phrases & twists & turnings. Wot 'appened was that I spent the whole weekend writing out the Pol. Int. report, so that I can hardly think or write straight now! Still, it was a good report, I think – dealing with Public Opinion on the Socialization of Basic German Industries, the Categorization of Nazis, the question of India, the coming Provincial Elections, and the starting up of the "Centre" Party, & Trade Union developments. The "Zentrum" is a Good Thing, as it will absorb a lot of the members of the C.D.U. who are not so right wing & reactionary, & leave a residue of true C.D.U. types, all very much easier to sort out.

... Mmm, I've reconciled myself, & am Now Quite Prepared to go to Spain – but – oh well, it was just a feeling of reluctance. You see, sweet – Madrid is my Home & it's a bit odd going back to it where things are so muddled now, & also I have got accustomed to another place as being home. Although I've moved about so much all my life I've never been without one place whither I always drifted & had a warm spot for – when I was at Wycliffe it was the Frenches (till Mrs. Fr. so very kindly slung me out), or Mother's rooms in Lampeter, or 45 Fairdene R (bless it), or your rooms (Mrs. Mason's) in Kettering. Wherever it has been, I've looked on it as having the <u>atmosphere</u> of home. But now I'm going to what is <u>officially</u> home & – oh, it's a bit muddling, that's all.

I am a selfish fellow – here you are chirpingly going without so much as a wee grouse... Darling, you're a very wonderful girl and will be a <u>terrific</u> person when you're 50. Wmk!

Mmm, I'm sure there's far more "Mental" adultery & growing apart than the physical sort.

... Ultra-womanly... ? Well, what I do rather regard with apprehension is women taking the view that only members of their own sex have any sense at all (which occurs rather a lot, I think) and Men are mentally Inferior – and, well, up-with-women-kind of gossip. I feel that I'd like you to belong to me, & never to any clique (I hate cliques) – in other words a man's woman rather than – oh that does sound rather mean, but do you see what I mean? Men may become ordinary (& I hope I won't) but women seem to forget completely what men's needs are & ridicule them & how important they are to them, just in the same way as the men <u>gloss over</u> & become insensitive to the needs of a woman, with all their little ins & outs.

[26.3.47]

... Oh sweet, don't talk about war, it would be so terrible. I don't think you realize quite how bad it would be – even if they didn't use Atomic bombs & things like that. It just <u>mustn't</u> come again – it wouldn't be just a matter of more bombed houses – it's the economic side which would be so disastrous – that, with its consequences. "British glossed it over" indeed – some bloody stupid twerps who write those letters don't realize what harm they do. Oh dear, if you could just see (you can't imagine it from any description of mine) the misery in Germany now – refugees living in real pig-sties, with open channels of sewers running through the middle of them, families in bits, Mothers wondering where their sons are, always hoping against hope they'll come back, farmers being hard & selfish towards the refugees, D.P.s, Poles stealing what little the refugees have left, mental agony, divorces, men beating their wives, stealing, lowest possible moral standards. Oh that doesn't give you any idea of it all. But just bring war onto that again? <u>No-one</u> in England suffered as these did & are because it's not just a question of goods, chattels or relatives being lost, but the very minds & innermost hearts of people being undermined and driven slowly <u>mad</u>. Worry, hate; hate, worry; worry, hate. No, it's not right, & mustn't be.

... Then this evening with the Youth Discussion Group Committee, then afterwards talking to Gussie about success in marriage – she's a very sensible person, I think. She said, amongst other things, that it's the woman's place, if she sees a quarrel brewing or leading somewhere serious, to quench it – her place because women see things instinctively right, whilst men have to work round to their views with a lot of reassuring etc. & never see the coming of a serious quarrel in time – which is quite true?

[28.3.47]

... Sweet, could you get me two or three pieces of thick leather? One sees it in Woolworths – square pieces about 1 ft × 9 ins, & ¼ inch thick. It's to sole some shoes for one of our maids, actually, she hasn't any leather & I said I would try & help. Please, Bear?

[30.3.47]

... I feel rather flat, too – dashed up to Bremervörde 'cos Karl said that Herr Schabbel was in prison (he'd only got a sentence before, & was still free pending the outcome of the appeal – but this is another charge brought against him) & so went there to see what I could do, to Stade this morning to visit him in Gaol (he's been there a week) and took him some sandwiches from Frau Schabbel – whereupon a fussy little German lawyer came round after a quarter of an hour & raised objections as he wasn't supposed to be visited, etc. So we had to go – could have stayed if we'd had a row, but it wouldn't have helped Schabbel much; & looked up the Court Officer of Mil Govt. & talked to him. The whole point about all this is that German Courts are dealing with the affair, and the English have nothing to do with it or have any power over it. The charge is that Schabbel requisitioned stored-away furniture – but he has proof that the Military Governor (Major Kennedy) told him to do that in view of the shortage of furniture. And in those days there was no German Court or law, so of course they now don't recognize the time before they came back into power & anything done then which is against their law (whether it was done by order or not). Oh the position is getting perfectly bloody. The Germans <u>aren't</u> capable of running a democracy – they just use its freedom to cut each others' throats. It's an appalling mess of inefficiency, chaos, rudeness, utter corruption, personal spite, & God knows what else. The Russians are <u>completely</u> right when they say we haven't carried out Denazification correctly (mind you, they haven't either!) & it's a horrible failure on our part.

... Well, apart from all that – I sat for an hour with Schabbel's defending lawyers – brilliant minds they had, & fascinating to listen to.

... Oh, & I have obtained a raincoat! Light grey, with silk lining – very smart & quite light in weight for – er – 500 cigarettes! This from Karl, to whom it belonged. And I'm hoping to get a suit too, and a shirt. The raincoat was a bit too big for Karl & fitted me quite well. Gosh, the things I've got from him. I hope you don't disapprove of all my Doings, sweet?! – but I've <u>decided</u> to get some clothes before I get back. We shan't be very rich at first, shall we, & if I don't need to buy clothes in England so much it'll all be to the good. Ho, but I'm not half as bad as some of the people here – which is no excuse, I know, but they deal in <u>thousands</u> of marks, which I don't!

Oh, & I went to Wiegmann's & looked at some paintings. There was a very nice one there, but it wasn't of trees, it was of cornfields. What do you think? And please could you get a fat tube of Zinc White (or Foundation White – oil colour) for me to give him, Bear – he's almost run out of white again. Eee?

[*1.4.47*]

... It's funny, our engagement's only been – let's see, only 4 months long, only counting the time with each other. And we haven't even had much time to get used to each other. But I <u>still</u> think letters have covered a lot of ground, one way & another – it's been very slow progress (or <u>development</u>) – but I believe that slow building-up is by far the best & rather like a river flowing out into the sea & depositing sediment at the mouth which slowly mounts & one day forms a delta.

... The reason why I don't say much about conditions in Germany to-day is that I get conflicting feelings within me. The greatest suffering of the Germans isn't their material condition so much as their mental vacuum. A French resistance leader who is beaten till he's half dead, the Dutch farmer who sees his lands flooded by the opening of the dykes, the Greek child hungering in the streets – they have still that warming feeling inside them "I'm doing this for France, so that better times will follow after the Germans are driven from our land", "Nevertheless, they'll have to leave Holland", "Better times are coming". But the German to-day lacks that: for many, the only hope is a war with Russia – a hope which in itself is but a perverted and deformed one. They play their petty politics, & must realize it's only a game. They aren't allowed to decide anything of importance. It's all very pathetic. There's the feeling that you're watching children playing with their toys, but playing with such intenseness and desperation that you feel awfully sorry for their illusions, knowing that it leads to nothing. The Germans are an intense people, & go from one extreme to another.

It's all rather sad, & much more so because of their lack of hope, lack of something to look forward to, lack of objective. The pathetic seriousness of those who say "We don't expect any more, but if we work hard, perhaps our children will have a chance", or the bewildered look of those who have lost everything but the old German Army uniform they have on, the unhealthily shining disillusionment of the ex. PW from England (a lot of whom want to go back, by the way - & nearly all of whom who would if they could take their families). And so on and so forth – and every time I think very much of it I feel ashamed I'm eating better than they, because that's all wrong. They have sinned as a people, yes, they have perpetrated terrible crimes, yes, they must be punished, yes, they must be controlled, yes, educated, yes, they had concentration camps, yes, & in a hundred years' time it's quite probable that you will be able to apply all that to England, why not.

... We very righteously hang a lot of people at Nüremberg, but do we then start hanging all the Russian, Czech, Polish and Yugoslav war-criminals? Then was it an International Tribunal? or what? It's all mess, mess, and continual popping of heads into sand so as not to see what one shouldn't. I'm not blaming anyone, & certainly not Russia – but Political Hypocrisy is about the worst there is, & the hard part is to pin the blame onto anybody anyway.

[4.4.47]

... Also enclosed a German Ration Card – note the '87ᵗʰ' period – T 62.5 grammes of butter weekly! This is a child's card..

[*15.4.47*]

... Yesterday morning I was interviewing all the time. In the evening Colonel Dent. Gussie, Dr. Knoll & I went to a Youth Discussion at Friesoythe. It <u>was</u> horrid, & so difficult. They were mostly roughs, & also arrogantly Nazi-minded – kept on getting up & interrupting the Colonel & saying "Bolshevism must be rooted out – there must be another war!" & one felt a hate such as there'd never been before. And so cynical & sneering, Ugh! Used hardly any reason whatsoever, & just said what their emotions prompted them to. I got terribly annoyed, & was venting my anger on my note book & writing it all down!

[*Douglas and Hazel met and stayed in Brussels during Douglas' leave of one week, followed by Hazel going to Paris where she met Unk – who then took her to Hendaye and on to Madrid.*]

[*7.5.47*]

My Darling Bear,

I received a telegram from Coulsdon to-day saying that you had arrived safely & was very relieved & pleased to get it. I've been feeling so odd to-day – do you know the sensation of being ultra-sensitive & <u>feeling</u> things very vividly. People's faces & the scum in a river, the dust in the street, & hats & voices & things.

... P.S. Payment for the worm powders came in the form of some material with which to make some pyjamas! Ho!

[*18.5.47*]

Darling Pooh,

And how are you to-day, I wonder? Two weeks since you arrived. Oh Bear, I am getting excited at the thought of coming to Madrid. Also very much too at the thought of September 6th – in fact very-much-in-a-state; since your Mother's letter telling me all about the preparations! It seemed so inconceivable that all that should be going on and that I'd be one of the centre pieces or rather that we'd be the kernel of it all. I think what staggered me most was that they're buying a Marquee! She was very sweet about my inviting everyone I wanted to, but I think my list will remain as it was. Oh sweet, I do wish I'd been to a wedding before, it's all so strange and bewildering, almost. I'd feel far easier if I were told I had to make a speech before a thousand people, even.

[23.5.47]

... Oh, & I received a reply from Eaton place, stating all the particulars (tuition etc. paid for + £195 a year & £110 for me – that's the maximum) and I can apply as soon as I know the date of my demob.

[26.5.47, Altenau, Herz Mountains]

Still I'm here, & enjoying it all so very much, & the weather has suddenly become very hot too...

... Nigel & I went for a long walk up the Burgberg, the castle mountain by Harzburg, & had such a wonderful view from the top! Looked at the Russian zone through my binoculars, but didn't see anything! The mountains here are so friendly, covered with woods & streams running through boulders at the bottom, & sheer faces of rock only in places, & friendly goats, a brown colour. Then crowds of German children, very clean, marching along arm in arm with guitars & singing.

[30.5.47]

Just a wee note to say that I shall be leaving for Brussels on the 2nd, get there the 3rd – try & get my visa by the 5th, & be at Madrid by the 7th. I'll wire Mother exactly what date when I finally get the visa & am all set. I have all my passes etc. ready except for my passport which I collect from Hamburg.

[*Douglas got leave to go to Madrid where he, Hazel and Lou were together till 19 June.*]

[*23.6.47*]

Everyone – well, both of us – is – are – waiting excitedly for the first letter from England – bless you for your telegram, sweet – it arrived on Saturday morning. And I'm writing this in order to catch to-morrow's plane. We've been having great fun just lately. Yesterday to the Corrida de Toros – so now I've been to one too! And I don't think I want to go to go to another! It was very exciting & all, and I more or less enjoyed it, feeling slightly sick at the same time. What made me rather more sick was the Bull's Last Moments, with it staggering around half on its knees, blood pouring from its mouth, & the Toreador patting it cheerfully on the back! Only happened once, that, actually, but as it was the last bull, it left rather a nasty impression. The horses got off quite lightly, though they were pushed over several times. The crowd is always most unsympathetic & difficult to please, isn't it?!

This corrida, though, was supposed to be quite a good one, & though they hissed at one of the matadors, another they cheered for ages, throwing coats, hats & leather bottles into the ring – gave him the bull's ears, & carried him off in triumph from the ring. The bulls were all extremely fierce & quite terrifying, or so it seemed from the fourth row from the front. We took some iced tea & scones along with us, so we had no need of 'gaseosa' or cerveza, bought an official programme nevertheless, also two cushions to sit on. Mother had her eyes closed for about ? of the corridas, bless her. We walked half the way back, & had a small & happy supper at home.

Later / Just received your letter from Dover, & we're both very pleased, bless you! It was a very nice ending to a perfect evening. We went to see a friend of Mother's (who wasn't in, actually) then to a café for an 'Apéritif' – being coffee & milk batitido & cakes & had a wonderful talk, all about you! It really was terrific. (Darling,

Mother really <u>does</u> love you, & appreciates you very <u>very</u> much, to the full, you know.) We went to a bookshop & bought a book of Goya's drawings – quite horrifying! – only 35 pts!

... Then at 11.30 we went off & found a big fair nearby – for the fiesta of San Juan! So had to look at that, & bought little botijos (er, I have <u>four</u> now, Dear) & jugs & peanuts & carnations & then as we came out – wonder of wonders, there was a free taxi complete with green light right in the middle of the road!! & so home!

[30.6.47]

Here I am! Back at Tilff – arrived at 5.0 last night, and slept from 11.0 to 10.30! Eee, what a long journey it seemed, though. Had a 1st class seat from Madrid to Irún as we couldn't get a sleeper after all – quite a good journey, however, and had a big lunch at the Hotel Terminus, crossed the frontier at 2.30 without any trouble – changed £1 into francs, then caught the 4.0 train, which didn't really fill up all the way to Paris! A few people got into the compartment at Bordeaux, but that's all. One a young reporter who had gone into Spain secretly in order to write an article about it! Very pro-republican...

At Paris we shared a taxi to the Gare du Nord – awful trouble getting onto the "Etoile du Nord", as I hadn't a reserved seat – spoke nicely to the lady at the barrier, however, equally nicely to the man stopping-people-without-reservations-from-getting-onto-the-train, & got a corner seat!! Took 3 ¾ hrs. to get to Brussels, & just caught the train to Liège by 3.20.

... Well, and so the happiest leave of all is over – sweet, I spoke to Unk the night before I went – very nicely & friendly-like, & got exactly the same answers as before except that he <u>wanted</u> to stay with Mother at the flat (with regard to the future), didn't want to leave the girl in the lurch, would like the affair to end, but wouldn't till she gave him up, & said that too much bitterness had come between him & Mother for them ever again to be as before.

... I <u>am</u> scared of hard-hearted & insensitive people. Mother & I talked about it a lot the last day, whether we should talk to him (I had already done so, the night before) as he was so pleasant & agreeable, & were still discussing when Mother suddenly got the impulse to & sailed right in. Bless her, oh I <u>do</u> hope she's feeling happier by now. Write to her often, sweet, won't you?

[4.7.47]

... I'm hot & slightly tired but have been thinking of you most of the day, & all the things we did together two weeks ago, & what fun it was being with you & the 'interim' period feeling... this was preparation and orienting ourselves a bit more – don't you feel?... I'm so glad you're not cold & sex-is-a-wicked-thing & ashamed of anything to do with it. I'm sure a lot of people are, & it can't make life any happier for them. It's quite right it shouldn't have a larger place than its due, but that doesn't mean it should have a smaller place either. Oh well, I'm rambling rather. But I do love you for being untouched, & anything we've learnt, we've learnt together, within each other & not from others. And I love you for being sincere about it & thoughtful & careful at the same time, & modest & sweet. <u>And</u> so happily glad that we came through up to now without touching the Do itself, & kept back to what we felt was right or on the other side of the wall.

... But I'll come straight to you when I'm demobbed anyway. Gosh it seems so queer to be going to be demobbed & come to Coulsdon for good – to you for always – it makes me feel odd inside, as if it'll be a very great changing point – which of course it will be – but not only the wedding but the demob too.

[9.7.47]

... Last night, I was suddenly called away to the Colonel, who was deep in a conspiracy in Gussie's new flat... Gussie showed me round it, including her bedroom, gleefully pointing out the big double-cum twin bed. I <u>nearly</u> said "Big bed for such a little girl", but didn't, as it wouldn't have sounded right & rather cheap – also she probably would have come out with something far worse. She has <u>no</u> shame whatsoever, Gussie ain't. Anyway, the conspiracy was this: a new chief official of the Kreis (the Ober Kreis Direktor) has to be elected. The C.D.U. party want to put a man in who is very favourable to them, a Herr Kern, refugee from East Germany. (Their idea being that the CDU will soon have had its day, and the sooner they can get in important permanent officials to their liking, the better.) Col. Dent, of course, favours the rival candidate, a native Cloppenburger. So we talked about how to do the others in the eye: he had heard that a special "informal" meeting was to be held before the regular Kreistag (Kreis parliament) sitting this morning. So we thought we'd go & turn up unexpectedly, for at the Kreistag, the new Oberkreisdirektor would be elected. So along we trundled at 8.30 this morning, & the blank look of fed-upness on their faces showed us that we'd come in on something interesting. It was, very. The Landrat (C.D.U.) had got together a group of those who <u>favoured</u> the <u>rival</u> candidate, & proceeded to "discuss" the matter with them, asking them not to vote against his favourite (Kern) – in this way he drew out <u>all</u> their arguments (which they would otherwise have used in the Kreistag) and left them feeling as if there wasn't much point in repeating themselves again! Also he prepared himself for any attacks or arguments they <u>might</u> make. <u>Very</u> clever thing to do, though he couldn't do it as well as he wanted to, as the Colonel, Gussie & I were sitting on a sofa nearby & staring glassily at him!

The outcome of this at the Kreistag was that they voted to postpone the election of an Oberkreisdirektor for another 14 days!

[*11.7.47*]
... The weather has been <u>so</u> awful – rain rain & more rain all the time. Fair brownin' off, but I'm very pleased to hear about Princess Elizabeth getting engaged, aren't you? I should have thought that

he [Philip] would have preferred life as a naval officer, though. Still, Mac [a friend in the Navy] says he's a very nice chap.

[*14.7.47*]

... On Saturday, Nigel & I went to Hamburg to collect Monica's printing blocks – which we did, & gave my own in to be done (ready by 2nd August) – paid for Monica's, took Gordon's passport application to the Consulate – had lunch at the Sergeant's club – bought some stamps (which I'll show you – very good they are), then went to see "Odd Man Out". Oh sweet, it is good, & I didn't feel it was too tragic at all – one left with a satisfied feeling, somehow – & so well done & wonderful acting. I like Kathleen Ryan, & those shots of alleyways in the dark with streetlamp reflections – eee, oh I loved it. I'd gladly see it again. Then we saw "The Seventh Veil", which I didn't think so good – it was quite different, the story more complicated yet more unreal – no, it wasn't so good.

After that the Sgts. club, & so on to Bremervörde, staying the night at Frau Schlichtings – saw Karl & all. Also went to the Schabbels – Herr S. is still in prison – 4 months there & not yet been tried or anything! It really is scandalous, and Mil Govt. can't decide whether the Germans should try him or not! And there's absolutely nothing to try him for, as during the time he was in prison a letter arrived that I witnessed & was sealed by a lawyer from the Mil Governor Explaining All! Oh dear. Pooh, the amount of wickedness in the world. Oh, I'll explain it all better when I see you, but this is a vicious country.

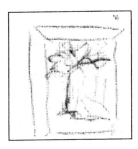

... On Sunday I spent the time seeing Frau Schabbel & exchanging stamps with the Old Herr Kausche. We left Bremervörde at 5.0 and went to Herr Wiegmann – got my two paintings: I shall be bringing three of his – one is already framed, of a tree, see. Then one is just stretched onto a frame – also of trees. Then the one I chose actually for your parents is just rolled up. Would you prefer to give them the framed one, or will there be time to get the loose one framed? Eee? (If you booked an order now...?) Herr W. said that if I would be so good as to send him the odd tubes of white or blue now & then (when I'm in England), he would send me from time to time a painting! So I said "Yes, you bet I'll send you some tubes of paint!" A very good idea, don't you think?!

Then after a cup of coffee we came back to Cloppenburg.

Pooh, don't get me wrong, but I've changed my mind about the coffee 'cos I said 4 lbs., & it was 4 lbs., but I'd quite forgotten that it will <u>cost</u> something more to have them [the blocks] actually printed onto cards. So can I have another two, making 6 in all? Or 600 cigarettes? There's my own Christmas cards to be done & printed & all (by the way, it's to be done in Postcard size).

Actually it would be best to send partly cigarettes because 6 lbs of coffee would be rather frowned on by the customs.

... There, & now we're back from the north of the Kreis, having seen the people we had to – it always tickles me when Germans (most of them, too) call us "The British Secret Service", when we're just Military Intelligence, or counter-intelligence. Now they're annoyed because the KRO goes out hunting with a former Nazi (not that he (KRO) knows that he was one, I'm sure). Mmm well, he's gone on leave so I'll see him in 2 weeks' time.

[*16.7.47*]

... Bless you for a <u>wonderful</u> letter (11th). It made me sizzle – honest! And I wondered how many other people were as happy as we are & have been these last three years & will be. Mmm, the times we've clicked have been very wonderful too, & in such a variety of ways have we done it – from the first visit to Brighton last July (when we walked along the undercliff walk – remember, & you got 'sprayed'?) – to the last night at Tilff, to the drawing room at Españoleto 13 – to that moonlight walk at Wentworth (mm, I think so, don't you?) to the various minor happy 'habits' we had, such as the British Restaurant at Rotherham (with those drawings on the walls, & where we always had salad) & walks in the park. Yet scarcely anything (except Tilff) to beat Rhosneigr. Sweet, it's been terrific fun when we've gone off on our own, hasn't it. I include Kettering too – most times – especially Peterboro' Cathedral, Fotheringay & driving suppers at Mrs. Mason's, & your room there, & watching you do your hair in bed at Mrs. Coley's, & driving out to Mr. Gislingham's.

... No, I think it's natural to grow into each other more, but the important thing is not to allow oneself to become insensitive to one's family – by not taking their advice truly to heart, or forgetting the attention or little habits they've become accustomed to from you. I'm sure that is what a mother misses most from her married daughter or son – not the fact that they have become united, but the expressions of Love that she used to receive, & confidence, that the son or daughter cease to give her. Which isn't necessary, because Love is infinite, and there's no need to cease asking advice or giving your confidence to your mother (or father, or brothers or sisters). And that's why I don't want us to change – 'cos we, of <u>all</u> people, just don't <u>need</u> to. Still, Bless you. Oh, there <u>is</u> a lot to talk about, isn't there.

[*18.7.47*]

... Mmm, I send my letters to you by airmail, that's why they cost 1½d – but letters are still free via surface mail – it was the free <u>airmail</u> service that they stopped.

... Last night I went to see Joop, who is back in the Control Commission as an Intelligence Officer Grade Three & very happy to be back. He had some perplexing times in London, when, as a complete stranger, he was wandering around trying to find out where to get a National Registration card, an Identity card, a National Health Insurance card, & an unemployment card! All required by the CCQ Authorities before he could become a fully-fledged Official! But they're lucky to have him, for he's a <u>very</u> good man, & excellent on his job. Dutchmen on the whole make very good Intelligence Officers, 'cos they're suspicious, & good businessmen.

Now Nigel's trying to persuade me to go on a raid on a Hostel at 3.0 a.m. to-morrow morning! And I am strongly opposing it – it's an anti Prostitute raid by the Police, & they invited us to be in on it in case there were any suspicious people there, etc. etc.

[*21.7.47*]

Tuesday / Sorry to break off! Last night I dreamt about the wedding & all I hope is that it won't be like that! Absolutely awful. I won't depress you with a description of it. Then there was a horrid article on weddings in some newspaper yesterday, a-meant-to-be-funny-one. Oh well, why haven't I been to one before, it's all so difficult to imagine, with things like dreams & newspapers as the only things in sight which one can lay ones' hands on!

Last night Ron came down from Westerstede, & Joop too as it was my birthday. I had to keep the promise to smoke a cigar before I was demobbed, & did & afterwards vowed I'd never do it again! Still, I brought a box of them along & made everyone else smoke one too! They went around 12.0. We had the 2 Colonels in, too – or rather, I invited one & the other invited himself.

Karl came to Cloppenburg for the weekend – very nice to have him here – and I heard from Bremervörde to-day that Herr Schabbel has at last been released! After 4 months without trial!

[*23.7.47*]

Just a note to say that D. Day is the 9th August! That is, I'll be arriving home on about the 10th. Our O.C. sent up a letter asking that I should be released as soon as possible as I was to be married!

... Don't panic about money – there is some coming from the Argentine, and Mother owes me £100 (though we won't ask for that). I think there'll be enough – really yes. I know it's the bread-boards & dishcloths that make such a hole, without counting Christmas, but it'll work out. We'll make some kind of budget – I love doing that, don't you? And if & when there isn't much, we can go without most things, 'cos we'll have grown a lot & can live off all our reserves.

... Darling, Goodnight. I say, do you know the painting-of-mine that I think I love best of all? The Christmas card of 1945 – it hangs over my bed, & looks so lucid & clear & serene.

[*24.7.47*]

Many thanks for your letter of the 21st all about the shopping Expedition, & the flat, & feeling-sleepy & so on. Bless you, I didn't know you quite felt like that about my stuff. Darling, I do collect things, yes. Perhaps I should have left them all at Auntie Ethel's or somewhere if only so that you wouldn't have got so overwhelmed & oppressed by them!

But dearest, you sounded serious, so let me be serious too, & explain the why-&-whereabouts of it all. Look I don't want any pity, & all that – but eleven years now I've been wandering around, more or less without a home – that is, ever since I left Spain during the civil war. I did go back for a few months in 1939, but not for long, really. So for eleven years I've carried my own home around with me (and I'm not talking of spiritual homes, which I've had with you, but material, general, absorbing homes – communal affairs), and in eleven years I've collected lots of stuff, yes sticky paper & bits & pieces, & used it pretty slowly, so that even to-day there's still a lot left of it. In those 11 years you, for instance, have had & collected just as much 'junk' as I have, only it's been used or absorbed into your home – 'cos you've had one, the same one, all the time. And that glue you bought in 1940, or that writing paper, or this wooden case, in 1937, and all these things have all been used, or worn out, or Just Disappeared.

[I've been more] homeless, & wandering from place to place with two kitbags & a trunk of all the material home I have – leaving bits here & there, yes, using the glue up & breaking the glass bottle, but packing the remainder when it's time to move, & on again to the next place & leaving it & coming back to it & sorting it out & being pleased & remembering each thing & the memories it has. Oh yes, maybe sentimental, but how much sentiment would you have for 45 Fairdene Rd. when you came back after 6 months? Or a year, or two years? I <u>know</u> I'm like a travelling caravan with pots & pans hanging all over the place, & things you don't think particularly necessary, but they're just part of the equipment & things that had to serve instead of a home, since 1936.

When I went back to Spain this time, my former belongings had gone their way – been absorbed into the home whilst I'd been away, & I wasn't particularly upset as that was probably what would have happened had I been there anyway. And lots of times I have cleared out my kitbags & things & chucked bits & pieces away & only kept what I liked especially much, or what might have been useful – all part of the wearing, absorbing & eliminating process. Don't look on my 'junk' without understanding it a bit – that it's the residue, even, of much wandering around & moving about – just equipment in substitute of a home.

And I will sort it out, I promise, & throw some of it away, & we won't have our two rooms being full of botijas! Oh Bless you, sweet. I collect things like that, I know, & small china animals & Field Marshals, just as you do books (well, dear, it's about my only weapon!), but <u>again</u> it's all part of that instinct that I can't explain, that's been formed by attempting to make myself a home wherever I went (for instance, the animals were for my room in Oxford, the porcelain Field Marshals for my room in Pau). Well, I've said enough about it.

... Bless you for being an honest Bear, though, I love you for it & think it's one of the nicest things about you. I feel I'll always know where we stand, & how we're feeling towards each other – which is Definitely a Good Thing.

... Sweet, we've both got an awful lot to learn, & realize. I to become more practical & less casual & less dreamy & less liable to get flustered, & less fits of absent-mindedness & less selfish! You – well – less sweeping & theoretical & more quiet, & less treading-on-toes & less flaps & more thoughtful & less noisy & more cautious. Oh dear, I hope you're not offended or fed up, I just let it trickle out of my pen, & I don't mean it all that deeply or seriously... I find it terribly difficult to explain & wish to God I had waited till I could speak to you about it.

You see, Humility is so important in Life – it's a sort of peculiar quality – cures everything, & builds everything too. It's bound up with what Jesus kept on saying "Except as ye become as little children... ", "The meek shall inherit the earth" & so on. It's the right basis of mind for Life – eternal Life – and helps us in all walks of this life as well as in our progress towards God along Christianity's road. It's what the rich man forgets, & what eventually any man forgets who believes so much in himself that he forgets God – lack of it is vanity, selfishness, greed, & all those peculiar things. Oh it's such a big thing & has relations with every good, every Christian act, thought & striving.

[27.7.47]

... I wrote such a Peculiar letter on Thursday evening, & have been wanting to write again ever since, & just didn't get a moment to do it. Pooh, you didn't get too offended, I hope, at my long lists of our faults, did you – 'cos there seemed to be much more about yours, & that isn't fair, 'cos you haven't got as many as I have. No, you haven't! Oh well, the letter is written, & posted, so sweet we can talk about it, week after next can't we. Gosh it's exciting. I can't believe it. I'm not really as excited as I generally am when I come on leave, though! Isn't that queer – for four years is a chunk out of one's life, & it's nearly that (well, over 3½) since I joined up. And all the time we've been together, darling, occasionally in person but always in spirit & one day I'd like to begin to tell you how much – terrifically much – you've done for me, keeping me

morally mentally & physically in one piece, & giving me something
to keep warm inside me & at the same time follow its light.

I've always been able to see the path I had to go by, because
you were always there, & faithful & true & giving all you had. I
never underwent any change or got mixed up with temptations,
and that again wouldn't have been so had not I had you to talk to
in my mind, & protect me. And though I never did anything at all
brave or out of the way, I always felt that there was something to
be over in France for, to be getting muddy for, & avoiding shells
for – 'cos you <u>were</u> there at home or in Kettering, and it was good
to know you were there to come back to. It sort of gave a point to
everything. I <u>do</u> hope I never get fat & contented & lazy and forget
all the hundreds of things you've given me like that.

... Dorothy asks masses of questions about wedding ceremonies,
& I seem to answer them as if I spent all my spare time attending
them!

We were wondering if, after we had both got married, we'd
change very much towards our friends. I thought of that thing of
E.M. Forster's of the glass screen that comes down. Bear, I don't
<u>want</u> to change towards anyone in the very <u>least</u>! & want to remain
exactly the same. Oh I do hope we'll remain as we are. I'm quite
content with us that way! Aren't you? I'm <u>determined</u> we're not to
change, anyway. One hears so much of people "not so jolly, more
bad-tempered, & worried-looking" after they had married...
"subdued & nervous" & all that tripe. Why <u>should</u> we, we're all
right as it is! If I'm to improve, or be improved, I'll do it slowly, &
not be rushed, & so will you, and we <u>won't</u> just have eyes for each
other & no-one else, & be doting & soulful at one another for the
first year & Indifferent for the next fifty-nine. We'll be normal <u>all</u>
the time & friendly towards each other in public & Rather more So
in private, & be a Quiet & Happy couple all our lives. <u>Yes</u>, and
never change, but develop & expand & give out. 'Cos surely that's
the best proof that we are as One, if we give out to others & not
spend the whole time giving to each other all the time?

[*31.7.47*]

... Darling, we're drifting into another ocean now, & this is one of the last letters to you, I expect. We'll be caught up in exciting streams, & violent little eddies, funny little plops, & blowing away confusedly at the froth from waves which are far bigger than us – as well as the wonders of the calmness of the sea, & the "witches' oil" at night-time, & the phosphorescence, & things & gentle breezes that put us onto quite different things to us & clouds in the sky...

And when we're there, & away from here – when we've left the old plodding sea, where we always had plenty of time to think things over, & could tear up letters if they seemed badly-expressed – where the wind was nearly always right, & the ground not too far away from our toes, & leave all that, & come to the Big Sea – sweetheart – don't let's forget too quickly the things we've learnt, even if they were safe, plodding & quietly-contemplative things – because I think we'll find that we've spoken out some of the wisest thoughts that we shall ever express. Not because we shan't grow wiser, but because they came from the best & truest we could give, & that is always something godly, & Good. Our thoughts (& one could call them theories) we mustn't forget, 'cos if we lived up to them always, we'd do well. And those thoughts were expressed carefully and quietly, in an ideal way & in such a way as perhaps will not be so frequent to come by during the first stages – who knows? Oh Dearest Bear – our Love has gone through some wonderful colours hasn't it – just like the Cybeles Fountain in Madrid, in a way – for all the colours were lovely. I know that I've changed colour for you since Madrid, & feel more realistic & wanting-to-be-closer to you & loving your forehead more, & hair – do you know, Madrid was a very long step forward. Yes, forward from Tilff indeed – not only because we came together so closely, but also because of Mother, & Spain, & my old home & Us being together there for the first time.

Tilff was so happy & wonderful & you were so very right when you said that it was the Real Ending & Peak of our engagement & Madrid was realistic, & swift & hot & practical & down-to-brasstacks (sorry for the silly expression!) Do you agree? The landing upstairs, or rather the threshold – just before we go up to the door and into the <u>living</u> room.

My Pooh, I <u>am</u> so happy about us! Mmm – <u>that's</u> what I really was getting at, & if we now go on into a haze, where the past seems blurred when we look onto it, we at least know inside us that our engagement was a Very Good Thing, & that we covered a lot of ground, & thought out a lot of useful things & put them in our bottom drawer ready for the Living Room – oh <u>Darling </u>Bear.

... I sent all my Ration Cards (spare) to your Mother as I heard that a new type has been introduced, so I hope she can manage to make use of them. I mean that the shops will accept them.

[5.8.47]

Just one last-ish letter to say that I still love you, & to thank you for yours of the 31st. <u>Bless</u> you, I <u>do</u> hope we'll settle down as quietly and happily as I am expecting us to... Things are so fluid just now. The next few evenings are going to be full of goodbye parties & things. Tonight the O.C., to-morrow night Germans, Thursday Bertelt, Friday Colonel.

Do you know what, I suddenly feel happy again! I was all muddled & apprehensive about coming home, & a black pall of Fear of the Unknown over everything, & now I feel miles better – in fact quite a different Pootle. 'Cos you as a Pooh are good-tempered & natural & normal, & your very bounciness is a joy to any weary person. <u>Bless</u> you – yes I feel very fine, now, & you must too. We won't change, & we won't be scared. I've neither grown a tail nor sport more spots nor have shaved my head nor let my fingernails grow. I'm quite the same, so are you...

It's all a question of whether the Demob centre functions on a Sunday. If it does, I ought to be in Coulsdon by Monday. If not, by Tuesday. I'll send a telegram as soon as I know. Oh <u>Bless</u> You. I love you!